Financial Justice

Financial Justice

The People's Campaign to Stop Lender Abuse

Larry Kirsch and Robert N. Mayer

Foreword by Congressman Barney Frank

 PRAEGER

AN IMPRINT OF ABC-CLIO, LLC
Santa Barbara, California • Denver, Colorado • Oxford, England

Library of Congress Cataloging-in-Publication Data

Kirsch, Larry.
    Financial justice : the people's campaign to stop lender abuse / Larry Kirsch and Robert N. Mayer ; foreword by Congressman Barney Frank.
        pages cm
    Includes bibliographical references and index.
    ISBN 978-1-4408-2951-2 (hbk. : alk. paper) — ISBN 978-1-4408-2952-9 (ebk.)   1. Consumer protection—United States.   2. Consumer protection—United States—Citizen participation.
3. Financial services industry—Law and legislation—United States.   4. Board of Governors of the Federal Reserve System (U.S.). Consumer Financial Protection Bureau.   I. Mayer, Robert N. II. Title.
    HC110.C63K57   2013
    332.70973—dc23   2012051588

ISBN: 978-1-4408-2951-2
EISBN: 978-1-4408-2952-9

17   16   15   14   13   2   3   4   5

This book is also available on the World Wide Web as an eBook.
Visit www.abc-clio.com for details.

Praeger
An Imprint of ABC-CLIO, LLC

ABC-CLIO, LLC
130 Cremona Drive, P.O. Box 1911
Santa Barbara, California 93116-1911

This book is printed on acid-free paper ∞

Manufactured in the United States of America

Contents

Foreword

It's not unusual for me to read a book where I am in very strong agreement with the basic argument, but have differences with some particular points. It is much less usual for me to be eager to write the foreword to the volume in question. The authors are very kind to me and somewhat critical of some of my colleagues, and I was concerned about the appropriateness of writing a foreword for a book that treated me so much better than a number of other people who I greatly respect. It is possible for Democratic members of the House and the Senate to disagree with the liberal position based on their views of good public policy, and not necessarily because they were influenced by campaign contributions. Substantively, I have one major difference. My opposition to the requirement that financial institutions work for a "plain vanilla" version of any financial product was based on my view that that would be wholly impractical, because I did not—and still do not—see any way to enforce that requirement. But this study of the adoption of the Consumer Financial Protection Bureau makes two very important points—one specific and one general—that far outweigh my disagreements.

The specific point is the importance of creating an independent bureau for the protection of consumers in the financial area. As I write this, the Bureau has already shown its worth, for example in recovering hundreds of millions of dollars for individuals who were mistreated by credit card companies. But the financial interests and their ideological allies in the Congress have not given up the fight against it, and this discussion helps make the case as to why it was needed and why it will be a great asset for our economy.

The broader point is that it shows that democracy can work, even in the face of strong opposition from powerful and wealthy interests. In this regard I welcome it as a refutation of a dangerous self-fulfilling prophecy that is too often uttered by people who would like progressive change in our society.

That prophecy is that politicians don't pay attention to individual voters because they are too beholden to the sources of campaign contributions. It is the philosophy that Elizabeth Warren cited when she said on the day that the Financial Services Committee passed the bill to create the Agency: "They told me not even to try this because the banks always win. But they didn't win today."

Of course, powerful economic interests have a great deal of influence on our political process. They have the money to hire lobbyists, make campaign contributions, and, more importantly than sometimes noted, organize campaigns of their employees. Money is unfortunately all too influential in congressional deliberations, and the outrageous Supreme Court decision in Citizens United has made it even more so. But while it is necessary to recognize that wealthy interests are politically powerful, it is a grave error to act as if they are omnipotent. It is emphatically a major strategic error for those fighting for change to propagate the argument that politicians are so influenced by the money that they will ignore public opinion.

Members of Congress will pay very little attention to opinions that are not expressed. It is also true that it is hard to mobilize the average citizen in many situations, giving the political advantage to those who have a large economic stake. But as this study shows, when individual voters and advocacy groups such as Americans for Financial Reform do express themselves in significant numbers, members of Congress listen.

The Consumer Financial Protection Bureau was established as a strong agency because my congressional colleagues understood that voting for it was better politics than either defeating it or voting for it in a substantially weakened form. This does not mean that it was only electoral considerations that led the members of the House and Senate to vote to create the Agency in 2010. A very large majority of those who voted for it did so because they believed in it strongly. The role of public opinion was not to coerce members who supported strong consumer protection to vote that way, but rather to give them the courage of their convictions, and in particular to enable them to withstand the political pressures being generated by the financial interests that opposed the bill.

The bad news is that money continues to have a significant effect on congressional deliberations, but the good news is that votes can beat money—if the voters are motivated to speak out. It is simply not the case that politicians will ignore a strongly expressed public opinion because big money has captured us all. And to the extent that repeating this argument dissuades citizens from speaking out to their members of Congress, it unfortunately strengthens the very tendency it bemoans.

Congressman Barney Frank

Acknowledgments

First, we extend accolades and appreciation to our interviewees, a remarkable group of public interest advocates, for pursuing their virtuous cause and for being generous with their time and patient with our ignorance. Their comments, we hope, will bring to life the crucial public policy episode covered in this book.

Several people provided valuable feedback on portions of the manuscript and/or assistance in selecting a publisher. Our thanks go to: Andrew Battista, Tom Beck, Betsy Burton, Bob Davis, Clara Greisman, Mel Gurtov, Neal Hirschfeld, Adolfo Lara, Robert Manning, Alan Mayer, Tom Morehouse, Eric Orner, Dick Rahm, Jerry Slepack, and Bob Weinberg. Special thanks go, as well, to Steve Catalano, our editor at Praeger. He believed in the book from the first time we approached him and helped shepherd it seamlessly through the intricate publication process.

No one, however, is owed a greater debt than our long-suffering spouses: Thanks to Karen Kirsch for her constant and uncomplaining support, her informed review of multiple drafts (with results always rendered with honesty plus a smile), and her intrepid advocacy of the lowly comma. And gratitude to Carol Blackwell for her encouragement to aim high and her understanding of the hours it takes to reach a lofty goal.

Introduction

Barney Frank, the left-leaning, straight-talking Jon Stewart of the Congress, once reprimanded allies within the consumer advocacy community for being "horseless headmen." The stinging message behind Frank's ironic rebuke was that just having policy smarts without matching political brawn amounted to a losing formula. Following a short but therapeutic spell in the cold tub, advocates stopped crabbing and began organizing. The successful campaign to enact the Dodd-Frank Wall Street Reform and Consumer Protection Act of 2010 was their vindication.

Had the devastating credit collapse of 2008 not sparked a full-blown people's campaign against reckless Wall Street financial practices, embattled borrowers would certainly have been scuppered even more seriously than they were. But consumer, labor, civil rights, fair lending, and community groups in Washington and across the country did come together in a way rarely, if ever, seen before in modern-day citizen politics. What ensued, in the populist narrative, was a pitched battle between newly cemented and sometimes unusual alliances advocating for the "people"—2000s' style— and the traditional leviathans of Wall Street and Big Business.

This book tells the story of a people's campaign to enact serious Wall Street reform and, in particular, to create an independent "cop on the block"—the Consumer Financial Protection Bureau (CFPB)—to safeguard consumers against predatory lending and other financial abuses. In the following chapters we set out to provide a sense of what AFR and its fellow advocates thought, did, and accomplished (and/or failed to bring about). We use a case study approach to illustrate some of the most significant advocacy efforts with respect to the independence, authority, and even existence of a new consumer financial protection agency.

The story is important because it says much about the prospects for successful progressive action in an increasingly sour political environment. It is a story about, and to a large extent told by, the people who made it happen. These activists were drawn largely from the consumer, fair housing, civil rights, and labor movements, and we had unparalleled entrée to them. Their candid on-the-record interview accounts provided us with insights that are rare in social movement and legislative histories. While our primary approach is to recount events through the eyes of the CFPB's advocates, we also try to recognize the views of people who opposed establishing the new, independent agency, relying on published material such as congressional testimony, statements to the press, and articles in law journals.

All authors have opinions and feelings about their subjects, and we gladly admit to ours. Even before writing the book, we were sympathetic to the idea of creating a new consumer financial protection agency. As we conducted research for this book, our prior admiration grew—both for the borrower safeguards enacted in Dodd-Frank and for the extraordinary group of advocates who helped make it a reality. We attempt to provide a fair accounting of all the political actors in this story, but we are clearly in tune with the worldview of the CFPB's champions. If you believe that government action is inevitably ineffectual and that *caveat emptor* is all the protection consumers ever need, then you may find yourself differing with our perspective.

In the course of the three years between when a new agency was proposed and when President Obama signed the bill establishing the CFPB, the names used to describe a new entity to protect consumers in financial transactions changed a number of times. To avoid confusion in the text, we consistently refer to the title of the proposed agency as the CFPB regardless of its name at a given point in the legislative process.

"History is written by the victors," Winston Churchill is supposed to have said with respect to military conflicts. The maxim applies to legislative battles as well. Winners crow; losers clam up. This is the story of the CFPB campaign as told largely by the winners . . . however tenuous their victory may be.

Chapter 1

How Did We Ever Get into This Mess?

At the beginning of 2007, the U.S. economy was like the animated cartoon character that runs off a cliff and floats momentarily in mid-air with legs spinning before plummeting to the ground. It's true that, nationally, housing prices had peaked in early 2006, but prices were holding steady in hot markets like California, Nevada, and Arizona.[1] It was, thus, unclear whether the drop in housing prices toward the end of 2006 and into 2007 represented a bump on what had been a dizzying upward ride or the beginning of a sustained national decline.

Some economic policymakers such as Federal Reserve Board chairman Ben Bernanke remained cautiously optimistic about short-term economic prospects. In February 2007, Bernanke reassured a Senate committee that weakness in the housing market had "not spilled over to any significant extent to other sectors of the economy."[2] A month later, he told the Congressional Joint Economic Committee that employment was continuing to expand, and the economies of the United States' major trading partners seemed strong as well.[3]

Soon thereafter, U.S. Treasury Secretary Henry Paulson leavened the forecast just a little bit more. He told an assembled group of business leaders that the housing market correction was at or near its bottom and that problems in the subprime mortgage market were unlikely to spread to the overall economy. In what has since proved to be a colossally incorrect observation, Paulson said: "I don't see [trouble in the subprime mortgage market] imposing a serious problem. I think it's going to be largely contained."[4]

Three Leaders

On May 6, 2007, the Kennedy School of Government at Harvard provided the venue for an academic workshop with the mundane-sounding title, "Managing Risk in the 21st Century." Participants might have found themselves admiring the expansive views of the Charles River on one side and a duo of striking, Oxbridge-inspired, undergraduate residential houses on another. Adding to the bucolic surroundings, there was also the makeshift volleyball court adjacent to the Kennedy School library that provided a relatively safe outlet for Harvard's spirited, highly competitive students and faculty. Inside, however, Harvard Law Professor Elizabeth Warren was anything but playful as she presented her research findings about the impact of abusive lending practices on families and what should be done about it. The name of her paper was "A Fair Deal for Families: The Need for a Financial Products Safety Commission."[5]

Warren's presentation was summarized a month later in a small circulation journal called *Democracy*.[6] The gist of her argument was that in the current environment, a very high percentage of middle-class, often dual-wage-earner, families was at substantial risk of experiencing some type of unexpected and unavoidable financial crisis serious enough to wipe them out. A medical emergency, job loss, or divorce could easily deplete their savings and force them to the maw of the banking and credit system in search of a financial reprieve.

The basic statement of the case presented that day by Professor Warren is not in serious debate; if anything, new studies provide additional evidence for her point that economic insecurity has become an ever more prevalent part of the American scene.[7] Household finances provide an extraordinarily fragile safety net for families facing financial emergencies. Almost half of all people surveyed by a team at the Brookings Institute reported that they would be unable to absorb the costs of even a very modest ($2,000) financial emergency if given 30 days to raise the funds.[8] Keep that number in mind when you reflect on the fact that the bill for a single emergency room visit to have your kid's chin sutured after a bike spill could easily come to $5,000 or more.[9]

The sobering conclusion of Warren's research can be summed up, roughly, in the following way: "Watch out, folks. Once you cross the threshold into the credit and finance system, the rules of the game are not consumer-friendly." Quite the opposite; lenders frequently employ sophisticated business tactics to "trick or trap" borrowers just when they are most vulnerable. And as if that isn't bad enough, Uncle Sam is doing a miserable job policing the marketplace.

Because the mission of the Tobin Project, the sponsor of Warren's workshop talk, is to produce transformative policy research (aimed at finding practical solutions to major societal problems), a highlight of Professor Warren's presentation was a proposal for a new, federal consumer financial protection agency to assure the safety of the credit system for borrowers.[10] Patterned, loosely, after Ralph Nader's 1965 book *Unsafe at Any Speed* and the consumer product safety improvements his exposé jumpstarted, Warren's mantra was basically that it made no sense for consumers to be secure from the hazard of exploding toasters but at risk of incendiary mortgages or credit cards.

One of the discussants of Warren's paper that day in May was Barney Frank, recently sworn in as chair of the U.S. House of Representatives' Financial Services Committee. Frank, a wry Bostonian and Harvard alum (who claimed, unabashedly, to have the longest uncompleted PhD dissertation in the university's history), was assigned the discussant's task of assaying the practical political challenges that would face enactment of a consumer financial protection agency should such a proposal be introduced.[11] Without in any way denigrating Frank's more than ample store of acumen, it would have taken a mind reader to predict the reception given to Professor Warren's proposal when it was actually introduced in Congress. Chairman Frank would soon find that out, first hand. More to the point, he would personally take charge of the Warren proposal and help steer it to final passage under the eponymously titled Dodd-Frank Act.

Shortly before Elizabeth Warren gave her presentation to the Tobin Workshop, Heather Booth, a leader and strategist for a variety of progressive causes, authored a blog post dealing with the future of progressive politics in America. Her basically optimistic article took off from a piece contributed by another Kennedy School faculty member and long-time activist colleague, Marshall Ganz.[12] Serendipitously, Booth's post dovetailed with some of the themes outlined in Elizabeth Warren's subsequent presentation.[13] If Warren played the part of the dramatist, evoking broad themes and sketching a justification for policy change, Booth was the stage director, transforming words into convincing images and carefully choreographed action. The main burden of Booth's remarks was that progressive political change, in the doldrums for such a long time, now enjoyed a better chance of success. This was due, in no small measure, to activists, themselves. By this she meant to suggest that activists had made important advances in building capable leadership, improving modes of communicating, mobilizing a broad membership base, and consolidating issue campaigning with electoral politics—in short, in organizing more effectively.[14]

Booth believed that the fundamental changes in power relations and structures sought by progressives would ultimately have to come about through some degree of engagement with the traditional political system. Therefore, to be successful, activists had to participate in the electoral and legislative processes through ground-level organizing blended with insider legislative lobbying work.[15] Activists needed to do more than identify issues and develop proposals standing on the sidelines of the political fray; they needed to jump in and become part of it.

This proposition, emanating from such a highly respected member of the activist community, would have surely cheered Barney Frank—an important progressive leader himself. Frank periodically found it necessary to goad activist friends and supporters into becoming more politically and strategically engaged—sometimes with brutal honesty. For example, in his comments about the participation of gay rights activists in the 2009 National Equality March, Frank, the first-ever gay member of Congress to come out as a matter of personal choice, told a TV interviewer, "[If activists] want to pressure Congress, I don't know what standing on the Mall on a weekend when no member of Congress is in town is going to do. All that's going to pressure is the grass."[16]

Based on decades of activist leadership, Booth argued that effective advocacy called for measures driven by generally accepted moral principles coupled with a clear demonstration that they would yield practical improvements on important issues in people's lives. And although upbeat about the historic opportunity progressives now had on key foreign and domestic issues, she was nonetheless realistic about the obstacles and opposition that would face any meaningful "democratic revival."

Clearly, the conjunction between the Warren and Booth arguments was very strong in a number of ways—none more important than the shared recognition that proposals for change would have to benefit people in ways which were meaningful to their lives on an everyday basis. For people to take concerted action as citizen-advocates, they would first have to feel the pain and then believe they had the power to do something effective to stop it.

As Elizabeth Warren later observed, while standing on the brink of her personal entry into electoral politics in Massachusetts, "I threw myself into that piece [the *Democracy* article] because I felt strongly that a new consumer agency would make the credit markets work better for American families and strengthen the economic security of the middle class."[17] Indeed, making credit markets more secure and increasing economic well-being for a broad swath of the population were the overarching, tangible goals that united the three leaders: the law professor with activist instincts, the community organizer with group mobilization skills, and the career politician with the position and credibility to drive the legislative process.

The Plascencias: One Family's Story of Lending Abuse

Although the story of the housing bubble has been recounted in great detail elsewhere, a thumbnail illustration of how lenders structured their mortgage products and transacted business with buyers helps to explain why Professor Warren concluded that the mortgage market was dysfunctional and defunct, and why a consumer financial protection agency was so vital.[18]

One typical case involves a couple, then in their mid-40s, named Melania and Armando Plascencia. The couple lived in San Leandro, California, just east of Oakland. The other key players included a California-based lender named Lending 1st Mortgage that issued a mortgage to the Plascencias; a Delaware company, EMC Mortgage, that bought and securitized mortgages from lenders including Lending 1st and sold them to investors; and a number of brokers, agents, and other unnamed players associated with the lenders.

Lending 1st Mortgage, a prototypical mortgage company, set out to design and sell home mortgages for which the monthly payment, not the size of the mortgage loan, was the chief source of appeal to a burgeoning market of folks like the Plascencias. Prospective borrowers included first-time homeowners who were not financially eligible for or willing to pay conventional market rates and, as in the case of the Plascencias, people who wanted to refinance their existing mortgage.

To achieve its sales objectives, Lending 1st used methods that were commonly found in the industry. It wrote Adjustable Rate Mortgages (ARMs) that offered time-limited, promotional (teaser) interest rates and low monthly payments.[19] The combination of low-cost terms and relaxed eligibility provisions earned mortgages like this one the sobriquet of "affordability products." (To other industry watchers, however, these products were sufficiently dangerous to warrant the term "neutron bomb"—signifying the most hazardous mortgage sold in the marketplace.)[20] When prospective borrowers considered the offer Lending 1st put on the table, the features marketers hoped they would observe most keenly included the low, teaser rate and the attractive monthly payment. Combined, these two features screamed "great deal."

The underlying value proposition floated by sellers was that spiraling home prices would continue, buyers would build equity, and refinancing would be easy to obtain when the initial loan terms became too costly. On its face, the basic sales pitch seemed plausible enough. Grievously, for the Plascencias and other borrowers, these assumptions and reality diverged. At a certain point, prices in the various local housing markets tanked and home values fell below the amount due on outstanding mortgages. As low cost, introductory interest rates wore off and were reset to market levels, borrowers began to face higher—in many cases, much higher—monthly payments they could not afford. And as home values fell and dragged owners' equity with it, the refinancing option many borrowers had come to count on was no longer available.

To compound matters, as the Plascencias claimed in a pending class action lawsuit, their lenders both fraudulently misled them and kept them in the dark about important financial provisions and onerous loan conditions. Among them were repayment features which made it virtually impossible for the Plascencias to pay-down the principal on their loan, prepayment penalties which effectively blocked them from canceling their mortgage and cutting their losses, and promotional interest rates which unexpectedly reset after 30 days instead of 2 to 3 years.[21]

The strategy of Lending 1st Mortgage reflected an approach to lending that was regrettably too commonly observed and was at the heart of the mortgage bubble: attract large numbers of borrowers; make loans without regard to the borrower's ability to repay them; offer products, terms and conditions that are not transparent, adequately understood, or fair to borrowers; charge outsize fees; and pass-through financial risk to investors. Elizabeth Warren argued, persuasively, that this business strategy was deformed. She and, later, Booth pointed out in their writings and other presentations that the broken commercial marketplace for consumer credit was unsafe and unfair to borrowers and was a prime contributor to economic insecurity and hardship.

The Failure of Financial Regulators

As unforgiving as Warren and Booth's indictment of mortgage, credit card, and Wall Street lenders may have been, their criticism of federal credit regulators such as the Federal Reserve and the Comptroller of the Currency was hardly more sparing. Their basic argument—and that of many other consumer and fair housing advocates—was that going back to the Reagan era, federal bank regulators, with limited exception, had pursued anticonsumer policies and had deliberately disregarded festering consumer protection problems within their jurisdictions.

In the case of the Federal Reserve Board, the Truth in Lending Act (TILA) enacted in the 1960s and the Home Owners Equity Protection Act of 1994 (HOEPA) conferred broad legal authority on the agency for a whole panoply of consumer safeguards. These ranged from on-site lender supervisory examinations to rigorous disclosure requirements. The laws also authorized compliance actions, rulemaking, and prohibition of unfair and deceptive lending practices and products. The Fed, however, explicitly chose not to enforce certain portions of the statutes within its jurisdiction. Selective enforcement meant, for example, that the Fed did not regulate nonbank subsidiaries of bank holding companies. Nor did it apply HOEPA's unfair and deceptive practices provisions to all lenders and credit products until 2008—after the housing bubble had broken. These were major shortcomings that stymied consumer protection.

Additionally, when it suited the Fed's purposes, the leadership simply dug in its heels. In one well known case dating back to the year 2000, Edward "Ned" Gramlich, a governor of the Federal Reserve Board and chair of its Consumer Affairs Committee, suggested that the Bank's supervisory staff be tasked to audit a sample of subprime lenders suspected of employing predatory practices.[22] Gramlich, sometimes called "the people's Governor," recommended that auditors be assigned to examine various lending practices in the field. His list covered: risk appraisal and underwriting standards; financial suitability determinations; borrower disclosures; and unfair and deceptive practices. Fed chairman Alan Greenspan rebuffed Gramlich saying that he did not think an investigation would be a good use of the Fed's resources, and Greenspan warned Gramlich that if the audit produced negative findings, the exercise could be counterproductive.[23]

The strong consumer-related concerns expressed by Gramlich could hardly have come as a shock to regulators. Indeed, Congress had created a Consumer Advisory Council (CAC) as far back as 1976 to advise the Fed on consumer protection issues. Since then, an uninterrupted line of highly competent experts from academia, consumer advocacy organizations, law, community development, public agencies, and the financial sector met regularly to advise top Federal Reserve officials and key staff on consumer issues. They included the structure of the subprime market compared with other market segments, predatory lending practices, and the role and practical limits of disclosure for consumer protection.

A good example of one highly controversial CAC topic was prepayment penalties. Consumer members of the CAC were deeply critical of prepayment penalties for locking consumers into exorbitant loans. Michael Calhoun, president of the Center for Responsible Lending and a CAC member appointed in 2008, commented that "[t]his is for us . . . the most important issue before the Board on these regulations."[24] Another CAC member, Sarah Ludwig, noted that over 70 percent of subprime loans incorporated a penalty of some sort for prepayment.[25] Originators who issued high cost loans relied on the penalty to discourage borrowers from refinancing in a lower cost environment and as a means of recouping their initial set-up costs.

Mike Calhoun, Professor Kathleen Engel, and legal services attorney Alan White, all CAC members, told the Federal Reserve Board that the prepayment penalties were defective for several reasons. First, borrowers did not understand them. The alternative of bundling the equivalent cost of the prepayment penalty into the interest rate would be more transparent and user-friendly, they argued. Second, borrowers who had the financial capacity to absorb the cost of the penalty tended to do so and refinanced their loans, but weaker borrowers had little choice but to stay with their loans.[26] Finally, the prepayment penalty was a feature of a two-tier market in which brokers and lenders targeted minority borrowers, thereby implicating issues of fair lending.[27]

Signaling something of a course correction after Alan Greenspan's term ended in 2006, the Federal Reserve partially accepted the consumer criticisms of the prepayment penalty when it promulgated final regulatory changes in July 2008. Later, in a speech to fellow economists in Atlanta during the 2010 annual meeting of the American Economics Association, Bernanke went further. There, looking through the rearview mirror, he allowed that "the best response to the housing bubble [on the part of the Fed] would have been regulatory, not monetary. Stronger regulation and supervision aimed at problems with underwriting practices and lenders' risk management would have been a more effective and surgical approach to constraining the housing bubble than a general increase in interest rates."[28]

That admission was probably as far as anyone could have realistically expected Bernanke and the Fed to go. But it was not nearly far enough. In a letter addressed to Sen. Chris Dodd, chairman of the Senate Banking Committee, 18 current and former consumer members of the Fed's Consumer Advisory Council expressed their "support for a strong and independent Consumer Financial Protection Agency." They wanted, in effect, a freestanding entity that—unlike the Fed—would not have "competing priorities that undermine its ability to strongly enforce consumer protections."[29]

A strong and independent consumer financial protection agency was to become the lodestar that guided advocates from July 2009, when Professor Warren's proposal was first introduced by Barney Frank in the House, through July 2010 when President Obama, with Frank at his left shoulder and Heather Booth close by, signed the Dodd-Frank bill into law. Advocates from across the spectrum of consumer, civil rights, labor, and fair lending had successfully mobilized to take on lending abuse and regulatory neglect despite extraordinary opposition from industry and entrenched regulators. This book tells this improbable story, leaning heavily on the perspective of the advocates most deeply involved.

Chapter 2

Elizabeth Warren Has a Notion

Elizabeth Warren, a Harvard law professor and doyenne of consumer financial protection, rarely misses an opportunity to tell the banking, consumer, and political audiences she regularly addresses that she loves capitalism and believes in free markets.[1] She comes to these preferences legitimately, having mastered the requisite intellectual material in law, finance, and socioeconomics. Beyond her acumen, according to Jared Bernstein, former economic aide to Vice President Biden, she is "maybe better than anyone walking the Earth, talk[ing] about financial markets and the complexities of our economic system in a language that people understand and that resonates with them."[2] What is perhaps most unusual, though, is her profound, gut-level understanding of the impact that financial and business practices have on real people carrying on with their everyday lives.

As an illustration of Warren's intellectual accomplishment, Katherine Porter, one of her former students and later a fellow commercial law professor, reports that Warren can get into the weeds and do the math on such abstruse financial transactions as mezzanine financing and securitization.[3] As to her instinctual concern for the effects of business practices on people's lives, it might be instructive to consider Warren's background as the child of a distinctly working class Oklahoma family where economic insecurity was a routine and persistent fact of life.

The first impression left by Warren can be her golly-gee demeanor and unfailing politeness. Yet, no one has been a more clear-eyed and unflinching critic of price gouging and the other "tricks and traps" that she regards as a persistent fact of life in today's financial services industry.[4] Her position in favor of market enterprise but against the abuse of consumers is just one of many reasons why Elizabeth Warren has been so difficult for political adversaries to pigeonhole and label as a knee-jerk liberal or worse. [5] According to her husband, fellow Harvard Law Professor Bruce Mann, Elizabeth's a "grandmother who can make grown men cry."[6] A self-described "cranky Okie," she just keeps asking the hard questions.[7]

The Financial Model Is Broken

Warren, an acknowledged expert on the adverse impact of overindebtedness on middle-class families, says she recognized just how broken the financial service industry's business model was when an executive of a major credit card company took her aside and told her that her vision of an independent entity designed to test, certify, and publicize clean credit cards wouldn't work.[8] The reason given was that it was at odds with the industry's basic incentive structure. Sitting on a plane returning from her meeting with the credit card company experts, Warren set out to sketch the outline of her germinal article, published in 2007, that would become the template for the CFPB legislation.[9] What was needed, she concluded, was an independent cop on the beat whose job description would be to secure consumer safeguards from all lenders—a sort of Consumer Product Safety Commission for banking and credit.[10]

Unsafe at Any Rate

Warren's vision of the independent cop on the beat was described publicly during the summer of 2007 in a 12-page paper published in the journal *Democracy*. The article, entitled "Unsafe at Any Rate," was a flattering reference to Ralph Nader's epochal critique of auto safety.[11] In her essay, Warren made several points that would soon become the essence of the lobbying campaign for an entity she initially called the Financial Product Safety Commission.

The most vivid point of the essay was the contrast between exploding toasters and imploding credit cards. Professor Warren juxtaposed the extraordinary safety protections individuals enjoy when they turn on their kitchen toasters in the morning with the wafer-thin safeguards they have when they put down a credit card for coffee in the afternoon. This homely comparison resonated with the financial insecurity that people feel when they are obliged to rely on credit for the basic necessities of life. One of Warren's main insights was that Americans, irrespective of class, race and level of financial self-discipline, are exposed to considerable financial risk when they take out a home mortgage or buy a car on time or put their groceries on a credit card.

Warren's publications dispelled the powerful myth that consumer credit practices were benign to borrowers with middle-class resources and only pernicious to the segment of low-income, minority borrowers and women. She showed that even solidly middle-class families with two wage earners, children, and a conventional lifestyle are stressed when a medical emergency or other unforeseen life event depletes their savings and forces them into the credit system. And she made the point that the at-home mom who once played a crucial role as the family's reserve earner against adversity is increasingly hard to find.[12]

Once consumers are involved with the credit system, lenders, according to Warren, all too often apply the finishing touches. They begin with practices that are hidden and one-sided. Then they deliberately conspire to fleece borrowers with interest costs and fees no longer held in check by national usury limits.[13] At the end of this cycle, the high cost, onerous credit terms, and predatory lending practices that many borrowers encounter ultimately push solidly middle-class families with kids into the bankruptcy courts.[14]

Warren's insights were grounded in empirical research done at Harvard as part of the Consumer Bankruptcy Project. In that work, she studied the risks and human consequences of bankruptcy for middle-class families. Describing her methodology she said, "I don't do library research; I talk to families who have worked hard and just slammed into a wall."[15]

In 2004, Warren co-authored *The Two-Income Trap: Why Middle-Class Mothers & Fathers Are Going Broke.* The book was written in collaboration with her daughter, Amelia Warren Tyagi, a Wharton School MBA, successful entrepreneur, and later Chair of DEMOS, a public policy think tank. In their highly regarded book, the two reported that 90 percent of personal bankruptcies in middle-class families stem from one of three causes: the loss of a job, a medical event, or a divorce. Specifically addressing the risks faced by women, Warren wrote (elsewhere) that:

> Bankruptcy exposes the economic vulnerability and insecurity of middle class women. . . . By the most overt criteria, the women who file for bankruptcy are, as a group, solidly middle-class. But at the time they file for bankruptcy, their incomes tend to hover only slightly above the poverty level, and they are deeply mired in debt. The women who file for bankruptcy played by all the rules, but they are still in economic freefall.[16]

Warren and Tyagi's interviews suggested that profoundly disruptive life events were often exacerbated by the credit system. Just as people depleted whatever savings they had accumulated in order to deal with the assaults on their lives, they found it necessary to tap into their credit cards or take out loans to meet basic nondiscretionary expenses. (A similar picture emerged from a national survey conducted in 2005 which showed that 70 percent of low- and moderate-income households used their credit cards for safety-net expenses like house and car repairs, medical expenses, and similar basics.)[17]

The lending practices spotlighted in Professor Warren's *Democracy* article are a high spot of her short course on the devastating impact of banking and credit policies on ordinary people. In a series of quick strokes, she revealed how incomprehensible provisions, buried in pages of mind-numbing, arcane contract language, are inevitably twisted in the lender's favor. She also demonstrated how loans, which on their face seem to be reasonably affordable, can effectively wind up costing upwards of 400 to 500 percent in interest and how people with good credit and high credit scores are often steered into high-cost subprime loans without ever knowing it.[18]

All of these questionable credit industry practices, according to Warren, are part of a deliberate business strategy driven by the calculus of financial gain. In Senate testimony presented shortly before her *Democracy* article was published, she told members of the Banking, Housing and Urban Affairs Committee that, in 2005, credit card companies earned $24 billion from basic lending and an additional $5 billion from cash advance fees and enhancements. She continued:

> But the credit card companies do not stop there. These companies know they can make higher profits if the customers finance their purchases over time, paying their credit card bills a little at a time—some of them for a lifetime. And the companies knew that they could make truly extraordinary profits if the customers stumbled and the company loaded up on default rates of interest and penalty fees. In 2005, *interest and penalty fee revenues alone* added up to a staggering $79 billion. (emphasis added)[19]

In the same hearing, Travis Plunkett, legislative director of the Consumer Federation of America, testified that the Government Accountability Office had recently reported that 35 percent of all credit card holders had paid at least one late fee in 2005.[20] That meant that over 60 million people were assessed late fees.

The Regulatory System Has Been Complicit

In an attempt to explain the ubiquity and grave personal impact of the "tricks and traps" on households, Professor Warren observed that the system we have for regulating financial abuses and keeping dangerous financial products and business practices out of the market is every bit as broken as the credit system itself. The regulatory system, she said, is fragmented and dysfunctional. Some states compete with others to provide shelter for the most costly, least consumer-friendly credit cards and mortgage loans while those with more rigorous consumer protection rules have been effectively forestalled from applying them by the Comptroller of the Currency, the Office of Thrift Supervision, and the Supreme Court.[21]

More insidious yet, Warren argued, the network of federal regulators with oversight responsibility for bits and pieces of the banking and credit system face what amounts to a fundamental conflict of interest. According to Warren, "[T]heir main mission is to protect the financial stability of banks and other financial institutions, not to protect consumers. As a result, they focus intently on bank profitability and far less on the financial impact on customers of many of the products the banks sell."[22]

In addition, Warren pointed out that the basic structure of regulation was maladaptive. Rules that permitted financial institutions to reincorporate and migrate from stronger jurisdictions to weaker ones naturally encouraged regulatory loopholes and timid regulators.[23] Using evocative terms, she expanded on this theme in an article published in *The Wall Street Journal*: "federal regulators played the role of lookout at a bank robbery, holding back anyone who tried to stop the massive looting from middle-class families."[24] A local thrift institution, for example, could readily convert to national bank status to take advantage of bank-friendly regulators, while national financial institutions could set up shop as state-level banks. Regulators had every incentive to protect their respective turfs by safeguarding the interests of their lender-clients.[25] The term of art Professor Warren drew on to describe this behavior was "regulatory arbitrage." The colloquial equivalent would be "race to the bottom."

An Independent Consumer Regulatory Agency

Elizabeth Warren's argument in favor of a new, independent, and expert regulatory agency with authority over all credit products and all issuers and with a single mission—consumer financial protection—was as bold as it was straightforward. Her basic stance may have been stated most succinctly in her hilarious one liner on *The Colbert Report*. Stephen Colbert (on the need to create another regulatory agency) put the question: "Why do we need a belt and suspenders? We've already got one set of bank regulators, don't we?" Warren: "The problem is they've got no pants."[26]

Warren pointed out that a new agency would not and could not be a panacea for the accumulated ills of the consumer credit system. She readily accepted the argument, oft-made by business leaders, that some traditional regulatory approaches killed innovation. At the same time, however, she offered an unapologetic argument for the legitimate social control of unsafe and abusive lending practices. And she suggested that a consumer financial protection agency would perform its consumer protection function directly, through product standards and marketing rules, and more subtly through research and other means.[27]

Most of all, Warren sought to find pro-consumer business practices that would support responsible behavior by individual borrowers. One of her most familiar illustrations dealt with product disclosures. "[T]he basic premise of any free market," she said, "is full information. When a lender can bury a sentence at the bottom of 47 lines of text saying it can change any term at any time for any reason, the market is broken."[28] In her *Democracy* article and elsewhere, Professor Warren's mantra was that clear and objective contract terms, divulged in transparent, consumer-friendly ways, are the most potent tools for bringing about well-functioning markets.[29]

For Warren, measures that support responsible borrower behavior were not limited to more disclosures by lenders. For example, she was a strong proponent of the plain vanilla mortgage proposal originally made by University of Michigan Law Professor Michael Barr (who subsequently held the position of Assistant Secretary of the Treasury).[30] The Barr proposal required that mortgage issuers offer one or more default products (e.g. 30-year, fixed-rate mortgages) side-by-side with ARMs and/or other more exotic loans sold to consumers. The underlying idea, advocated by behavioral economist Richard Thaler and President Obama's former law school faculty colleague, Cass Sunstein, was that less sophisticated borrowers could be nudged by choice alternatives toward products that were more likely to suit their needs.[31] If policies such as plain vanilla could make markets function more efficiently, then command-and-control-type regulations, like product bans or recalls, could be avoided.[32]

As zealous as the case Professor Warren made out for consumer protection was, it seems clear, in hindsight, that the links between consumer protection and financial safety and soundness could have been drawn even more explicitly. As Professor Eric Gerding has written, making that link would have demonstrated that "consumer financial protection is not antithetical to, but, in fact, represents a critical tool in mitigating systemic risk."[33]

Indeed, that precise argument was made by Sheila Bair, chair of the Federal Deposit Insurance Corporation. In June 2007 (just as Elizabeth

Warren's *Democracy* article was being released), Chairwoman Bair told the House Financial Services Committee, "Activities that are harmful to consumers also can raise safety and soundness concerns."[34] Expanding on the same point several months later, Bair testified:

> [T]he events that have led up to the recent market disruptions and problems in the mortgage market demonstrate how weak credit practices in one sector can lead to a wider set of credit market uncertainties that can affect the broader economy . . . they underscore my longstanding view that consumer protection and safe and sound lending are really two sides of the same coin. Failure to uphold uniform high standards in these areas across our increasingly complex mortgage lending industry has resulted in serious adverse consequences for consumers, lenders, investors, and, potentially, the U.S. economy.[35]

The Political Agenda: Elizabeth Warren as a Policy Entrepreneur

As skilled as Professor Warren was as an analyst and communicator, she was equally formidable as a policy entrepreneur. She was able to move her ideas onto the political agenda at the very highest levels. In less than two years, Warren's ideas had sprinted from journal article to legislative proposal; at the three-year mark they were enacted as a title of the Dodd-Frank bill authorizing a new, independent consumer financial protection agency.

Writing in *The Washington Post*, Ezra Klein labeled Warren's *Democracy* piece the most influential policy article of the decade.[36] And Michael Tomasky, who assumed the editorship of *Democracy* two years after Professor Warren's article appeared in the journal, commented on his blog that: "I've been doing this sort of work for a quarter-century, and I can tell you, it's extremely rare that an idea goes from being an article in a small-circulation quarterly journal to becoming law of the land in three years. It's a serious accomplishment."[37]

Trying to unravel all of the strands leading from her *Democracy* article to the enactment of the Dodd-Frank Wall Street Reform and Consumer Protection Act would involve the deconstruction of numerous personal and professional influence networks and more. Nevertheless, several factors provide important insights into the fast tracking of Professor Warren's big idea.

The first is that Professor Warren skillfully and successfully helped inject consumer financial protection into the 2008 Democratic presidential primary campaign. Bankruptcy, foreclosure, and economic insecurity—the main inspirational sources and framework for Warren's work on consumer financial protection—became the grist for campaign proposals advanced by the leading Democratic candidates. She held that bad, ultimately unrepayable mortgages and other consumer loans were not only a disaster for borrowers but also a major contributor to the gathering global economic crisis.[38] This connection made the issue that much more compelling to candidates and policymakers.

Several years before passage of Dodd-Frank, from her perch on the Harvard campus, Warren wrote, debated, advised, and testified tirelessly in the Senate in what turned out to be an unsuccessful attempt to defeat the 2005 Bankruptcy Act Prevention and Consumer Protection Act. As some reflection of her importance to the debate, John Edwards, former senator (and 2004 presidential aspirant) told Warren's law students in April 2005 that:

> Like a lot of Democrats, I voted for a bankruptcy reform bill before. I can't say it more simply than this: I was wrong. The bill is supposed to crack down on irresponsible borrowers. That's the right thing to do. The problem is that this bill imposes big burdens on families who did everything right but went broke just because they lost a job or lost their health insurance. . . . Thanks to Professor Warren, we now know that half of families going broke suffered illnesses or high medical costs. . . . We need to stop the abuses by the credit card companies and the predatory lenders. We need to make sure all families, and especially those who are poor, can build their savings and assets so they have some security if something goes wrong.[39]

Returning to the same theme late in June of 2007, Edwards, then a candidate in the presidential primary race, delivered a major address in the Dialog Series at The Cooper Union in lower Manhattan. In it he enthusiastically endorsed Warren's newly published proposal for an independent consumer financial protection watchdog agency.

> As Elizabeth Warren has pointed out, you can't buy a toaster that has a one-in-five chance of burning your house down—consumer protections prevent it. But you can easily get a mortgage that has the same one-in-five chance of putting the family out into the street—and the lender doesn't even have to disclose the risk. . . . It's time we did more than say "buyer beware" while millions of families go broke every year. We should put in place the same consumer protections for financial products that we have for everything else Americans can buy. And when I'm president, I'll do just that.

John Edwards labeled his brand of the Warren concept the Family Savings and Credit Commission.[40]

Warren responded immediately in a blog posted on TPMCafe.com: "Senator Edwards is moving middle class economic issues front and center. It's time. . . . The centerpiece of the proposal is a Financial Product Safety Commission—renamed as a Family Savings and Credit Commission. This means more than outlawing any specific credit practice because, if done right, it would be the gift that keeps on giving—the reform that can provide consumer protection to match new products that the credit industry invents later on." And in an obvious invitation to go viral, Warren concluded with this challenge: "John Edwards has stepped up. Will other candidates join him?"[41]

In January 2008, Hillary Clinton took up the call with a position paper she called Fair Credit for Families. In it she focused explicitly on credit card abuses. Her announcement pointed out that "Professor Elizabeth Warren notes that credit products are 'regulated by a tattered patchwork of federal and state laws that have failed to adapt to changing markets.' "[42] In direct response, Senator Clinton proposed the creation of a Financial Product Safety Commission, the streamlining of regulatory responsibilities at the federal level, and greater emphasis on compliance and enforcement including concurrent regulation of national banks at both the state and federal levels. The centerpiece of her proposal was a hard, nationwide 30 percent cap on credit card interest rates—in effect, the resurrection of usury limits.

A month later, Sen. Barack Obama outlined his basic economic program at a General Motors plant in Janesville, Wisconsin. In that presentation he addressed the debt spiral, credit cards, and reform of the bankruptcy laws. In a tone laden with populist outrage against unfair credit practices, Obama pledged to "establish a Credit Card Bill of Rights that will ban unilateral changes to a credit card agreement; ban rate changes to debt that's already incurred; and ban interest on late fees." The senator opined: "Americans need to pay what they owe, but they should pay what's fair, not what fattens profits for some credit card company."[43] In a passage dealing with bankruptcy laws, Obama vowed to "make sure that if you can demonstrate that you went bankrupt because of medical expenses, then you can relieve that debt and get back on your feet. And I'll make sure that CEOs can't dump your pension with one hand while they collect a bonus with the other. That's an outrage, and it's time we had a President who knows it's an outrage."[44]

Professor Warren clearly appreciated Senator Obama's message on the link between lending practices, bankruptcy, and family financial insecurity, and she responded accordingly.

So far as I know, he is the [only] candidate to discuss consumer bankruptcy in a general election. I can think of many reasons that bankruptcy is a terrible subject for someone running for president. It is very technical (hard to wedge into a sound bite). It is depressing (no one wants to think about going bankrupt). It will annoy big-money interests (financial services gave big money to pass the current bankruptcy laws). So why would he take it on in a high stakes campaign? First, he understands that bankruptcy policy is an integral piece of economic security for families. When all else goes wrong, bankruptcy is the ultimate safety net. . . . Second, Obama has history. He voted against the bankruptcy bill. He voted in favor of the amendments that would have eased the effects of the amendments. But his real history is deeper. He was a community organizer who saw first-hand the effects of aggressive lending. He was a state legislator who felt the impact of federal preemption on his ability to protect the citizens he represented.[45]

All said, by February 2008 Warren's independent consumer agency proposal had gained enough traction to win the endorsements of presidential candidates Obama and Clinton and the support of John Edwards (who by then had dropped out of the race in favor of Senator Obama).

The next step was to engage Republican policymakers. In March 2008, the Bush Treasury Department under Secretary Henry Paulson issued a Blueprint for a Modernized Financial Regulatory Structure. One element of the Treasury Blueprint was the creation of an umbrella Conduct of Business Regulatory Agency (CBRA) that would be "responsible for business conduct regulation, including consumer protection issues, across all types of firms, including the three types of federally chartered institutions."[46] Under the rubrics of "consistency" and "business competitiveness" (and without mentioning Warren or any of the other proposals for an independent consumer financial protection agency), the Treasury Blueprint said the CBRA would have responsibility for "the development of national standards for disclosures and business practices" for the entire range of retail financial products and services and for all federal and state licensed or chartered institutions.

Although the Republican Blueprint was plainly oriented toward structural efficiency, regulatory consolidation, and competitive business environments, it did share some features with the Warren proposal. The most important was an independent regulatory agency with a consumer protection mandate and powers of enforcement.

Some critics of the Paulson Blueprint, such as Damon Silvers of the AFL-CIO, were distrustful of proposals to carve up agencies like the Securities and Exchange Commission and the Commodity Futures Trading

Commission. "It was a formulation that was not appealing to me. It seemed to be a recipe for an overall weakening of financial regulation."[47] And though the Blueprint embodied other features Democrats opposed, the simple fact that the Bush administration had created a place for consumer protection in its overall program meant that Republicans could not totally ignore the issue and claim it was a pure invention of the Democrats.

Professor Warren: The COP

On November 14, 2008, Senate Majority Leader Harry Reid nominated Elizabeth Warren to serve on the Congressional Oversight Panel (COP or Panel), created to monitor implementation of the $700 billion Troubled Asset Relief Program (TARP). At the first meeting of the COP in late November, Warren was elected Chair. She served in that capacity until her resignation the following September. Damon Silvers, associate general counsel of the AFL-CIO was elected as deputy chair.

In a special report issued on January 29, 2009, the Panel majority made a very strong statement to the effect that problems of transparency and unfair and abusive market practices had destabilized American families, deluded investors with inaccurate risk signals, and contributed significantly to the financial meltdown. "Unfair dealings affect not only the specific transaction participants, but extend across entire markets, neighborhoods, socioeconomic groups, and whole industries. Even when only a limited number of families in one neighborhood have been the direct victims of a predatory lender, the entire neighborhood and even the larger community will suffer very real consequences from the resulting foreclosures. As those consequences spread, the entire financial system can be affected as well."[48]

The policy recommendations adopted by the Panel majority included Elizabeth Warren's original proposal for a single consumer regulator with a full panoply of rule-making, investigative, and enforcement authorities dedicated exclusively to a mission of consumer protection. The Panel majority also recommended that federal consumer protections serve as a floor, leaving space for individual states to implement stronger rules if they chose to do so. In policy circles, this is referred to as the "federal preemption issue."[49]

Although New York State Banking Commissioner Richard Nieman, House Speaker Nancy Pelosi's appointee to the COP, joined Warren and Silver in support of the January Report, he issued a separate comment opposing an independent consumer agency and proposing, instead, the integration of consumer protection and financial safety and soundness in a single regulator. He also came out in favor of the majority's recommendations with respect to preemption.[50]

The Republican appointees, Congressman Jeb Hensarling and former U.S. senator John Sununu, dissented from the report and inserted a joint statement opining that "[r]egulation can . . . harm consumers in the form of higher costs, less innovation, and fewer choices."[51] Their dissent also suggested that consumers deserved blame as much as new protections: "While the vast majority of borrowers continue to honor their commitments and pay their mortgages, for many of those who put little or no money down their mortgages became a 'heads I win, tails you lose' proposition."[52] Ultimately, the appointed Republic members opted against formulating any alternative to the majority's proposal.

Publication of the COP's Special Report two weeks into the Obama presidency sharpened and consolidated the specific mortgage and consumer credit recommendations that were the bedrock of Professor Warren's earlier work. The Panel gave particular priority to restoring the policy of legal deference for strong state consumer safeguards and to the creation of a single, fully competent consumer financial product safety regulator.

At the same time, the Panel expanded the scope of financial reform by combining consumer protection with programmatic provisions for investor safeguards, systemic risk regulation, and other substantial changes. By expanding its agenda to include the shadow lending system, executive compensation, and the special problem of institutions deemed "too big to fail," the Panel successfully enlarged the number of stakeholders who had a significant investment in its agenda.

Beyond reaching out to traditional consumer organizations, the Panel's strategy attracted the involvement of unions, civil rights organizations, fair lending organizations, community organizations, and other groups with a general commitment to progressive politics. Union interest was cemented out of concern regarding threats to the security of employee pensions, access to affordable mortgage credit, the safety of the financial system, and durable global macroeconomic conditions. Civil rights, community, and fair lending organizations were attracted out of deep anxiety for the effects of racial disparities in lending practices and the severe impact of predatory credit practices on the loss of wealth in communities of color.[53]

One of the points most central to Professor Warren's argument might, ironically, have presented a stumbling block to attracting broad-based support for the COP agenda. Her conclusion that abusive lending practices and the breakdown of financial protections were a problem of middle-class families might have put off some groups representing non–middle class communities. Civil rights, fair lending, and community groups could have balked at this characterization given the extensive evidence of racially disparate lending practices and outcomes dividing social classes—a phenomenon often referred to as the "dual credit market." While the Panel's Report recognized racial targeting and race-linked injury, it did so in a single sentence.[54] Furthermore, Professor Warren's *Democracy* paper did not mention race-based lending practices at all.

In a prior law review article, however, Warren was explicit about racial differences in financial practices and outcomes.[55] Although primarily reporting on racial differences in bankruptcies among middle-class families, she also turned to the credit sector. Among other things, she found: "The connection between predatory mortgage lending and race is unmistakable: predatory lenders target black and Hispanic homeowners. They are, of course, glad to take a subprime mortgage from anyone, but they redouble their efforts to saddle families they see as vulnerable with burdensome mortgages, and that includes black and Hispanic families."[56] Warren also quoted a loan officer involved in a Citibank case settled by the Federal Trade Commission who testified, "If someone appeared uneducated, inarticulate, was a minority, or was particularly old or young, I would try to include all the [additional costs] CitiFinancial offered." Racial steering was just one of many discriminatory practices cited by Professor Warren.

Janis Bowdler, director of the Wealth-Building Policy Project at the National Council of La Raza, the largest Hispanic civil rights advocacy organization, was asked whether she felt the middle-class narrative drowned out the case for discrimination against people of color—the dual credit market—and, if so, whether it had deterred groups like hers from providing full support for Professor Warren's proposal and the campaign to pass financial regulatory reform.

> Question: So when people like Elizabeth Warren are always talking about the middle class, does that bug you or do you see that as sort of an entrée into a discussion of issues more relevant to low-income people and minorities? Or do you see that term, "middle class," as encompassing everybody except for Wall Street?
>
> Answer: No, I see it as an entrée, and I think that Elizabeth Warren has established a lot of credibility among civil rights institutions and my peers, and so people trust her that it is an entrée and not simply lip service. If it were somebody else delivering a similar message, I'm not sure that they would get as much juice as Elizabeth Warren has.[57]

Next Step: The White House

The COP Special Report on Regulatory Reform was issued just days after Barack Obama assumed office on January 20, 2009. After the inauguration, work began almost immediately at the Treasury Department and elsewhere to produce comprehensive proposals for financial regulatory reform, including consumer protection. In the same time frame, Sen. Dick Durbin and six liberal cosponsors offered S. 566, the Financial Product Safety Commission Act of 2009. On March 10, with a generous tip of the hat to Elizabeth Warren for her conceptual outline of the bill, Durbin introduced the measure with the formal backing of over 50 consumer, labor, and civil rights groups ranging from the AFL-CIO, the Leadership Council on Civil Rights, and the Consumer Federation of America to the Kentucky Equal Justice Center.[58] S. 566 represented the first legislative proposal to establish a consumer financial protection agency to be introduced in Congress.

The following week, having been in the Oval Office for less than two months, the president went on *The Tonight Show with Jay Leno* to announce that consumer financial protection would be part of his coming comprehensive "finreg" proposals.[59] Appropriating Warren's vivid image of the exploding toaster, Obama literally took consumer protection to the country in front of a late night audience of over 5 million people. The week after, on March 26, Treasury Secretary Tim Geithner formally told the House Financial Services Committee that the administration's proposals would be forthcoming within weeks.[60] They ultimately arrived on June 17.

Chapter 3

The Magic Moment for Reform

It would take more than a compelling message and messenger to translate Elizabeth Warren's idea of a consumer financial protection agency into reality. Once before, in the early 1970s, consumer advocates were confident that the combination of a Democrat-controlled Congress and a supportive president would result in a new watchdog agency for consumers (although one quite different from the CFPB), only to see their hopes dashed. The advocates were led by Ralph Nader, then one of the most admired people in the United States. On several occasions, a bill was nearly passed, but effective lobbying by the business community ultimately proved too much.[1] Fast forwarding to 2009, advocates of a consumer financial protection agency knew that they faced a heavy lift.

Certainly, the planets seemed aligned for the CFPB. There was an economy brought to its knees by the financial sector; intense pain among workers, investors, homeowners, and consumers; a new president who stood for change; and a Democratic Congress raring to notch some victories.[2] Moreover, advocates and their congressional allies had momentum from a recent legislative success—the passage of the Credit CARD Act in the spring of 2009.

Nevertheless, establishing something like the CFPB was not going to be a trifling task. First, it would take overcoming the opposition of, arguably, the strongest political force in the country—the financial services industry.[3] Second, the advocates of financial reform were drawn mainly from social movements that had been in decline. Third, supporters of reform were going to have to compete for attention and resources with advocates for other important goals, especially President Obama's top priority, health insurance reform. Finally, advocates would have to counteract any implication that consumer gullibility and irresponsibility were the root causes of the financial meltdown.

F.I.R.E. Power

The U.S. economy has become dominated by the so-called F.I.R.E. industries—finance, insurance, and real estate.[4] Whereas jobs and profits once came primarily from manufacturing, the U.S. economy has become increasingly reliant on the financial sector for growth. As part of the shift to a service economy, jobs in the financial sector grew from 7.46 million in 1998 to 8.15 million in 2008, peaking at 8.35 million at the end of 2006, according to the U.S. Bureau of Labor Statistics.[5]

Employment data understate the economic importance of the F.I.R.E. industries. At their peak in late 2001, the financial services industries accounted for almost 45 percent of all U.S. corporate profits, according to the Department of Commerce's Bureau of Economic Analysis.[6] The percentage declined thereafter but remained over 25 percent for the decade, with the exception of the depths of the recession from late 2007 to early 2009. By the fourth quarter of 2010, the percentage had bounced back up to 29 percent, or $57.7 billion in profits.[7]

Economic dominance wrought political power.[8] Back in the 1970s and 1980s, the brokerage firm E. F. Hutton ran a TV commercial in which conversation at a dinner party ceased when one person mentioned the name of his broker. The tagline was: "When E. F. Hutton talks, people listen." The same can be said about Goldman Sachs, the Bank of America, or Morgan Stanley. When they talk, congressmen listen. The same applies to financial trade associations such as the American Bankers Association, Mortgage Bankers Association, Alternative Investment Management Association (for the hedge funds), American Financial Services Association, and Financial Services Roundtable.

According to data compiled by OpenSecrets.org, the financial industry—broadly conceived—spent nearly a half billion dollars lobbying in 2008 at the federal and state levels.[9] All this spending did not include campaign contributions, which accounted for another half billion dollars in the 2008 election cycle.[10] According to OpenSecrets.org: "The financial sector is far and away the largest source of campaign contributions to federal candidates and parties. . . . The sector contributes generous sums to both parties. . . . The sector gave at least 55 percent of their contributions to the GOP from 1996 to 2004, but actually gave a slight majority of their donations to Democrats in the 2008 cycle."[11]

The traditional nexus of the financial industry's political clout was the House Financial Services Committee. It was known as the "cash committee" because serving on it guaranteed copious campaign contributions for Republicans and Democrats alike.[12] The result, according to U.S. PIRG's Ed Mierzwinski, was that for years, consumer advocates couldn't lose a vote in this committee—they couldn't get a vote at all.[13] After the 2008 election, the Democratic leadership used the committee "as an ATM for vulnerable rookies" from conservative-leaning districts.[14] When the 71-person committee convenes, members sit in tiered rows, with newer members in the front rows. The result, according to veteran committee member Luis Gutierrez (D-Ill.), was an "unreliable bottom row" (and a second row that was not much better) when it came to voting out financial reform legislation.[15]

The influence of the financial industries on the Senate Committee on Banking, Housing, and Urban Affairs was also considerable. Taken as a whole, members of this committee received 2.3 times the amount in campaign contributions than members of the Senate as a whole in the 11 months after the 2008 election.[16] The chairman of the Committee, Christopher Dodd (D-Conn.), would eventually play a sufficiently key role to merit his name being in the title of the final bill, but advocates of financial reform did not initially consider his commitment to be rock solid. Some may have been influenced by Ralph Nader's earlier characterization of Dodd as the "Senator from Aetna" because of the insurance companies headquartered in his state.[17] And if Dodd was the senator from Aetna, then his Democratic colleague Tim Johnson (D-S.Dak.) was the "Senator from Citibank," since South Dakota's lack of a usury law regarding interest has made it the favored address for credit card companies.[18] Charles Schumer (D-N.Y.), a leading liberal, was also sympathetic to the concerns of his Wall Street constituents and the leading recipient of their campaign contributions during the 2009–2010 election cycle.[19] The defection of just one or two Democrats in the Senate Banking Committee could doom a financial reform bill.

During the two decades preceding the financial bubble's bursting in 2007, the financial sector was supremely powerful. No president, congressman, or regulator wanted to rain on its parade. Actually, government officials were blowing up the balloons. And when the parade veered violently off course, the government was there with $700 billion in roadside assistance in the form of the Troubled Asset Relief Program. What were the chances government would fully commit to reining in Big Finance having just bailed it out so generously?

Just in case the voice of the financial industry wasn't loud enough, companies led by Goldman Sachs built a revolving door of influence through which their executives took top posts in government agencies such as the Treasury Department and the Securities and Exchange Commission.[20] The movement from business into government was common in the legislative branch as well. As of December 2009, 16 of the 86 staffers of the House Financial Services Committee—most of them senior lawyers—had previously been lobbyists.[21] More often, the door swung the other way, with former government officials exploiting their knowledge and contacts as current employees of financial companies.[22] A 2010 study by Public Citizen and the Center for Responsive Politics found that investment firms and other financial companies employed almost 1500 former lawmakers, congressional aides, and executive branch employees as lobbyists just since January 2009.[23] It's called a revolving door because the process is continuous. According to House member Brad Miller (D-N.C.), "They tend to go out and come back and go out again. It really does create a set of financial incentives, whether conscious or not."[24]

Above and beyond the substantial political power of the financial sector, any effort to create the CFPB would have to face the additional clout of two trans-industry organizations, the U.S. Chamber of Commerce and the Business Roundtable.[25] The Chamber alone spent almost $92 million on lobbying during 2008. Only a small portion of the 2008 spending addressed financial issues, but there was nothing subtle about the Chamber's feeling about the CFPB. Ryan McKee, a senior official at the Chamber said, "We are going to kill the [CFPB] bill."[26]

David on His Back

The image of David vs. Goliath has become a cliché in describing battles between modestly funded and staffed public interest organizations and powerful corporations. In the fight over establishing the Consumer Financial Protection Agency, the image of Goliath that was commonly invoked to describe the F.I.R.E. industries was apt enough, but the advocates of the Agency were not young shepherd boys dressed in simple tunics. For the most part, they were aging professionals in business suits who had grown accustomed to working pragmatically for incremental change. The social movements they represented—consumer, fair housing, labor—were waning in terms of their passion, momentum, and public appeal. A major go-for-broke campaign might exceed their capabilities. On the other hand, winning such a campaign might be a chance to regain relevance.

The consumer movement's heyday was the late 1960s and early 1970s, a period during which advocacy efforts resulted in the establishment of new agencies and the passage of dozens of landmark laws.[27] This spurt of activity was actually the third time in a century that consumer activists had prompted major policy advances. The first era of the consumer movement was part of the Progressive Era at the turn of the 20th century. The second occurred between the two World Wars.[28] If the roughly 30-year interval between each of these eras has any significance, a fourth era of consumer activism should have occurred before 2009, but no one was holding their breath.[29] The days when Ralph Nader attracted young law students to Washington, D.C., to serve as "Nader's Raiders" were long past. As of early 2009, the heads of the three major consumer organizations—Consumers Union, Consumer Federation of America, and Public Citizen—averaged 68 years of age.[30]

The vigor of the fair housing/community reinvestment movement was also open to question. Passing landmark legislation, such as the Fair Housing Act of 1968 and the Community Reinvestment Act of 1977, had given way to the less glamorous work of handling complaints and ensuring adequate enforcement. Fair housing and community reinvestment advocates were under constant barrage by critics who saw their goals as obsolete and their methods as counterproductive.[31] These organizations were put further on the defensive by a series of scandals involving the Association of Community Organizations for Reform Now (ACORN), the final one resulting in the organization's dissolution.[32]

The historic power and accomplishments of the labor movement dwarfed those of the consumer and fair housing movements, making its decline that much more dramatic. In 1970, the influence of organized labor was manifest in the passage of the Occupational Safety and Health Act. Eleven years later, though, President Reagan was able to break the air traffic controllers' strike. While it is important not to read too much into this one loss, the decline in union membership tells a more objective story. Union membership in the United States declined by 360,000 between 1970 and 1980, a drop that continued unabated.[33] Between 1983 and 2010, union membership among men fell by almost one-half.[34] When commentators spoke of the decline of the U.S. middle class, they typically pointed to the loss of private sector union jobs.[35]

To put it mildly, the condition of the various nonprofit organizations that would have to lead any effort to establish a consumer financial protection agency was not optimal. They faced an opponent in the F.I.R.E. industries whose public image had reached a new low in 2009 but whose economic and political resources were largely undiminished.[36] The public interest advocates might have been excused if they had focused on winning a limited or purely symbolic victory. The consumer organizations could have waited to see what would become of the Durbin-Delahunt bill to create a Financial Product Safety Commission. The fair housing groups could have continued their attempts to strengthen the Community Reinvestment Act, while labor organizations could have devoted themselves to passage of the Employee Free Choice Act. The battle with the F.I.R.E. giant, however, was both an outsized risk and a momentous opportunity. If won, the fight could re-energize or even re-define these flagging movements.

Issue Clutter

The U.S. Congress is typically incapable of taking decisive action on one major policy issue, let alone multiple ones. The Obama administration and the 111th Congress made health insurance reform their signature issue, "sucking the air out of the room" for other hot issues such as immigration reform, climate change, and financial reform.[37] The bill that eventually became the Dodd-Frank Wall Street Reform and Consumer Protection Act was officially introduced on December 9, 2009. This was two months *after* the House of Representatives had passed the Patient Protection and Affordable Care Act, and only two weeks before the Senate passed it.[38]

The suffocating effect of the health insurance debate on consideration of financial reform was not just a matter of competing demands on the time of government officials. The health insurance debate also dominated the agendas of many of the same groups that were the logical advocates for financial reform. This applied especially to the labor unions. Bill Ragen, a veteran organizer for the Service Employees International Union, remarked: "There was a balancing act, trying to do two things at once—health care reform and financial reform. We had to weigh how much we were going to push Senator So-and-so on this as opposed to that. And I would have to admit that, although I would have liked my campaign [on financial reform] to get all the attention, health care really was a bigger deal for us."[39]

The same problem of allocating scarce political resources faced other large organizational members of the AFR coalition, such as Consumers Union, the world's largest consumer organization, and the nonprofit behemoth AARP. In the case of smaller organizations like the National Council of La Raza, the resource pinch was even tighter. Janis Bowdler, deputy director of La Raza's Wealth-Building Policy Project, described the difficulty of finding the resources to simultaneously lobby for health insurance reform, immigration reform, and financial reform: "There were some tough months in terms of mustering all of our internal resources. Sitting at the

AFR table, we heard there were at least a couple of our peers who were in a similar position where their campaign staff, their organizers, maybe even their media team were pulled for health care reform and had to finish that before they could focus fully on Dodd-Frank."[40] Until health care reform was a done deal, it was going to be a challenge for advocates of financial reform to get attention from the media. Advocates were either going to have to be very patient or find a way to cut through the issue clutter.

Blame Game

Overcoming the opposition of the F.I.R.E. industries and competing for attention with other worthy issues may have been the most obvious barriers to creation of a consumer financial protection agency, but there was a more subtle obstacle as well. The country was embroiled in a debate about the causes of the mortgage meltdown that sparked the broader financial crisis, and not everyone agreed that consumers were innocent victims. Advocates offered a narrative in which unscrupulous brokers and lenders offered consumers toxic mortgage products that brokers and lenders knew would blow up in the face of consumers if housing prices ever stabilized, let alone fell. The mortgage lenders, in turn, had an unlimited line of credit from Wall Street firms that craved mortgages—any mortgages—that could be bundled into securities and sold to investors.[41]

There was a competing narrative in which consumers, while not the primary cause of the mortgage mess, were far from blameless. According to this narrative, consumers had been offered virtually free money and had forgotten the TANSTAAFL principle—there ain't no such thing as a free lunch. Homebuyers were eager to believe assurances from brokers that rising home prices would make virtually any mortgage an affordable, good investment. Credit card users had focused on the monthly minimum payment rather than their outstanding balance. In short, this narrative had consumers taking the bait and forgetting about basic economic reality.

The view that consumers deserved a healthy share of the blame for the financial crisis was typically articulated by people on the right side of the political spectrum. Conservative commentator Sarah Elizabeth "S.E." Cupp wrote in October, 2008:

> Almost everyone, it seems, is afraid to point a finger in the mirror—and, at least in part, that's where it needs to go. The role of consumers in the housing crisis has been largely ignored by the candidates and their Washington contemporaries. And it's a huge oversight. We are overextended. We grew

accustomed to getting something for close to nothing. We counted on housing values to rise indefinitely. Just as our government kept borrowing from foreign sources to fund its profligate spending, we stopped buying only what we could actually pay for.[42]

Cupp approvingly cited Eric Salzman, a blogger on financial matters: "The borrowers have to accept that they were part of the problem. Many subprime borrowers, especially in 2005, 2006 and 2007, were putting little to nothing down on homes that they had to know they couldn't afford. These people may not have been finance whizzes, but they weren't mentally incompetent."[43]

Some academics also pinned the blame on consumers. The libertarian economist and best-selling author Thomas Sowell wrote that people "were *not* trapped by circumstances beyond their control but . . . chose risky ways of getting money and lost."[44] New York University economics professor Richard Sylla, speaking on the television program *Nightly Business Report* on October 30, 2008, said, "The American public is responsible [for the financial crisis] . . . because the American public . . . went on this borrowing binge. You know there have to be two parties to a loan transaction. Somebody says yes I agree to borrow it and the other person says I agree to lend."[45]

Several years earlier, in the unsuccessful fight to resist anticonsumer changes to the bankruptcy laws, consumer advocates faced a similar challenge of avoiding a "blame-the-consumer" mentality. Then, advocates of leaving the bankruptcy laws largely unchanged argued that the majority of bankruptcies were due to factors beyond an individual's control, such as illness, unemployment, or divorce.[46] Those favoring major changes in the laws portrayed bankruptcy filers as deadbeats who imposed the equivalent of a $400 annual tax on responsible consumers.[47] According to Ed Mierzwinksi of U.S. PIRG, "The bankruptcy fight was difficult for us because the industry made a very compelling case . . . that people who don't pay their bills are irresponsible. I don't agree with that, but it sells on Capitol Hill and with the public."[48]

Advocates for the CFPB faced the challenge of winning an ideological battle about the role of consumers in the mortgage debacle and thereby avoiding a replay of the bankruptcy campaign failure. They had to make sure that recognition of any consumer role in mortgage abuses did not obscure the far greater role of lenders and thereby derail reform. Advocates of a new agency would have to rebut any claim that consumer greed, addiction to credit, and willingness to just walk away from loans gone sour were the root causes of the financial meltdown and paint any such arguments as blaming the victim.[49] Conversely, if advocates of a consumer financial protection agency could win this argument, making the case for a new agency would be that much easier.

Winning Is Possible: Lessons of the Credit CARD Act Campaign

The possibility of overcoming the political muscle of the financial lobby, cutting through the clutter of competing issues, and keeping opponents from pinning consumers with the blame for financial problems became apparent in early 2009. For decades, consumer advocates and their allies had been decrying a number of practices in the credit card industry but getting nowhere. The list of anticonsumer practices of credit card issuers was long. There were garden-variety irritations associated with annual fees, late fees, over-the-limit fees, cash advance fees, and balance transfer fees. There were outrageous practices as well. Under "universal default," one credit card issuer would increase a person's interest rate because of a missed payment or other misstep with respect to *another* creditor. To make things worse, when a person's interest rate increased, the higher interest rate might be applied to the entire existing balance, not just any new charges.

The various credit card industry "tricks and traps" turned Elizabeth Warren from a researcher on the subject of bankruptcy to a full-fledged consumer advocate. With Warren's help, reporter Lowell Bergman pulled the pants down on the credit card industry in a 2004 *Frontline* television program.[50] However, public anger regarding credit card practices had not yet reached a boiling point. It was virtually impossible to get a sympathetic hearing from a congressional committee. Long-time consumer advocate Ed Mierzwinski recounts this story:

> We got a hearing in 2001 but only because [Mike] Oxley [R-OH] owed the ranking member, John LaFalce [D-NY], a favor. [On an earlier bill] LaFalce had agreed that the Democrats wouldn't be obnoxious and have an all-day or two-day markup, which is very possible on a seventy-member committee. So in return Oxley said, "Well, okay, what's your chip?" And LaFalce says, "I want to have a hearing on credit cards." The credit card industry apparently went ballistic and supposedly cut off—again, this is all third-hand—Oxley's campaign contributions for three months or six months as punishment for having a hearing.[51]

By 2008, the credit card industry was on the defensive, and consumers had found a champion in Representative Carolyn Maloney (D-N.Y.).

Representative Maloney introduced the Credit Cardholders' Bill of Rights in February 2008 and fought hard for its passage. Using her position as chair of the Financial Institutions and Consumer Credit Subcommittee of the House Financial Services Committee, she held hearings to high-light the need for reform. Instead of inviting a token consumer represen-tative to testify, Maloney invited a cavalcade of consumer advocates. On March 13, 2008, Elizabeth Warren had her turn.[52] A month later, Ed Mierzwinski of U.S. PIRG, Travis Plunkett of the Consumer Federation of America, and Linda Sherry of Consumer Action got their chance to speak.[53] Industry abuses had become so numerous, pervasive, and outrageous that spokesmen for the industry didn't dare argue that the problems were the result of consumers who lacked the self-discipline to pay their bills on time. Instead, industry spokesmen had to fall back on the argument that any restrictions on its conduct would drive up the overall cost of credit and drive low-income consumers into the arms of payday lenders and other "fringe bankers."[54]

Maloney's bill passed the House overwhelmingly in September 2008. The Senate never took a vote on the bill, knowing that President George W. Bush was opposed to it.[55] In December 2008, the Federal Reserve (in co-operation with Office of Thrift Supervision and the National Credit Union Administration) belatedly finalized a set of rules aimed at curbing credit card company abuses.[56] The Fed's action was likely a last ditch effort to retain its regulatory authority.[57] Congressman Barney Frank had issued a warning to the Fed in June, 2007. He told a member of its board of gover-nors: "With regard to your rulemaking authority: use it or lose it."[58]

For the 111th Congress that convened in early 2009, Representative Ma-loney had a new and renamed version of her bill—the Credit Card Ac-countability, Responsibility and Disclosure Act (Credit CARD Act). When it came to lobbying this time, consumer groups were part of a broad coali-tion. They were joined by labor unions (AFL-CIO, SEIU), fair lending and civil rights groups (ACORN, National Community Reinvestment Coali-tion, NAACP National Leadership Conference on Civil Rights), and even the National Small Business Association as supporters of the legislation.[59] The Credit CARD Act was passed by the House in April 2009, followed by the Senate three weeks later. President Obama happily signed the Credit Card Accountability, Responsibility and Disclosure Act (Credit CARD Act) on May 22, 2009.[60]

Consumer advocates drew several lessons from the passage of the Credit CARD Act. First, at least one segment of the financial services lobby could be defeated. This was a revelation in itself. Not since passage of the Fair

Debt Collection Practices Act in 1978 had the might of the financial sector been effectively challenged.[61] The victory over the credit companies in early 2009 suggested a new game, one in which the financial industry did not hold all the cards.

Second, consumer advocates had potential allies who might be willing to work in a formal coalition. In February 2007, an organization was launched—Americans for Fairness in Lending (AFFIL)—that brought together consumer, civil rights, faith-based, and grassroots organizations to "raise awareness of abusive credit and lending practices and to call for re-regulation of the industry . . . using a unified and consistent national message."[62] AFFIL's approximately 20-member organization not only included the usual suspects from the consumer movement (Consumer Action, Consumer Federation of America, Consumers Union, National Association of Consumer Advocates, Consumer Law Center, Public Citizen, and U.S. PIRG) but also champions of low-income communities, fair housing groups, and organized labor.

AFFIL folded its tent in September 2010. Located in Boston rather than Washington, D.C., AFFIL was never in a position to lead the lobbying effort for credit card reform. It did, however, shelter a wide variety of organizations under its umbrella, enlist the analytic support and collaboration of academics, and help underscore the viability of a coalition approach to financial reform.

The final lesson for advocates of the Credit CARD Act experience was less foreseeable. Rather than validating a piecemeal approach to financial reform in which specific abuses in specific industries were addressed by specific legislation, the campaign yielded a different conclusion. Advocates realized that it had taken them decades to successfully address an accretion of credit card–related problems. The resulting legislation, which was only an amendment to the ancient Truth in Lending Act, had 40 sections, each taming a particular abuse, requiring a disclosure, or mandating a study. There had to be a better way than playing what U.S. PIRG's Ed Mierzwinski described as "a game of Whack-A-Mole" in which specific abuses are addressed, only to find that the lending industry has already figured out ways of nullifying any new protections.[63] Plus, if it took this much lobbying work to defeat an industry that virtually everyone hated, what would be the chances of success in taking on banks, insurers, investment firms, or real estate companies? Advocates concluded that they needed a more "structural" solution in the form of an agency that could respond quickly to both abuses themselves and industry efforts to evade new rules.

What If You Had a Party and Everyone Showed Up?

With the election of President Obama in November of 2008, it was clear to both labor and consumer organizations that they needed to be ready to push for the changes they believed in. Initially, labor and consumer groups met in parallel fashion with respect to financial reform. The two types of groups had collaborated informally on issues such as credit card rights, foreclosure prevention, and investor protection, but they were hardly in lock step.[64] When it came to organized labor's top legislative goal, enactment of the Employee Free Choice Act, the most important consumer organizations—notably Consumers Union and the Consumer Federation of America—chose to sit on the sidelines.[65] The two movements weren't even working together on health care reform. Mainstream consumer organizations (with the exception of U.S. PIRG and the National Consumers League) were not members of the Health Care for America NOW!, the coalition through which organized labor expended most of its energy toward passage of the Patient Protection and Affordable Care Act.

Building on a limited history of working together, small, informal meetings took place involving leaders of labor and consumer organizations in late 2008 and early 2009. According to Gary Kalman, director of U.S. PIRG's federal affairs office in Washington, D.C., "there was a point at which Ed [Mierzwinski] knew that SEIU was interested in trying to pull together a larger coalition, and so he invited Steve Abrecht from SEIU to our offices. They had a conversation about trying to bring together groups that had not really worked together before."[66] Barbara Roper, director of investor protection at the Consumer Federation of America, and Maureen Thompson, a consultant with close ties to AARP, had experience working with labor leaders and facilitated additional meetings.

Maureen Thompson recalls having functioned as a sort of marriage broker:

> Very early on when it became obvious that there was going to be an effort to do a Wall Street reform [and] consumer protection bill, I was asked [by someone at SEIU] to start the process of bringing together the variety of groups that would be interested in financial reform broadly defined. . . . I tend to kind of work across them because I do work for a number of different clients. But because our work can often be done in silos, the concern was that, with such a powerful financial services industry working to basically kill everything as a corporate community through the Chamber of Commerce and others, it would be far more effective to have all of the organizations that

have any interest in this issue working together. . . . And that was really the early stages and the genesis of Americans for Financial Reform.[67]

Eventually there were two pivotal meetings, both of which took place at AFL-CIO headquarters. Ed Mierzwinski sent out an email to a variety of advocacy groups. Without any real follow-up, representatives of about 50 organizations showed up. A second meeting took place shortly thereafter, and it was standing-room only. Elizabeth Warren and John Sweeney, then president of the AFL-CIO, addressed the attendees. It was at this point that the participants realized that a broad coalition was possible, essentially marking the birth of what would become Americans for Financial Reform. David Arkush of Public Citizen attended the first organizing meeting. He recalls:

> The turnout for the initial meeting was incredible, easily filling this very, very large room. It was surprisingly easy to get everybody to agree that we needed something that hadn't existed before. We needed a very broad-based coalition to get people out of their silos because there was nobody who had enough expertise on the full range of issues to do a good job by themselves. We needed a broad range of constituents, and we needed a broad range of expertise. We needed as much organizing power as we could muster because it was gonna be a tough fight.[68]

The second organizing meeting was larger than the first and was energized by the presence of Elizabeth Warren. Susan Weinstock, who was about to join the Consumer Federation of America as its financial reform campaign director, was not at the meeting but strongly approved of the cross-movement collaboration that was taking shape:

> I thought it was awesome. I thought it was great. In my years doing utility advocacy I had tried to get the unions to work with us, and I could rarely do it. So I was excited that this was a great coalition of people all working towards the same goals. And since it was such a massive undertaking, financial reform with all its various parts, you needed that breadth of folks to cover all the different issues.[69]

It was one thing for advocates to have energy, talent, goodwill among themselves, and the political winds at their back. It was another to have an explicit set of goals, the lack of which often dooms broad coalitions.[70] In this instance, not everyone was immediately convinced that the people in the room shared the same goal. This was likely due, at least in part, to the "silo effect" whereby Washington interest and advocacy groups tend to specialize in particular issues and to work in semi-isolation from one another. In this case, for instance, the AFL-CIO focused on issues of corporate governance, derivatives and shareholder rights; AFSCME was especially interested in fiduciary duties in conjunction with its pension funds; and many of the consumer and civil rights groups had a history of specializing in credit markets and consumer regulation.[71] Thus, identifying shared goals would be a challenge.

Lisa Rice of the National Fair Housing Alliance (NFHA) expressed the trepidations of one of several constituencies within the coalition—groups that traditionally represented low-income and minority communities.

> All the groups in the room were a coalition with a small *C*, and we [NFHA] were trying to figure out if we wanted to become a coalition with a capital *C*. We said very pointedly at that meeting that our goal remained unchanged: we wanted to eliminate the two-tiered financial system [in which low-income consumers pay higher prices] that has existed in America forever, and that if that wasn't a main goal of the entire coalition, that we would not be participants in the broader coalition. We would just keep our civil rights coalition that had already existed for years and years. The other groups— CFA, U.S. PIRG—and Elizabeth Warren said, "Absolutely. This is a major goal. We have to eliminate the unfair sort of separate-and-unequal financial system. Everybody is on board with that. It will be explicitly stated in the policy document that forms the coalition." That's "coalition" with a big *C*.[72]

In the search for unifying and explicit goals, Steve Abrecht of the SEIU recalls recognizing that manna had already fallen from heaven on January 29, 2009, in the form of the general principles for financial reform articulated in the Special Report on Regulatory Reform of the Congressional Oversight Panel (COP).[73] The five-person panel was headed by Elizabeth Warren, with the AFL-CIO's Damon Silvers as its deputy chairperson. In early April, Abrecht told Ed Mierzwinski and Gary Kalman to "forget about drawing up a mission statement and just take Elizabeth Warren's road map and say this is what we agree on."[74] Abrecht was referring to the eight general recommendations contained in the COP Special Report. The result was a "Call to Action" issued on April 8 and signed by more than a hundred consumer, labor, civil rights, community, and responsible investing organizations. The document called for "bold action" to deal with "a full-blown global economic crisis."[75] The Call did not refer explicitly to a consumer financial protection agency, but the Call provided indirect support because the COP Special Report pitched the creation of a "single federal regulator for consumer credit products."

Magic Moment

The spring of 2009 was a magic moment for advocates of financial reform. The economy was in shambles, and Democrats controlled the presidency and Congress. Advocates in the consumer, fair lending, and labor movements had different priorities with respect to financial reform, but they recognized the power of a consolidated effort. All advocates needed now to advance the cause of financial reform, including creation of a new agency to protect consumers, was a lobbying vehicle and someone to steer it.

Chapter 4

Activists Need Leaders, Too

In June 2009, history came as close to repeating itself as it ever does. In both 1978 and 2009, a group of progressive organizations created a formal coalition to take on the most powerful industry in the country in response to a national economic crisis. Both coalitions were headed by a woman trained in community organizing. Indeed, both coalitions were led by the *same* woman, Heather Booth.

On June 16, 2009, the launching of a new organization, Americans for Financial Reform (AFR), was announced via a call-in press conference. Its stated goal was to "fix our financial sector and make sure it's working for all Americans." Representing AFR were its executive director, Heather Booth, as well as three members of its 18-member steering committee (Jim Carr of the National Community Reinvestment Coalition, Rob Johnson of the Roosevelt Institute, and George Goehl of National People's Action). Lisa Donner, while not at the conference, was aboard as AFR's deputy director.[1]

A Veteran Leader

Heather Booth may be the most accomplished community organizer you have never heard of. Her life is a short course in the various progressive social movements from the 1960s to the present.[2]

Booth (née Tobis) was born in 1945 in Mississippi, where her father was stationed with the army during World War II, but spent most of her youth in the New York City area.[3] What propelled Booth toward a career devoted to the pursuit of social justice? She acknowledges the role of her family, religious heritage, and childhood experiences. Her parents believed in equality and "taking action for what is right."[4] Her Jewish background reinforced these values. Booth reports wanting, as a youth, to become a rabbi but being told that women were ineligible.[5]

Her early years were spent in Brooklyn, but Booth went to a suburban high school where she felt a bit out of place. She was active in school clubs, but she quit a sorority when she realized the members "didn't accept anybody who wasn't conventionally pretty. I'd been on cheerleading, and I quit that because they weren't letting blacks onto the team. I was ready for the sixties, and the sixties weren't here."[6]

Booth enrolled at the University of Chicago in 1963. She chose the school, in part, because it had no sororities and college sports didn't dominate the scene.[7] As a university student, she headed the Chicago Area Friends of the Student Non-Violent Coordinating Committee.[8] In support of the civil rights struggle in the South and in Chicago, she helped organize the Chicago "Freedom Day" school boycott to protest against segregated and inferior schools for African Americans as well as tenant strikes.[9] The Chicago school boycott, which saw roughly half of the children in the Chicago public schools stay home and attend classes in churches instead, was a mirror image of the protests by Southern whites in response to court-ordered school desegregation.[10]

Given the temper of the times, the logical next step for the socially conscious Booth was to head to Mississippi and participate in "Freedom Summer" in 1964.[11] The Freedom Summer project was a response to the historical denial of rights to blacks, especially their exclusion from voting. The goal of the project was to register as many blacks as possible. Participation in the project was deadly for some—notably, Northerners Michael Schwerner and Andrew Goodman who were murdered in Neshoba County along with Mississippian James Chaney.[12] Booth, fortunately, returned safely to the University of Chicago.

In 1965, Booth's sophomore year, an ex-boyfriend told her that his sister, who also had been in Mississippi, was pregnant and needed an abortion. Booth contacted the Medical Committee for Human Rights, a team of physicians who supported the civil rights movement, and was able to put the young woman in touch with Dr. T.R.M. Howard, a leading civil rights activist. Coincidentally, Dr. Howard was from Mississippi but had left in 1955 under pressure from the Ku Klux Klan.[13] Over the following months, Booth received additional pleas for help. Eventually, she told people that they should ask for "Jane" when they called.[14] With the help of other women, Jane eventually helped approximately 11,000 women obtain abortions in the days before the 1973 *Roe v. Wade* Supreme Court ruling legalized abortion nationwide.[15]

Booth met her eventual husband Paul Booth in 1966 at—where else—a sit-in against the Vietnam War. Paul wasn't just another college kid who opposed the war. He had been an early leader of Students for a Democratic Society (SDS), serving as its vice president.[16] In 1965 Paul helped organize the first antiwar march on Washington, D.C.[17] That same year, he led a sit-in at Chase Manhattan Bank to protest its business activities in South Africa and thereby its complicity in apartheid.[18] By 1966, Paul was national secretary of SDS, working out of the organization's headquarters in Chicago. After meeting Heather at a protest, the two decided their stars, values, and commitments were aligned; marriage and family followed soon thereafter.[19]

Heather Booth was one of several feminists who found an incongruity in the low status of women in the socially conscious movements to protect workers from exploitation, advance civil rights, and end the Vietnam War.[20] At the sit-in at which Heather first met Paul, she and Naomi Weinstein shared their unease about how few women were speaking.[21] They were giving voice to a general alienation felt by women in the face of patronizing and even hostile treatment at SDS meetings and other meetings of New Left organizations.[22] As Booth's friend Amy Kesselman observed, women in the New Left were tired of "feeling judged and humiliated by the male heavies."[23] Booth felt that if women and men were going to work together for a better society, they also needed to change the culture of the movement so that women were treated as equals.[24] As a first step, Booth and about nine other women formed their own organization, the West Side Group.[25]

In 1969, many of the same women, including Booth, founded the Chicago Women's Liberation Union (CWLU). The Jane abortion counseling service that Booth had originated was folded into the CWLU, alongside campaigns against sexism in employment, health care, and sports. CWLU also championed the rights of lesbians.[26] The CWLU remained active until 1977.

The various strands of Heather Booth's political activism came together twice during the 1970s—first with the establishment of the Midwest Academy and later in the creation of the Citizen Labor Energy Coalition. Booth was a guiding force in both organizations, and, in retrospect, both experiences set the stage for her direction many years later of Americans for Financial Reform.

Midwest Academy

The establishment of the Midwest Academy in 1973 stemmed from the community organizing activities of both Booths in the Chicago area, as well as the ideas of master organizer Saul Alinsky that suffused that city.[27] The

Booths were instrumental in the formation of the Chicago Citizens Action Program. The organization was initially titled the Campaign Against Pollution. Its first campaign was in 1970 and targeted the filthy air emanating from a Commonwealth Edison power plant. The result was enactment of stricter emissions standards by the city.[28] Flushed with its success, the organization changed its name to Citizens Action Program in 1971 "to reflect its organizational growth and its advocacy of other issues like redlining."[29] The organization's signature achievement occurred in 1973 when it helped stop construction in Chicago of a cross-town expressway, Mayor Richard J. Daley's pet project.[30]

Convinced of the power of citizen activism but unsure about some aspects of Alinsky's training organization (the Industrial Areas Foundation), Heather Booth (with Steve Max) founded the Midwest Academy in 1973. The purpose of the academy was to train leaders and staff members of community organizations, reinforce interorganizational and intermovement cooperation, and, in the long run, build a broad-based movement in support of the American goals of freedom, democracy, and justice for all.[31] Booth provided the initial funding for the academy; it came from a successful lawsuit against a former employer who had fired her for complaining about the conditions under which the company's secretaries worked.[32] Within 10 years, more than 16,000 people had attended training sessions provided by the academy.[33]

Three defining features of the Midwest Academy approach are the pursuit of economic justice, formation of coalitions in which member organizations retain a great deal of autonomy, and a willingness to work through mainstream political channels (including elections).[34] The Illinois Public Action Council (IPAC), an organization that was assisted by the academy, exemplified these features. Launched in 1976, IPAC had 130 member organizations by 1984.[35] IPAC sought both immediate economic benefits for working- and middle-class people, such as lower utility bills and taxes, as well as the longer-term advantages of electing candidates sympathetic to these constituencies. Decades later, Americans for Financial Reform under Heather Booth's leadership would embody the same principles of seeking economic benefits, building a flexible coalition, and seeking change through traditional political channels.

Citizen/Labor Energy Coalition

By 1977, with the Midwest Academy operating smoothly, Heather Booth was looking for another challenge. "After exploring interest in a national coalition on jobs, which didn't catch on, and later a coalition on the military budget, which also failed to raise much excitement, she settled on the issue of energy."[36] She would create a national coalition of unions, civil rights organizations, farmers, churches, senior citizens groups, and local community groups around the issue of affordable energy. The result was the Citizen/Labor Energy Coalition (C/LEC), with Booth as its executive director.

The story of C/LEC has been told elsewhere.[37] For our purposes, what's interesting is the coalition format and leadership of Heather Booth as precursors of Americans for Financial Reform. In both cases, the country faced an economic crisis. During the 1970s, the United States (and most of the world) experienced two major increases in the price of oil and the loss of its ready availability. The first price shock, in 1973, was due to an oil embargo organized by many of the major Arab oil-producing countries in response to their displeasure with Western support of Israel during the Yom Kippur War.[38] The second oil shock occurred in 1979 when the Iranian Revolution disrupted global oil supplies. Many people who lived through that period remember having to wait hours at the gas station to fill up their cars. From 1973 until the end of the decade, the United States suffered from high rates of inflation, unemployment, or both in the form of stagflation. While inflation was not a problem during the Great Recession of the late 2000s, the level of unemployment was deeper and more persistent than in the 1970s.

Beyond the similarity in the economic conditions underlying the formation of C/LEC and AFR, both coalitions brought together citizen groups, public interest groups, and labor unions. Heather Booth's partner in setting up C/LEC was William Winpisinger, president of the International Association of Machinists (IAM). "Wimpy," as Winpisinger was called without any disrespect, believed strongly that the labor movement should be part of broader coalitions for social and economic justice.[39] C/LEC was one such vehicle. "He helped plan and chaired its founding conference, recruited unions and solicited union funding for C/LEC, and committed considerable financial and in-kind resources to it."[40]

Yet another similarity between C/LEC and AFR is the use of both national and local lobbying. At the national level, C/LEC advocated a variety of federal policies to avoid future energy price spikes, including a more competitive oil industry achieved via forced divestiture, reimposition of price controls on natural gas and crude oil, grants and tax credits to subsidize energy costs for low- and middle-income consumers, and tax incentives for energy-efficient building and retrofitting.[41] AFR's primary goal was passage of broad-based financial reform and consumer protection, as eventually embodied in the Dodd-Frank Act.

Both C/LEC and AFR tried to enlist local organizations to support their national goals as well as undertake local initiatives. C/LEC gradually formed energy coalitions within 25 states,[42] and AFR signed up almost 160 state or local groups as members.[43] One comparison between the two organizations' grassroots activities is particularly striking. In 1981, C/LEC—with the assistance of National People's Action (NPA)—sponsored a "Showdown Chicago." The protest event drew 5,000 union members, senior citizens, and consumer activists to the annual meeting of the American Petroleum Institute.[44] The street protestors chanted slogans like, "Freeze prices, not senior citizens" and "Stop natural gas decontrol."[45] In 2009, AFR took the place of C/LEC in teaming with NPA. They pulled together about 5,000 people from the same constituencies for a "Showdown in Chicago." This time the venue was the annual meeting of the American Bankers Association in response to the mortgage foreclosure crisis.[46] The people chanted, "ABA, you're the worst! It's time to put people first!" and carried signs saying, "We didn't break the banks. The banks broke us."[47]

Electoral Politics

Relative to more dogmatic members of the New Left, Booth always had a pragmatic streak. Although she had an ideologically informed vision for transforming society,[48] her actions spoke of someone who was willing to work within the system for concrete gains. At the Midwest Academy, she complemented its training programs on community organizing with ones on electoral politics, from campaign management and fund-raising to voter registration.[49] Hence, it is not surprising that many of Booth's activities after 1983, when C/LEC was absorbed into a larger organization pursuing a broader range of issues, were devoted to strengthening the progressive wing of the Democratic Party. In 1990, she directed the Coalition for Democratic Values, a progressive, issue-advocacy organization of leading left Democrats, such as Sen. Howard Metzenbaum, Congressman John Lewis, and Boston mayor Ray Flynn. The organization served as a counterweight to the centrist Democratic Leadership Council.[50] In 1992, she served as director of field operations for the successful senatorial campaign of Illinois Democrat Carol Moseley-Braun.[51] In 1993 Booth worked for the Democratic National Committee as its training director. In 2000, Booth directed the NAACP's National Voter Fund. From 2007 until early 2009, Booth directed the AFL-CIO's Health Care Reform Campaign.[52]

Thus, it was not entirely surprising that Booth, the activist rooted in the zeitgeist of the 1960s and the New Left, would end up leading a coalition of mostly progressive-leaning organizations in pursuit of legislation crafted by a centrist president. She did so because of a belief that the time was right to achieve progress. Speaking on February 26, 2009, Booth stated, "There is an opening for change that is precious. We have not had a time like this for 40 years."[53]

Spring 2009

The spring of 2009 was heady for liberal interest groups and busy for Heather Booth. Advocates finally had the ear of the president and his staff.[54] This new access applied in particular to consumer groups. They found themselves being invited to sessions with Obama administration powerbrokers, from chief economic advisor Larry Summers on down. Pam Banks, policy counsel for Consumers Union, couldn't help but remark on the new environment: "For a long time, there were few consumer groups that had seen the inside of the White House or the Treasury. Now sometimes you go to these meetings, and they say, 'Tell us what's on your mind.' And then *they* start taking notes."[55]

Whereas labor, health, consumer, education, and environmental groups all had their own legislative priorities, these organizations shared a common interest in the passage of the first Obama budget. The budget was submitted by President Obama on February 26th, 2009. Shortly thereafter, Heather Booth began directing a nongovernmental organization, Rebuild and Renew America Now, devoted to passage of the first Obama budget.[56] Before that campaign was over, though, Booth was approached by Gary Kalman of U.S. PIRG and Steve Abrecht of the Service Employees International Union. They told her that there had been three meetings of groups interested in a financial reform campaign. There was enormous potential, but the organizing effort wasn't advancing. "And if it wasn't advancing, people were going to leave."[57]

According to Kalman, Booth wanted to know whether the campaign to enact financial reform would be serious, that is, whether there would be adequate funding for it. He responded, "No. Not only don't we have a little bit of money, we don't have any money. So, if we hired you, we couldn't actually pay you." To Kalman's delight, Booth turned back to him and said, "You know, this kind of economic issue, the restructuring of financial systems, is why I do what I do. I can't *not* work on this issue. I will do it."[58] The opportunity to rein in the banks and other financial institutions that had crashed the economy and destroyed so many people's lives was irresistible for Booth.[59] And it helped, as the always-colorful Ed Mierzwinski put it, that Booth was "between gigs."[60] Abrecht assured Booth that AFR would be adequately financed. According to Booth, every member of the Steering Committee was expected to contribute funding, and did.[61] More important, $900,000 in foundation funding was lined up within a few months (Arca, $200,000; Atlantic Philanthropies, $550,000, Panta Rhea, $150,000).[62]

With initial funding committed, Booth had to recruit a deputy director. She found one in Lisa Donner. Donner, whom Booth had not met previously,[63] came from a younger generation of organizers but had activist credentials that would have appealed to Booth. After graduating from Harvard, Donner cut her political teeth as an organizer for the Service Employees International Union, spending most of her time on the Justice for Janitors campaign in Washington, D.C. As the campaign name suggests, it was a city-by-city effort begun in the mid-1980s to improve the working conditions and remuneration of janitors. For the next 11 years (1995–2006), Donner worked for ACORN. While ACORN eventually succumbed to one scandal too many, for most of the organization's four-decade history it was respected as an effective mobilizing force for low-income and minority communities.[64] While with ACORN, Donner headed its Financial Justice Center, tackling such issues as payday lending, refund anticipation loans, and subprime home loans.[65] In 2006, Donner founded and codirected the Center for Working Families, where she advocated for fair taxes, family-friendly workplace policies, and green jobs. Beginning in August of 2008, she directed the Half in Ten Campaign, a project with the goal of reducing poverty in the United States by half. With such an ambitious target, Donner must have been relieved when Booth recruited her in May, 2009, to "only" tame Wall Street and the Big Banks.[66]

Donner brought to AFR knowledge about financial issues that Booth lacked, and no one recognized this more strongly than Booth. Booth said, "Lisa knew far more about [housing and consumer] policy than I ever will know and probably as much overall as anyone inside the organization."[67] Heather McGhee, the director of the Washington, D.C. office of Demos, a policy research and advocacy organization, was one of AFR's policy task force chairs. She too was impressed by Donner's experience, knowledge, and guts. McGhee observed that Donner is "very smart and a very quick study. She could quickly go toe-to-toe with anyone on the issues. She's kind of a sponge mentally and commands a lot of respect and trust from everyone."

Booth's confidence in Donner's abilities allowed the normally detail-oriented Booth to back off a bit. Heather McGhee recounted that "[Heather Booth] delegated [being on the task force phone calls] to Lisa. Lisa, as deputy director, was pretty much on every single task force call so that she could always have a really incredible bird's-eye view as to what was going on in every piece of the bill and in every part of the coalition."[68]

Organizing the Organizers

The hiring of Booth and Donner reflects the aspiration that AFR would be a highly professional operation. Yet, coordinating a diverse set of organizations, some of which were themselves composed of many organizations, was going to be a bit like herding cats. To build an effective coalition, Booth and Donner would have to engineer consensus with respect to campaign goals and strategy, build a resilient organizational structure, and develop a culture of trust and sacrifice.

Chapter 5

Coalescing the Coalition

By 2009, the facts on the ground were roughly as follows: The U.S. economy had tanked. At mid-year over 14 million people were unemployed and the unemployment rate had jumped from 5.8 percent to 9.3 percent in just 12 months. Home mortgage foreclosures were running at record rates. Average household incomes declined by $5,800 between September 2008 and December 2009, and the value of household assets invested in stocks and homes dropped on average by almost $100,000 over the same period.[1] Heather Booth, fresh from a stint working on the campaign to pass President's Obama's first budget, latched onto these indicators as explicit signs of a unique and transformative opportunity for progressive change. True to her pragmatic nature, she observed: "Here we're facing a crisis, and we need to do something about it."[2] Thus in June 2009, even before AFR's staff, budget, salary support, and the other necessities could be put in place, Booth committed herself to organizing a Wall Street Reform campaign.[3] Arriving on the scene in June 2009, with a mandate to help address these problems by launching a nationwide citizen's campaign for financial reform, Booth found a considerable amount of enthusiasm and a strong sense of the urgency to begin. Equally important, however, she encountered profound uncertainty about the roadmap for moving forward.

The immediate challenges on her plate were daunting and were seriously compounded by the immediacy of congressional timelines for action. Her to-do list included: distilling a shared mission and creating a platform that would attract the support of diverse organizations having varied interests and priorities of their own; creating a durable organizational infrastructure; developing an inside-outside strategy of congressional lobbying and grassroots mobilization; and developing a strong organizational culture.

Agreeing on a Mission and Campaign Platform

Informal soundings begun in late 2008 by a small group of organizers including Travis Plunkett, Ed Mierzwinski, and Maureen Thompson uncovered a strong inclination among progressive-leaning groups in Washington to support a campaign for comprehensive financial regulatory reform.[4] These leaders established that there was provisional support for a campaign to address housing, fair lending, financial systems reform, consumer and investor protection, and related matters.

Many of the groups contacted by Plunkett and the others had recently participated in a successful legislative campaign championed by Rep. Carolyn Maloney (D-N.Y.) to reform credit card practices. But even this stand-alone piece of financial regulatory reform was 10 years in the making and exhausted the energies of all involved. Plunkett, the legislative director of the Consumer Federation of America, recalls a telephone conversation with Elizabeth Warren in which she asked, "Aren't you tired of fighting these one-off fights going issue by issue—struggling?" And then Plunkett observed, "She was completely in tune with how I was feeling, struggling for these significant victories, but struggling nonetheless."[5]

There was a clear preference within AFR's constituencies for attacking financial reform in a strong, across-the-board manner instead of the usual piecemeal way. Despite the widespread feeling that "we had better all be in this time," it was not self-evident that all the organizations that had evinced a preliminary interest in a coalition-style citizen's campaign were necessarily on the same page.[6]

Yes, there was agreement at the conceptual level with the broad principles for financial reform laid out in the Congressional Oversight Panel's Special Report released in January of 2009.[7] The members of AFR's multi-organization steering committee had no difficulty recognizing that if AFR was to build a powerful membership list and energize its core group, it would have to mount a full-scope campaign that took ownership of the entire range of issues presented.[8]

At the same time, there were inevitably some tensions that had to be worked out. Given the diversity of interests, priorities, and styles of the groups coming to the table, there was a certain degree of uncertainty about how the agenda would play out as the campaign progressed. These concerns were sometimes stated quite explicitly. If, for example, the problems of low income and minority consumers were not adequately addressed by the entire coalition, some groups indicated they would not be inclined to jump in.[9] Other issues were not as sharply defined but they were palpable nonetheless. Many arose out of the unfamiliarity and lack of working experience some of the players had with one another. When it came to working together on a day-to-day basis, would there be sufficient common purpose and commitment among players representing such diverse organizations?

Focusing on the CFPB

The importance of consumer protection was a good example of how the varying priorities of AFR's members lined up. Whereas establishment of a new, strong, and independent regulator was ranked as the number one goal for many of the groups involved in discussions, there were a number of others with different interests. Consumer protection and an independent consumer agency were at the top of the list for the Center for Responsible Lending (CRL), Consumers Union, the Consumer Federation of America, the National Consumer Law Center, U.S. PIRG, AARP, the National Association of Consumer Advocates, Public Citizen, and a host of other national and state and local groups.[10]

Establishing a new consumer protection agency, however, was a lower priority for the AFL-CIO and other labor organizations including the SEIU and AFSCME. For these organizations, structural issues, such as corporate governance, and investment provisions, such as shareholder rights and fiduciary obligations, achieved top billing.[11] The same was true for the National Community Reinvestment Council, the National Fair Housing Alliance, and other fair lending and community development organizations for which reauthorization of the Community Reinvestment Act was at the head of their priority lists.

Still, virtually all of AFR's members realized that the idea of a new consumer-oriented agency would be appealing to the public. Opinion polls, for instance, showed that Americans were enraged that big banks, CEOs and other financial actors were getting off scot-free after causing severe injury to many millions of consumers, small businesses, and the economy. And they found it outrageous that lenders were receiving bailouts as compensation for scamming borrowers in everyday transactions involving credit card accounts and mortgages.[12] Cora Ganzglass of the National Association of Consumer Advocates picked up on the strength of popular outrage and the inherent opportunities for channeling it:

> As an organizer you always want to tie in to the overall sentiment, and people were just outraged by the kinds of bonuses that banks were getting, and then the bailout, and where were everyday Americans? And that's . . . where our

coalition came together because we represented it and we framed ourselves as representing the everyday American . . . Big banks and corporations are getting billions of dollars in bailouts and still giving these officials, or their presidents and whatever, outrageous bonuses. What about all these hard-working Americans?[13]

Reenter Elizabeth Warren. Given the priority that many (if not most) of the AFR partner groups shared, the Consumer Financial Protection Bureau, as identified in the Administration's White Paper on Financial Reform, was destined to become a headline feature.

As expressed in Professor Warren's original *Democracy* article, the idea behind the CFPB was predicated on that homeliest of images—the kitchen toaster. Warren's toaster was potentially unsafe and, without suitable regulation, it ran the risk of exploding on the breakfast table. Of course she drew analogies to the danger of exploding home mortgages, credit cards, student loans, and other credit instruments—financial products which she famously suggested were full of tricks and traps. And, as with the toaster paradigm, she connected the dots to consumer product regulatory mechanisms that offered buyers protection. If the big banks, payday lenders, and auto finance agencies put out deceptive products and treated customers unfairly, CFPB would line up as the tough cop for the little guy.

At a conceptual level, the CFPB appeared reasonably easy to understand and to explain. It would be an independent, consumer-friendly regulator—a Consumer Cop on the Block—with broad jurisdictional authority, adequate and sustainable funding, and sufficient tools to tackle a myriad of credit safety problems. It would mean that borrowers would have their own regulator, free of competing priorities and potential conflicts of interest.

Even so, the problem of breaking through off-putting, arcane language and complex concepts in order to reach ordinary consumers was not an easy one to solve. So too was the growing disconnect between voter preferences for progressive plans and their heightened cynicism and distrust of government. As Democratic pollster Stan Greenberg observed, it is increasingly difficult for political messages to break through to voters who are inclined to turn off these communications as "just words."[14]

In making the case for the CFPB to the public, AFR's principals knew they would face opposition from business lobbies, such as the U.S. Chamber of Commerce, which would be intense. David Hirschmann, head of the Chamber's Center for Capital Market Competitiveness, fired off a warning shot, saying that proposals for an independent consumer financial protection agency resembled "lead balloons," not silver bullets. At the same time,

Chamber CEO Tom Donohue announced the launch of a $100 million campaign to defend "economic freedoms" (presumably against intrusion from the likes of a CFPB).[15]

AFR's Infrastructure

Booth envisioned the creation of a highly disciplined, sufficiently financed, and professional campaign organization. This would be a truly rare commodity in the world of public interest lobbying where most campaigns are put together with dribs and drabs of funds and with volunteer, part-time management contributed by members. The AFR organizers, on the other hand, realized this campaign was far too important and complex to be run the old-fashioned way.

AFR developed an organizational structure that blended inclusion and participation with streamlined decision making. The coalition had a six-member Executive Committee and an 18-person Steering Committee, with Booth holding membership on both. The Steering Committee, as AFR's primary decision-making body, had the role of approving the organization's policy positions and letters to the Hill. If time was short, the Executive Committee would serve as the rapid response team. The original members of the Executive Committee, other than Booth, were mainly selected to represent the key constituencies within the coalition:[16]

Stephen Abrecht—Service Employees International Union
Gary Kalman—U.S. Public Interest Research Group
Nancy Zirkin—Leadership Conference on Civil Rights
Lisa Rice—National Fair Housing Alliance
Rob Johnson—Roosevelt Institute
James Carr—National Community Reinvestment Coalition

The major activities of AFR—legislative policy, field mobilization, and communication—were organized as task forces. David Arkush, a young but accomplished attorney at Public Citizen, was the initial coordinator of the Policy Task Force. This task force was in turn divided into eight mini task forces. The one most relevant to the proposal to create a Consumer Financial Protection Agency was called the Consumer Protection Task Force, with Ed Mierzwinski as its coordinator. Other task forces included: Systemic Risk and Resolution Authority; Derivatives; Corporate Governance/Investor Protection; and Foreclosure/Housing.

Within a few weeks of AFR's debut, groups began meeting to produce position papers. Seven such papers were eventually produced. Although the seven final papers did not correspond exactly to the eight mini task forces, the papers, when taken as a whole, represented the collective wish list of AFR's members. The lengthiest of the seven position papers, and the one that engaged the most people in its formulation, had the opaque-sounding title, "Restoring Oversight and Accountability to the Financial Markets." Within this roughly 8,000-word document, the members of AFR devoted three paragraphs to calling for a new agency to protect consumers. Additional paragraphs called for two other reforms. First, AFR proposed an Office of Consumer Affairs in the White House to "give consumers a voice in the administration and provide some balance to the influence enjoyed by Wall Street." Second, the document championed a government-chartered consumer organization created by Congress to represent consumers' financial services interests before regulatory, legislative, and judicial bodies.[17] Upon a complete reading of AFR's laundry list of policy preferences, one might identify with the movie character Austin Powers when he said, "[I want] a toilet seat made out of solid gold, but it's just not in the cards now, is it?"[18]

The existence of so many specific policy objectives must have been a major leadership challenge. It was one thing for the members of AFR to believe that they stood a better chance of achieving their goals by working toward an omnibus piece of legislation. It was quite another for each organization to feel that its goals were central to AFR and wouldn't get jettisoned if the going got tough.

The Two-Way Strategy

Having decided to embrace a comprehensive platform and to make the CFPB one of its centerpieces, the AFR was now able to turn to strategy. Two basic questions needed to be settled at the outset: How ambitious should AFR's legislative demands be on each of the items addressed, and should AFR be willing to trade off one piece of the legislation against another?[19] Doubts about AFR's resolve and capacity were expressed almost immediately. In an outrageous smackdown that coincided with AFR's launch, Jane Hamscher, a left-leaning political activist, film producer and blogger, must have consulted her astrologer as the basis for proclaiming AFR to be just "[a]nother group that will redouble every mistake made by every such liberal group since the 1970s. . . . They're utterly and completely useless, and pose absolutely no threat."[20]

AFR's strategic concept called for a combination "inside and outside" approach.[21] The "inside" strategy would focus on direct and ongoing contacts with legislators and their personal and committee staffs. AFR would provide an umbrella for setting lobbying objectives as well as supporting teams made up of AFR staffers, members of Washington-based partner organizations, and their local members. These would be augmented by outside subject matter specialists, paid consultants, and cooperating direct action groups.

It mattered enormously that Wade Henderson, the highly respected president and CEO of the Leadership Conference on Civil and Human Rights and formerly director of government affairs for the NAACP, decided to jump into this campaign with both feet. Together with LCCHR's executive vice president, Nancy Zirkin, generally reputed to be one of the savviest lobbyists in Washington, the two sent a message that neither adversaries nor allies could ignore. When Henderson was first approached, his reaction was that LCCHR needed to join the coalition, not merely as a rank-and-file member, but as one of its core players.[22] LCCHR's participation was pivotal. Not simply did it contribute invaluable professional expertise; it brought the credibility and organizational support of the entire civil and human rights movement with it.[23] Many dues-paying members of the organizations that affiliated under the LCCHR umbrella had been personally affected by the housing and credit crisis, and thus their organizations had more than a casual interest in the issue.

Zirkin promptly assumed leadership of the campaign's lobbying team. Not only did she bring years of personal experience and access to many of the legislators and Hill staff most prominently involved in the various aspects of the Dodd-Frank matter, but she also had the organizational and leadership skills critical to the coordination of lobbyists and field organization volunteers calling on their representatives. This called on her diplomatic skills since many of the lobbying staff remained on the payrolls of AFR member groups and the volunteer field workers were primarily responsive to the various organizations with whom they were affiliated. The lobbying effort was also informed by Zirkin's pragmatism and shrewd ability to judge the odds of success in a dispassionate way.

In practical terms, Zirkin's influence meant that members of the lobbying operation were not tripping over one another or approaching the Hill with dissonant voices. It also meant that the coalition was using its resources most efficiently. As an example, Hill lobbyists were tethered to scattered research and policy staff by cell phone and Blackberry. Thus, technical questions raised during a legislative visit could often receive an immediate, real-time response—having previously been vetted for policy as part of AFR's internal review process. Similarly, during the final debate in the Senate and in Conference Committee deliberations, Zirkin mobilized a team that positioned some coalition members, including Travis Plunkett and Ed Mierzwinski, just outside the hearing room and backed them up with a War Room at LCCHR's office plus a virtual War Room in other organizations—all of which could feed legislators and staff talking points, arguments, and factoids of various sorts.[24]

The "outside" game adopted by AFR had two components. The first sought to capture and channel what organizers perceived to be the deep popular rage felt by individuals and groups at the local level. Given limited funding, a decision was made to concentrate on certain states and localities and to develop clear messaging directed toward opinion leaders ("grasstops") that would focus, especially, on big banks and predatory lending practices. The second involved linkages between AFR's efforts and those implemented by the White House and the administration.

AFR's executive director Heather Booth had extensive experience mobilizing members of the general public, but given her other leadership responsibilities, Booth needed help. It came in early July, 2009, when AFR hired Eileen Toback to lead its field operations and serve as a liaison to other direct action groups.

Toback practically had consumer advocacy in her genes. Her father, Jack Toback, had worked as a product tester for Consumers Union, the publisher of *Consumer Reports*.[25] Long before Elizabeth Warren used the analogy of the exploding toaster to sell the idea of the CFPB, Eileen Toback's father was trying to make sure that consumers did not buy toasters that were unsafe. The younger Toback had ample experience in grassroots organizing. She worked as national field manager for the Children's Defense Fund, as a political organizer for the AFL-CIO, and as special projects manager for the United Steelworkers.[26]

A principal focus of the field strategy was to maintain a constant drumbeat for reform via grasstops and grassroots lobbying. The grasstops strategy involved contacts initiated by local influentials such as union officials, the clergy, friendly business leaders, and the like. It aimed at providing information and helpful personal channels to legislators in their districts and in Washington. In one typical case, a grasstops contact with a wavering senator provided important reassurance that a particular vote was safe in his district.[27]

The grasstops effort also required maintaining ongoing liaisons with news media: meeting with editorial boards, offering insights about conditions in regional credit markets and current developments in the Congress, and presenting victims of outrageous lender activities. "[T]he minute that the banking lobby sensed that this was gonna fall out of the media, that people weren't paying attention, that's when they come to win," reported Gary Kalman of U.S. PIRG.[28]

Ongoing, local grasstops activity was to be complemented by grassroots efforts. Street demonstrations and special events would be spearheaded by progressive direct action groups such as USAction, PICO (a faith-based organization), and National Peoples Action.[29] These groups maintained large e-activist lists and could be called upon to organize substantial street-level protests in different venues. As Alison Maurice, a canvasser for the Maine People's Alliance put it, "Maine people have seen that some Republican senators are still trying to protect their banker friends, stalling the process and trying to insert loopholes for special interests. They want senators Snowe and Collins to have no part of that."[30] To facilitate local collaborations, AFR planned to offer small cash grants to help defray expenses. These events were often cosponsored by other AFR membership groups such as various SEIU locals.[31]

Both the grasstops and grassroots elements of the field strategy required a compelling and consistent message. As Toback recalls matters, the messaging for the overall campaign came together "fairly quickly . . . somewhere between July and September of '09, and it pretty much stuck. We kept to it. It didn't change all that much, with the exception of tweaking for what was happening [at a given time]."[32]

Highlighting the CFPB was central to AFR's messaging strategy, Toback said: "First of all, people understood it. I think even the field people who were selling it understood it. I think also the general public understands it. . . . It was the most sexy cornerstone of [the campaign], if you're going to call financial reform sexy, and it was just the easiest thing for people to understand."[33]

Toback thought that the financial derivatives reform provisions might have been "the most important element of the bill as far as true financial reform was concerned," but these provisions were far more difficult to explain to members of the public than the virtues of the CFPB. Toback allowed that even she wasn't sure she completely understood derivatives, even after a year on the campaign: "I knew what I needed to know [about derivatives]. That's about it. It's kind of like cramming for a test. I got it for just that moment, and then the day after that test, I'm like, 'What?' "[34] The other prong of the outside strategy—networking with the White House, the Office of Public Liaison, the National Economic Council and the Treasury Department—primarily involved a mix of technical work, policy consultations, and a review of lobbying and communication strategies aimed at the Congress and the public. This component of the outsider game was important albeit controversial at times. It presented a tricky balancing act inasmuch as some members of AFR were adamant about preserving the organization's independence on all issues. At the same time, coalition members were always cautious about undermining the president's stance on the economic agenda. This concern was resolved through an understanding that allowed AFR to collaborate with the White House on issues both could agree on while preserving AFR's independence and license to pressure the administration on issues in contention. When AFR functioned as a critic, it often proved helpful to have a field operation that fed in intelligence and opinion from outside the Beltway.

The concept of linking popular advocacy with electoral politics was wholly in keeping with Booth's strongly held view that the chances of progressive reform were strengthened by a merger of the two. Having enjoyed recent success with an inside-outside campaign to stop Social Security privatization, Booth sought to sell the approach to some skeptical organizers of the AFR coalition. The skeptics were gravely concerned about the appearance of partisanship and the risk of tying AFR too closely to the Democratic Party and the White House.[35] As Booth recalls her initial meeting with AFR organizers, there was "an intense argument" about even having "regular conversations with people inside" (referring to the administration). She was asked, "You want to do that? It'll make us too close to them."[36] The essential assurance sought by virtually all of the advocates at the table was that AFR would stand up for its own priorities even if it meant brooking occasional disagreement with the administration.[37]

A good example of the sometimes sensitive relationship between AFR and the White House was reflected in the so-called Common Purpose Meetings. These regular weekly sessions were set up by the White House to network with progressive supporters of the Obama administration. According to some critics, the meetings also served a disciplinary function. At one of these confabs, Rahm Emanuel was alleged to have called some advocacy groups "f@#king retarded" for using radio ads to attack certain Blue Dog Democrats for their weak positions on health care reform.[38]

The meeting was given the snarky nickname of "the veal pen" by Jane Hamscher. According to Hamscher, the essential feature of Common Purpose was to put "rock star" members of the administration (e.g., Larry Summers, Rahm Emmanuel) side by side with liberal funders and progressive organizations (like AFR) . . . and presto! Skeptics appeared to be convinced that AFR would become excessively beholden to the White House for largesse. While this concern never amounted to anything, the issue of sufficient independence from the Obama administration remained an on-going concern for some AFR members.

Supporting the Campaign

Booth, Donner, Toback and their colleagues knew that, to support the in-side game, they needed to build an effective grassroots field operation under the AFR umbrella.[39] This would be a tremendous test of their organizing skills. In part it was a question of resources. Booth soon came to under-stand that many of AFR's core DC-based organizations had no field orga-nizations of their own. Others had very sophisticated field operations and could potentially provide great value to the campaign, but not at the cost of sacrificing their operational autonomy.[40] This was agreeable to Booth whose coalition management style generally favored independence and autonomy rather than tight integration of field organizations with central staff.[41]

Janice Bowdler of the National Council of La Raza, a group with a devel-oped field organization, described how it worked on the ground:

> So we considered everything that we were doing to be aligned with AFR and we would try to time things as best that we could. But we were also setting our own field strategy. . . . So for example, if there was a big call-in day in a certain state, we would be sure to let our members know. . . . In certain cases there were field calls in certain states, and so we'd make sure they had those numbers and try to get them involved as best we could. And that was one way that we supported the field effort. But in another way, we branded our own campaign out to the field, and often would link back to AFR materials either directly or through cross posting. And so we did our own national calls, really making the case of why from civil rights and within our com-munity's perspective, we had to be pushing for XYZ, this particular limit and provision or these market provisions. And then that would—we saw that as feeding into the broader AFR efforts.[42]

The other component of the grassroots mobilization challenge had more to do with expectations. The poll results, focus groups, and other data gath-ering strongly suggested that people across the country and in all demo-graphic categories were scared and infuriated about Wall Street practices. Campaign planners understandably took this as a sign that the grassroots could be educated, activated, and effectively mobilized for political action.

In retrospect, some people who have taken a fresh look at the evidence have concluded that getting the base to coalesce and act on its emotion was far more difficult than anticipated.[43] David Corn, among others, has asked: "So where's the wrath?"

Having consulted polling and political consultants across the political spectrum, Corn uncovered a number of plausible explanations for why the grassroots did not coalesce to produce an explosive popular upsurge. One was that people hated Wall Street but thought it was far too dangerous to undermine it at that moment in history when the economy was so fragile. Tim Fernholz writing in the *American Prospect* chimed in that, in light of Obama's TARP bank rescue plan, the fear narrative made sense. But it was undermined by the obvious contradiction between an administration excoriating Wall Street in one breath and bailing it out in the next.[44]

Internally, AFR leadership believed resource limitations represented an important barrier to the mobilization and expression of popular opinion. Although coalition partner organizations were able to fund three cable TV ads during the campaign, AFR did not have a sufficient budget to place paid TV advertising. To increase its impact, AFR had to rely instead on the echo chamber effect of having various partner organizations broadcast the identical message.

A second hypothesis was that the problem seemed far too complicated for ordinary people to engage with. How could you possibly expect ordinary people to rise up against something called derivatives or even predatory lending? And a third explanation put forward by the Gallup poll was that while people don't like big business they distrust government even more.[45] This was subsequently stated in a slightly different way by Barney Frank: "The government doesn't produce good results, so the people get angry at the government. So they elect people who hate the government, and then the government is unable to produce results."[46]

Organizational Culture Based on Trust and Accountability

The decision to adopt a comprehensive campaign with a broad-based platform was inseparable from the commitment to build an inclusive coalition. By definition, the breadth of the agenda would effectively require an alliance between consumer groups concerned with predatory lending practices; trade unions focused on systemic issues and financial practices; and fair lending, community development and civil rights organizations involved in issues of discriminatory practices and community impact.

One of the biggest risks posed by adopting a "big tent" strategy, however, was that it could just as easily devolve into discord as harmony. Judging precisely how an inclusive membership policy bridging racial, ethnic, and economic fault lines would work out was perilous at best. Since many of the groups coming to the table, especially grassroots organizations, did not have a history of campaigning side by side, building trust was an early challenge. In addition, making an assessment of each organization's willingness to collaborate and devote resources to a coalition effort would be fraught with even greater uncertainty.

Elizabeth Warren's approach to framing lending abuse as a problem of the middle class was intuitively congenial to the "big tent" inasmuch as its intent was to be open and inclusive. As a practical matter, however, there could be no guarantee that advocates for the poor or for racial or ethnic communities would necessarily trust that their issues and interests would receive high enough priority from the group as a whole.

In a meeting before AFR was formally constituted, Lisa Rice of the National Fair Housing Alliance was reassured by Elizabeth Warren and others that elimination of the two-tiered (separate and unequal) financial system would be a major goal of any coalition. Janice Bowdler of the National Council of La Raza also sought assurance that the problems of minority consumers would not be lost in efforts to present financial reform as a middle-class issue. She became convinced, however, that the middle-class frame could be a definite plus instead of a minus. She observed that: "Leading with the existence of the dual credit market from a policy perspective is not always a winner, as opposed to leading with fraud and scams that broadly affect the middle class, and not exclusively low-income, low-wealth or communities of color. It's more compelling and draws more people in. So in some ways what we're really talking about is message and style, and not so much substance."[47]

Building trust meant smoothing divisions beyond income, ethnicity, and economic class. Recalling her first meeting with AFR organizers Booth said, "When I came into this, there was electricity in the room, and very thick tension, I would say. Many of the people did not know each other, did not trust each other. . . . Why do we need these think-tank people in the room? What do they contribute? Won't they just slow us down?" Correspondingly, other people were asking why they needed "some specific grassroots organizations in there?" Booth's view was: "We needed both kinds and more."[48]

Although others who attended the early meetings did not comment directly about distrust between groups, many acknowledged the veritable silos that had encapsulated people working on different aspects of the financial meltdown. There were consumer protection silos and systemic risk silos and other issue-related silos. There were also cloisters of attorneys and compounds of economic researchers. Some segments tended to address issues in an incremental way, while others were more comfortable with a structural approach. It was a polyglot community. People working on similar issues spoke completely different languages and had divergent expectations of what could be and should be done.

Booth described the process by which AFR members came to trust each other:

> There were uncertainties about how a [coalition approach] would play out. There were a lot of conversations and a lot of staffing time put into trying to establish trust. The process was totally transparent. There was nothing that wouldn't be shared about our budget, our conversations, who was talking to whom. There were not going to be any secret meetings. Of course, there were some times when meetings wouldn't have proceeded if we hadn't respected other groups' confidentiality, but we were very transparent.[49]

Other initial commitments and evolving aspects of AFR's work style promoted group cohesion. Perhaps most important, AFR members assured each other that the coalition wouldn't trade off one organization's major priority in favor of another's. This relieved the concern of being sold out in the endgame and encouraged groups to work for mutual benefit. In addition, when lobbying Congress, AFR members were expected to be somewhat interchangeable. So, for example, a lawyer focusing mainly on the rules governing auto financing had to know enough about the macroeconomic aspects of "too big to fail" when s/he was on the Hill and was asked a question. This "got-your-back" work style was just one of a number of expressions of a cooperative mentality that helped overcome potentially divisive organizational forces.

Hard Work and Accountability

Quite apart from building trust, committing to a comprehensive platform and large coalition would call for substantial resources in terms of money, staff, and time.[50] As one example, probably none of the people involved in the campaign had comprehensive knowledge of the entire range of issues outlined in the January 2009 COP Report. Certainly, no one person or organization had the level of expertise needed to match their industry counterparts when lobbying at the highest levels. Thus, it would take an appreciable investment of time and effort for advocates to educate themselves and each other and to identify sympathetic outsiders in the academic community and think tanks.

To make a credible showing, member organizations and the AFR would have to step up in ways that had frequently eluded prior campaigns. To fulfill their commitments, partner organizations would almost certainly have to siphon staff, money and resources away from other projects and activities and to add to their existing workloads.

Booth and Donner built an organization in which hard work was rewarded. According to Booth, "We were absolutely work-focused; if you did work, you got listened to. If you didn't do work, you weren't listened to."[51] Booth and Donner led by example, and their example rubbed off on others. Michael Calhoun, the president of the hard-charging Center for Responsible Lending, recalled Booth's amazing work ethic:

> She was a stickler—you come into the meeting and there will be a written agenda. There will be notes that go out immediately after the meeting. These practices are both effective and necessary in the context of a coalition to minimize misunderstandings or conflicts. What a lot of people would think were overly restricted ground rules and procedures, in practice everyone appreciated. It was not this casual you call a couple people or you check here or there. There were very explicit and carefully followed procedures. There were sign offs. There were task forces on every issue with designated people to run those task forces. They had set schedules for when meetings would be. Heather Booth worked at a level that few people could match in terms of both duration and intensity.[52]

Bill Ragen of the Service Employees International Union, a dynamic organizer himself, described Booth as a "real force of nature."[53]

Looking back, Booth could joke about how hard she and Donner worked. Their work day would start at 8:00 A.M. Still working at 1:00 A.M., "we would send each other emails that finally say, "Look, good night, go to sleep." Whereas Booth and Donner appreciated that the people they were coordinating were donating time from their full-time jobs, they would joke about working two shifts themselves. According to Booth, "Almost for a year, I'd go out to parties [but] I basically couldn't take a drink, I'd say, 'I can't. I gotta go to the night shift.'"[54]

Perhaps because Booth worked so hard herself, she wasn't bashful about asking other people to join in the work. David Arkush of Public Citizen remembers Heather Booth lining him up for a job the very first time they met. Arkush was in the lobby of the AFL-CIO headquarters in Washington, D.C., when Booth walked up to him and said, "Oh, I'm Heather Booth," and told him that she might be playing a role in a coalition. She said to Arkush, "I heard you get work done. Could I get you to chair a task force possibly on policy?"[55] It was incredibly savvy on Booth's part. Among consumer groups, Public Citizen is typically the most unwilling to compromise. By having Arkush serve as the task force's chair, she virtually assured that Public Citizen would be an integrator rather than an instigator.

Janis Bowdler of the National Council of La Raza was very circumspect about being drawn too deeply into the work of AFR. She had a day job after all. As a favor to Ed Mierzwinski, Bowdler attended some of the early organizational meetings. When Mierzwinski told Bowdler that AFR was going to be staffed, she replied, "Okay, keep me posted." Then Bowdler starting getting phone calls from Heather Booth, whom Bowdler had not met but knew of as an effective coalition leader. Booth asked Bowdler to be on AFR's steering committee, but Bowdler resisted.

> I don't know that I outright turned her down at first, but I told her, "We're not funded for this," and my time was tight and my team's time was tight. I just felt cautious about what I felt we could commit and still be fair to everybody else at the table. And then, after a couple of phone calls, she'd worn me down. She did promise me a lighter meeting schedule, which did not actually happen.[56]

In fact, La Raza and many other organizational members of AFR would end up providing tens or even hundreds of thousands of dollars worth of staff time to the coalition effort.[57] In the case of La Raza, approval from an external funding source allowed them to reallocate funds and staff to the Dodd-Frank campaign. According to Bowdler, the funder agreed with the proposition that "this is where we needed to be."[58]

Booth and Donner built an organizational culture in which hard work yielded influence and recognition. With respect to writing the position papers for AFR, David Arkush was in charge of the important Policy Task Force. At a meeting, he was slowly trying to get people to volunteer to write on the subjects on which they had expertise. Then, Booth stepped in and just started assigning people to subcommittees for the writing. Arkush was skeptical that Booth's approach would work. He felt it necessary to exhort people to hold themselves accountable and follow through on their commitments.[59] Arkush was pleasantly surprised: "What was amazing was that people would turn around in a day or two and produce a two-to-five-page paper."[60] Led by Booth and Donner, people were far more inclined to hang together than hang separately.

Attracting Allies

With the formation of AFR, the CFPB was no longer the abstract brainchild of a Harvard professor or one of many proposals from a newly elected president. The new agency had a formidable phalanx of supporters with AFR at its center. AFR claimed as full-fledged members (sometimes referred to as partners) of its coalition, 250 advocacy groups. They ranged from mainstream organizations like the AARP (with 40 million members) and the Consumer Federation of America (whose constituent organizations have a combined 50 million members) all the way to state and local entities such as the 1,000-member Rocky Mountain Peace and Justice Center. Although not formally members of AFR, there were numerous organizations, ad-hoc groups, public entities, and individuals who also functioned as advocates for Dodd-Frank or one of its substantive titles. These entities included: The Military Coalition, with approximately 35 membership groups of active and retired military and their families; an informal group of law professors convened by Professors Jeff Sovern and Norman Silber; roughly half the state attorneys general, including Lisa Madigan of Illinois and Tom Miller of Iowa; members of the entertainment community such as director Ron Howard; and, of course, Elizabeth Warren. Some of these individuals and groups focused on a single issue and partnered with AFR to support it. The Military Coalition, for instance, played a vital role on the issue of auto loans, while Lisa Madigan was an invaluable ally on federal preemption. Others were important niche players, helping out with particular contacts or tasks (e.g., gathering data, maintaining complaint files, garnering media exposure, or fund raising). Still other individuals or groups played a broader role. Elizabeth Warren, for instance, was a very close and consistent partner of AFR throughout the legislative process.

While it might have been advantageous in some ways to more fully integrate certain of the allies (e.g., the Navy-Marine Corps Relief Society and the Military Coalition) into the AFR structure, creating informal working collaborations was certainly a less complicated and perfectly functional approach. As retired admiral Jan Gaudio explained, the cultural differences and political orientations of the respective organizations would have made it difficult to formalize a full-fledged partnership arrangement but did not interfere with a more limited, issue-specific collaboration.[61]

Challenges Ahead

Having created a general framework and infrastructure to advocate for financial fairness and borrower safety, the AFR campaign was approaching show time. The House Financial Services Committee chaired by Barney Frank, a gruff, irreverently funny, and brilliant career politician from Boston, was their first stop. The committee, Frank himself, and the other key stakeholders involved in the debate represented challenges and opportunities that AFR strategists would need to sort out as they began their legislative work. The conclusions they reached would say a lot about their assessment of the prospects for eventually passing a bill and making sure it was strong enough to repay the tremendous effort it would require to pass it. It would also provide an early indication of whether the advocates had enough juice to produce.[62]

Draft legislation released by the Treasury Department on June 30, 2009, was largely adopted as a starting point by the House Financial Services Committee. A bill initially introduced by Frank on July 8, the Consumer Financial Protection Act of 2009 (H.R. 3126), represented a strong and comprehensive view of the Consumer Financial Protection Bureau and its regulatory authority. It was basically consistent with the earlier COP report that had been embraced in AFR's platform.[63] According to Booth, the consumer protection features in H.R. 3126 were "where the administration, Frank and Dodd, and our coalition largely started on a common page." There were differences—importantly, AFR wanted the Community Reinvestment Act and loans in low-income communities covered—but the key players were in agreement on most consumer issues. Booth recalls: "The original language was very strong, and we all would have wanted an equally strong measure, if we could get it."[64]

Shortly after the bill's introduction, however, a new reality began to set in. The large and polarized committee chaired by Barney Frank was highly susceptible to special interest pleadings by powerful interests within the lending community. Thus, preserving the original intent and text would be a very demanding task for the advocates.

In addition to the business-friendly orientation of many Democrats on the House Financial Services Committee, there was the problem of spillover from the ongoing health care reform debate. As the House began to consider financial reform in early July 2009, the bruising battle over health care was at its midpoint. Attempting to deal with both health care and financial reform, simultaneously, created enormous pressure on members of the House and Senate and their personal office staffs and made it more difficult for Congress to complete its work. This was especially true for people like Kay Hagan (D-N.C.), Jeff Merkley (D-Ore.), Bob Menendez (D-N.J.), and Chuck Schumer (D-N.Y.) since these senators had committee assignments that required work on health care and financial reform, concurrently.

Another complication arose because the health care experience put some legislators on edge and made them more risk-averse than they might have been otherwise. As one example, Eileen Toback, who headed field operations for Americans for Financial Reform, recalled that one Democratic senator was avid for reassurance that the CFPB would not turn into a "death panel" fiasco in his state.[65] In addition, the problem of overlapping agendas also complicated the political equation. Some of the most contentious issues arising during the health care debate soon had counterparts in financial reform. For example, the question of whether government should be allowed to mandate the purchase of health insurance or require insurers to cover patients with preexisting conditions was not so different from requiring mortgage lenders to issue standardized, plain vanilla loans or desist from charging prepayment penalties.

The overlapping health care and financial reform agendas also complicated matters for the advocates. Pam Banks of Consumers Union recalled that CU had adopted an aggressive approach during the health care campaign and encountered some pushback from a few readers. While fear of alienating subscribers did not fundamentally alter the way CU intended to deal with financial services, it remained a vivid reminder for the organization's legislative strategists and leadership.[66] The ultimate question was whether a bitterly divided Congress, a new president, and coalitions of citizen and business advocacy groups involved in political and policy campaigning had the capacity to deal simultaneously with two extraordinarily complex, crisis-driven reforms.[67]

Effectiveness = Independence + Authority

Despite the many challenges, advocates for the CFPB were not pressing for the mere establishment of a new agency but for one that would be effective in protecting financial consumers. Effectiveness, in turn, depended on two things: the powers of the new agency, and its inclination and ability to use these powers on behalf of consumers. Both of these qualities were summarized with adjectives such as "strong," "robust," "aggressive," and most often, "independent."

Appearing on the talk show *Charlie Rose* in early March 2010, Elizabeth Warren discussed the need for an independent consumer protection agency in her characteristically pungent fashion. Referring to the CFPB's organizational placement and its funding and authority, she said:

> Bloated, inefficient, and either ignored and ineffective, or captured by the large financial institutions. A fractured, bloated, overly fat regulatory system is what we've got now. It works very well for the large financial institutions because it means no effective regulation.
>
> You've got to have an agency that's ultimately independent, whether it's located within the Fed, within Treasury, the Department of Agriculture, or whether it sits in its own separate place. The key is whether or not it is

functionally independent. Does it write its own rules, does it enforce those rules, and does it have access to a budget that's independent of the folks who want to smother it?[68]

In contrast to issues of independence (which involved agency structure, location, and funding), issues of authority centered on the new agency's ability to carry out its mission. What regulatory tools would it have at its disposal, and who would be subject to these tools? Key issues of authority were the new agency's specific rulemaking and enforcement powers, the lenders over which it would (and would not) have jurisdiction, and the relationship between the CFPB's powers and those of individual states.

An independent agency with adequate authority—this was the basic template that AFR and its partners could (and did) get behind. It was also the edifice that opponents tried to obliterate or weaken, brick by brick.

Chapter 6

The Battle in the House

Ed Mierzwinski, the quick-witted director of consumer programs at U.S. PIRG, likened the struggle to enact Dodd-Frank to the confrontation in the original Star Wars movie. There, you will recall, the ragtag Rebel Alliance clashed with the seemingly invincible Galactic Empire.[1] When comparing the resources of those who were for and against financial reform, advocates like Mierzwinski had reason to feel that they were attacking the Galactic Empire's Death Star super-weapon with water pistols. Nevertheless, the members of Americans for Financial Reform and their allies were inspired by a collective vision of how a new federal agency, with the independence and authority to protect consumers, could tame Wall Street and overcome the persistent financial abuse of borrowers.

The legislative saga of the CFPB had two elements of suspense: would there be a new agency at all and, if so, would it be endowed with sufficient independence and authority to merit the support of AFR and other advocates? Although the advocates wanted to preserve flexibility and thus were hesitant to define independence and authority in too hard and fast a manner, these were, in fact, the main criteria they used to evaluate the bill as it worked its way through the process.

To increase the likelihood of success, the advocates supporting the CFPB needed to reconcile their unique capabilities with their equally genuine limitations. They also had to determine the most effective ways to collaborate with each other as well as with the Obama administration. This was not always easy inasmuch as groups could sometimes be reluctant to get too close to one another and/or to sacrifice their independence.

Although dealing with the interplay among the various groups and with the administration was important for the advocates, the more demanding tasks ultimately had to do with their relationships with Congress. One task was to strengthen the resolve of their main congressional champions, especially when they seemed to falter under pressure or to give in to the normal inclination to sidestep important but divisive issues. A second was to fend off weakening amendments or delaying actions taken by their congressional adversaries (both Republicans and some centrist Democrats).

This chapter and the next track the CFPB proposal, from the House to the Senate and then to the Conference Committee. Assuring the new agency's independence was particularly important to the CFPB's advocates. Two later chapters focus on the role of the CFPB's advocates in struggles over the new agency's authority—its powers, jurisdiction, and policy tools.

The Importance of Independence

Having an independent CFPB was high on the priority list for virtually all the member organizations of Americans for Financial Reform as well as its allies. Without independence carved into its infrastructure as well as its funding stream, the new agency would lack the freedom to stand up for consumers. To the advocates, "independent" and "strong" were essentially synonyms.[2]

While the CFPB's supporters agreed that the agency needed to be independent, they did not make any one specific feature of agency structure or funding into a drop-dead issue on which they could not rethink or negotiate. AFR's initial position paper on the CFPB avoided an overly precise definition of independence. With respect to funding, it read: "Agency funding should be structured in a manner that provides stable, adequate resources that are not subject to political manipulation by industry."[3] Later in the campaign, AFR updated its statement of desiderata, adding a structural component: "It would be equally impossible to assure the necessary degree of independence for a CFPA if its rules were effectively subject to veto by a political appointee such as the Secretary of the Treasury, at the behest of a banking regulator."[4]

While AFR and its allies remained flexible on questions of precisely how the CFPB's independence would be achieved, they never lost track of the ultimate prize. Intermittently, the CFPB's supporters engaged in serious debates on specific legislative proposals pertaining to structure and funding. To be sure, these debates produced a certain amount of heartburn within the coalition. In prior campaigns, tensions like these over issues of structure and funding might have undermined all forward progress; in this matter, however, to the credit of the coalition and the management of

AFR, these tensions were never allowed to fracture the coherence of the alliance.

Making a Good Showing in Congressional Hearings

Between late June and early September, 2009, both the House and the Senate scheduled many rounds of hearings on financial reform. Many of these hearings focused on predatory lending abuses and the idea of establishing a new consumer financial protection agency. The first such hearing took place on June 24, 2009, a mere week after the release of the Obama administration's White Paper on Financial Regulatory Reform and a week before the Treasury Department released its draft legislation on a new agency. The first challenge for advocates of the CFPB, therefore, was to prepare testimony . . . and fast.

Congressional hearings are rarely "ah-ha" moments for bringing new facts to light; nor are they occasions for carefully examining all sides of an argument or offering innovative solutions. More often, hearings serve as political theater—opportunities for members of Congress to get TV facetime, to demonstrate their concern, or vent their ire about some hot public issue. Testimony serves as a backdrop for these theatrics.

The tenor of congressional hearings may be strongly influenced by the chair of the relevant committee or subcommittee. Under Republican chairs, a token representative of the consumer, civil rights, or labor communities might be invited to balance multiple witnesses from the business community. This time around, with sympathetic Democrats like Barney Frank and Mel Watt in the leadership, the advocates of financial reform and the CFPB had a much better shot at getting star billing. Still, the number of witness slots was finite, so advocates were under pressure to wrangle invitations for their most persuasive spokespeople.

Between June 24 and September 30, 2009, there were nine congressional hearings devoted in whole or in part to the CFPB—two in the Senate and seven in House. At these hearings, the roughly two dozen pro-CFPB witnesses had to offset testimony by a similar number of witnesses representing important industry players, including the U.S. Chamber of Commerce and the Independent Community Bankers Association, who testified vehemently against a new standalone agency.

The identities of the pro-CFPB witnesses provide important insight into the breadth of its supporters. Congressman William Delahunt, who earlier in the year had sponsored a bill to create a new consumer agency, was given the honor of being the first witness at the first hearing. He was followed by

Elizabeth Warren. Of the 23 additional pro-CFPB witnesses, 12 were identified with AFR or AFR partner organizations.[5] They included Travis Plunkett of the Consumer Federation of America and Ed Mierzwinski of U.S. PIRG, both of whom were invited to speak on two separate occasions. The 11 witnesses not directly affiliated with AFR were either academic experts, mostly from the field of law, or government officials. The latter included Treasury Secretary Tim Geithner, Assistant Treasury Secretary Michael Barr, FDIC Chair Sheila Bair, and FTC Commissioner Jon Leibowitz. These pro-CFPB government voices were especially important as a counterweight to several key government officials—most notably Comptroller of the Currency John Dugan and Fed Chairman Ben Bernanke—who expressed strong reservations about the CFPB in their testimony.[6] For Dugan and Bernanke, creating a new agency would only underscore their own failure to protect consumers.[7]

The CFPB's supporters framed a limited but core set of tasks at the congressional hearings. One was to lay out a convincing narrative about the causes of the mortgage meltdown, linking them to the broader financial crisis. Another was to show that creating a consumer financial protection agency was the right policy response to these underlying causes. They also used the hearings to rebut the main objections to the CFPB raised by the other side's witnesses.

Fortunately for the advocates, they found themselves in broad agreement with the contents of the administration's White Paper and the Treasury's draft legislation for the CFPB. Instead of having to create a bill from scratch, they could sign onto the administration's proposal and explicit justifications.[8] Regarding the causes of the financial crisis, the administration's White Paper stated that "gains [in access to consumer credit] were overshadowed by pervasive failures in consumer protection, leaving many Americans with obligations that they did not understand and could not afford. While this crisis had many causes, it is clear now that the government could have done more to prevent many of these problems from growing out of control and threatening the stability of our financial system."[9]

The solution, the White Paper argued, was to give consumer protection "an independent seat at the table in our financial regulatory system."[10] This seat would be in the form of a new agency whose sole mission was, in the words of the Treasury draft legislation, "to promote transparency, simplicity, fairness, accountability, and access in the market for consumer financial products or services."[11]

Anticipating objections to the idea of curing a regulatory failure by creating yet another government bureaucracy, the White Paper stated that the administration's objective was "not [to] propose a new regulatory agency because we seek more regulation, but because we seek better regulation."[12] The CFPB would end the fragmentation of consumer protection among seven federal agencies, not to mention between federal and state regulators. It would pull together enforcement of existing statutes on consumer financial protection as well as have "the ability to fill gaps through new rule-making."[13]

With the White Paper as their outline, the job of the advocates was to create a narrative that combined populist passion with intellectual heft. Elizabeth Warren made the argument that the "tricks and traps that are robbing American families every day" aren't limited to a few working-class families.[14] In a TV interview with Roland Martin, Warren said: "What we're talking about with this crisis is we're just taking a bunch of middle-class people, hardworking people, people who played by the rules, and we're just knocking them out of the middle class. We're saying, 'You go back down to the lower class.' "[15] To a large degree, the problem, according to Professor Warren, was excessive complexity exacerbated by a failure of transparency. Testifying in Congress, Warren observed:

> Everyone in this room recognizes the problem. Consumers cannot compare financial products because the products have become too complicated. Make a comparison between four credit cards, put the papers on the table, and you would have more than 100 pages of dense, fine-print text to work through. And, quite frankly, even if you invested the hours to do it, I don't know if you would be able to understand it. I say that only because I teach contract law at Harvard Law School, and I can't understand many of the terms.[16]

Other witnesses contributed further important dimensions to the picture. Hilary Shelton of the NAACP testified that a new consumer financial protection agency was needed to address the "systematic discriminatory and abusive lending practices and the resulting wealth-stripping, ruinous effects."[17] Janet Murguia, president and CEO of the National Council of La Raza, described a "two-tier financial system" in which "frauds and scams are rampant." Consumers in communities of color, in particular, "are routinely . . . steered toward expensive products regardless of their creditworthiness . . . [and] creditors trap borrowers in cycles of debt."[18] The effect of abusive financial practices was to rob low-income consumers of the chance "to move firmly into the middle class."[19]

Virtually every pro-CFPB witness also made the point that the ruinous lending practices that lay at the heart of the financial crisis were at least partially attributable to government regulators who neglected consumer protection. Nancy Zirkin, executive vice president of the Leadership Conference on Civil and Human Rights and AFR's most experienced Hill lobbyist, testified that "the efforts of civil rights and consumer advocacy organizations to enlist the help of federal banking regulators fell on deaf ears."[20] Michael Barr, a University of Michigan law professor who was then serving as assistant secretary of the Treasury, added: "Today's consumer protection regime just experienced massive failure. . . . It cost millions of responsible consumers their homes, their savings, and their dignity. And it contributed to the near-collapse of our financial system."[21]

But it was Ed Mierzwinski of U.S. PIRG who presented a root and branch indictment of regulatory failure:

> We have a system that is broken. . . . First, the Fed had 15 years in which it did not write rules about HOEPA [the Homeownership Equity Protection Act]. Second, the OCC [Office of the Comptroller of the Currency] spent most of its time and energy preempting the States for 15 years instead of enforcing the laws. . . . On credit cards, we know the answer to that one. [Regulators] slept while the credit card problem got worse, and Congress had to step in and solve the problem. The Fed has allowed a shadow banking system of prepaid cards outside of the current financial protection laws that target the unbanked and immigrants. The OTS [Office of Thrift Supervision] allows bank payday loans to continue on prepaid cards. The Fed has refused to speed up check availability. The list goes on and on. . . . These regulators do not look at consumer protection as something that they should be doing.[22]

The conclusion the pro-CFPB witnesses drew was that a new agency, not a patched-up retread, was needed to protect consumers. Kathleen Keest of the Center for Responsible Lending testified that it "should be an independent, stand-alone regulator with the primary mission of consumer protection . . . should have rule-making, supervision and enforcement authority over all providers of consumer credit, deposit and payment systems . . . and be funded in a way that ensures its capacity, strength and independence."[23]

According to supporters, the new agency should educate consumers and provide them with better, easier-to-use information, but its job should not stop there. Ellen Seidman, a fellow at the New American Foundation and executive vice president of ShoreBank, the country's largest community development financial institution at the time, testified: "We have to stop relying on consumer disclosure as the primary method of protecting consumers."[24] The new agency should be able to require certain contract features to safeguard borrowers and to ban others it considered unfair, deceptive, or abusive. Seidman's position was compatible with AFR's Policy Platform which said: "The agency should have a strong mandate to move away from disclosure-based 'consumer protection' to the prohibition of harmful, unfair, deceptive or abusive products and practices."[25]

A specific approach backed by the administration and Elizabeth Warren required lenders to offer mortgage products that were simple, low-risk, easily understood by consumers, and comparable on an apples-to-apples basis. The so-called Plain Vanilla proposal was incorporated in the bill first introduced in the House on July 8, 2009. It called for lenders to make available to prospective borrowers a Plain Vanilla loan contract such as a 30-year, fixed mortgage, with the proviso that people could opt-out and select other mortgage products that were accompanied by full disclosure.[26] The role of the CFPB would be to create pre-approved contract templates lenders could choose from—not to dictate the particular choice any lender was required to make.[27]

Finally, the congressional testimony of CFPB's supporters had to rebut arguments that the proposed agency should not be created at all. Among the objections, the most common and serious was that consumer protection should not be separated from prudential regulation, that is, the supervision of financial institutions for the purpose of "safety and soundness."[28] The fear, articulated by lenders and their existing regulators, was that a stand-alone consumer protection agency might undermine the safety and soundness of the lending business.

Advocates responded to the safety and soundness concern in two ways. First, they argued that under the current regulatory system, safety and soundness had not co-existed with consumer protection; it had drowned it out. The ironic result was a set of unwise lending practices that created the greatest threat to safety and soundness since the Great Depression. Nobel Prize–winning economist Joseph Stiglitz put it most forcefully in testimony before the House: "[I]t was the subprime mortgages, irresponsible loans made to uninformed individuals beyond their ability to pay, designed to generate bankers fees as they robbed the poor of their life savings, that began the unraveling of our financial system."[29]

The work of the CFPB's supporters in front of numerous congressional committees during the summer of 2009 was taxing, but testifying was relatively familiar territory. Advocates were experienced at the inside baseball of Washington, D.C. politics. They had connections and credibility within congressional offices, especially with the staff of the key House and Senate committees chaired by Barney Frank and Chris Dodd. The advocates had compiled a respected body of work on prior campaigns, and they had the ability to produce research papers that supported their positions. What came next, though, would test their ability to fight in the court of public opinion.

Taking the Campaign to the Public

Initially, Elizabeth Warren was the chief public relations weapon of the pro-CFPB forces. During 2009, she received a great deal of publicity by virtue of her high-profile leadership of the Congressional Oversight Panel for the Troubled Asset Relief Program. She was a guest on *The Daily Show with Jon Stewart, Real Time with Bill Maher,* and *The Colbert Report.* And she was not averse to using her celebrity to promote the CFPB to the general public. In mid-July, she posted a video on YouTube. Appearing at her professor's desk at Harvard attired in a pale pink blouse, she began by mentioning that she had testified before Congress on President Obama's plan to create a new agency for consumers. Now, she wanted to share her "thoughts directly with anyone who wanted to hear them."[30] Warren explained that the job of the new agency would be to "set up basic rules so that no one gets tricked or trapped again." She concluded by urging viewers to tell their representatives in Washington: "Tell them you support change. Tell them you want a consumer agency, someone in Washington who's on your side."

Shortly thereafter, Warren penned a magazine article for *BusinessWeek* magazine. The piece stressed that a new agency would cut rather than increase the regulatory burden on businesses "by transforming fragmented, cumbersome, and complex regulations spanning seven federal agencies into a coherent set of smarter rules."[31]

That same week in late July, Warren posted an essay on the Internet addressing critics of the CFPB. She attempted to rebut "three myths about the consumer financial product agency": it would limit consumer choice and industry innovation, add another layer of regulation, and threaten the financial soundness of lending institutions.[32] The essay's defense of the proposal for a new agency was a possible sign of progress: her ideas had achieved sufficient legitimacy to elicit critics.

During the summer of 2009, Warren was not alone in making the case for the CFPB to the public. AFR weighed in on June 29 with a press release.

A Consumer Financial Protection Agency (CFPA) as proposed today by the President would provide a critical check on deceptive or unfair consumer practices, such as those that led to the foreclosure epidemic and ultimately to the economic crisis we are all experiencing today. Opposition to the Agency from the U.S. Chamber of Commerce, Wall Street bankers and the financial services industry is a slap in the face to the millions of Americans who played by the rules and got burned by predatory products, and those now suffering under the broader economic crisis. It is particularly galling when many of Wall Street's lobbyists are essentially being paid with taxpayer dollars advanced to prop up the broken financial system.[33]

In September, 74 legal scholars—led by Jeff Sovern and Norman Silber—sent a letter to congressional leaders, urging them to create a consumer financial protection agency. As one might expect from legal scholars, more space was devoted to footnotes than the main text, but the message was clear: the CFPB was the right way to correct past mistakes that had undermined the country's financial stability "and toward a better future for consumers and the nation."[34]

All the testimony, press conferences, letters, and blogging began to pay off for CFPB's advocates in the form of editorial support from some prominent columnists and leading news outlets. Syndicated columnist Bob Herbert described the financial industry's opposition to the newly proposed CFPB as "chutzpah on steroids." Herbert was appalled: "These malefactors of great wealth . . . developed hideously destructive credit policies and took insane risks that hurt millions of American families and nearly wrecked the economy. Then they were bailed out with hundreds of billions of taxpayer dollars, money that came from the very people victimized by the industry's outlandish practices."[35] Herbert concluded that the financial industry viewed "an informed consumer as Public Enemy No. 1. The last thing in the world that they want is a fair marketplace, which is why the Consumer Financial Protection Agency can't come fast enough."

Supportive words from the editors of *The New York Times* were not a surprise.[36] Approval from *USA Today* and the *New York Daily News* was less predictable.[37] Public opinion also seemed to be falling in line for the CFPB. In September, the Consumer Federation of America released a poll showing that 57 percent of a national sample of respondents supported the idea of creating a new federal agency to protect consumers of financial products and services. Support was notably high among young adults, African Americans, and low-income persons.[38] In October, Lake Research Partners concluded that public support for the new agency was strong even in relatively conservative Democratic districts and swing states.[39]

Survey research conducted by the CFPB's opponents yielded results less favorable toward the CFPB. In what might be viewed as using polling to influence rather than gauge public opinion, "word doctor" Frank

Luntz posed the following question: "Which of the following, if true, would concern you most about the creation of a Consumer Financial Protection Agency?" From a long list of possible answers, respondents were asked to choose three. The most common answers were "cost hundreds of millions of dollars every year," "creation of more government agencies," and the *non sequitur,* "filled with lobbyist loopholes."[40] Issues of polling bias aside, the early polling results seemed promising, if not conclusive, to the agency's advocates.

The Opposition Bites Back

While AFR and its allies were making their case to the public, the CFPB's opponents were doing the same. If a major hurdle for proponents of the CFPB was to make the case that government regulation of the financial industry would really work this time, opponents of the CFPB had their own problem. They couldn't deny that a problem existed with consumer financial protection, so they had to both describe the CFPB as the wrong solution and offer a credible alternative.

Many of the lobbying activities of the CFPB's opponents mirrored those of its proponents. The case against the CFPB was stated in congressional testimony, letters to Congressmen, op-ed pieces, and briefing papers from academics. There was the standard tack of playing for time, as exemplified in a July 20, 2009 letter to the House Financial Services Committee from 23 business trade associations: "While we commend your commitment to passing comprehensive financial regulatory reform legislation, including enhanced and effective consumer protection, we are very concerned that this legislation could advance without sufficient time to fully assess the cost to consumers and impact on businesses from all sectors of the economy."[41]

Similarly, John Courson of the Mortgage Bankers Association said the nation faced "a once-in-a-generation opportunity to improve the mortgage lending process," but "proposals should not be rushed through."[42] The slow-walk strategy of the CFPB's opponents made perfect political sense during a Democrat-controlled congressional session. Even if financial reform could not be delayed indefinitely, anything that contributed to procrastination increased the pressure on Democrats to make compromises.

In its communications with congressmen, the CFPB's opponents painted a picture of a massive and unaccountable bureaucracy with sweeping powers to create unnecessary and burdensome regulations. Edward L. Yingling, testifying on behalf of the American Bankers Association, complained that under the CFPB: "All current financial consumer protection laws, carefully crafted by Congress, [would be] rendered largely moot—mere floors. The CFPA can do almost anything it wants to go beyond those laws, as well as into new areas, to regulate the terms of products, the way in which they are offered, and even the compensation for offering them."[43]

Prior to the CFPB campaign, the groups that comprised AFR were accustomed to being outspent 10 to 1 by their opponents. The differential spending was usually confined, however, to lobbying directed at congressmen and other political decision makers. Advocates of the CFPB had less experience counteracting a highly professional advertising campaign aimed at influencing public opinion.[44] In this case, the U.S. Chamber of Commerce unleashed a $2 million advertising campaign based on the claim that the CPFB would "punish" small businesses. In September, 2009, print ads appeared in the Washington, D.C. area. The overall theme was: "It's a tough economy. The CFPA will make it tougher." One ad featured a butcher with the tag line: "Virtually every business that extends credit to American consumers would be affected—even the local butcher and the credit he extends to his customers."[45] Additional print ads displayed a baker and an orthodontist. The theme common to the campaign, which included television and web ads as well, was that the proposed agency would be an uncaring bureaucracy intruding into even the smallest businesses.

The Chamber's advertising campaign was smart. The Chamber knew that the public had little sympathy for the banks and other large financial institutions; however, the common man and woman could sympathize with the owner of a small business. If Elizabeth Warren was going to lay claim to the middle class as consumers, the Chamber would appeal to the same group as actual or potential small-business owners.

The Chamber's advertising blitz began in early September, 2009. While it is difficult to quantify the impact of the ads, it is plausible that they contributed to eventual carve-outs for small businesses and auto dealers in the final CFPB legislation. In the fall of 2009, however, the long-term impact of the Chamber's advertising efforts was not the most pressing problem for the CFPB's supporters. Their more immediate concern was some unsettling developments in the House Financial Services Committee.

Fending Off Weakening Amendments in the House

AFR and its allies never expected to run the gauntlet of the legislative process without having to fend off threats to the CFPB's authority, independence, and its very existence. Given the power of the industries that opposed them, legislative efforts to weaken the new agency's independence and authority were inevitable. These efforts not only threatened the proposed agency; they also challenged the cohesion of the AFR coalition. Some partner groups might abandon the coalition if a particular provision near to their heart was stricken from the bill; other groups might decide that the bill was so freighted with half-baked compromises that it was no longer worth supporting.

The first major compromise occurred when Chairman Frank introduced The Consumer Financial Protection Agency Act on July 8. The Obama administration's White Paper had proposed that enforcement of the Community Reinvestment Act (CRA), a law designed to ensure access to financial services in underserved communities, be moved to the CFPB.[46] When Frank introduced his bill three weeks later, there was no mention of the CRA in it.

Frank was well aware of how irritating the CRA was to banks and had already begun to hear opposition to placing the act's enforcement in the hands of a new and vigorous CFPB.[47] Recognizing this political reality, Frank saw the CRA as just too controversial. The press release announcing his bill said that CRA considerations would be taken up "at [a] later time."[48] Frank told Ed Mierzwinski, "It just gives us another thing to fight about."[49]

This was a pivotal moment for the brand-new AFR. For many of the civil rights and fair lending groups that were charter members of AFR—groups like the National Community Reinvestment Council and the National Fair Housing Alliance—strengthening enforcement of the CRA was their very top priority. They viewed existing enforcement of the CRA as weak, fragmented, and inconsistent.[50] After seeing their number one priority dropped from Chairman Frank's bill, the first response of several civil rights and fair lending groups was to challenge the move.

John Taylor of the National Community Reinvestment Coalition led the charge of those seeking reinstatement of CRA enforcement in the CFPB bill. In a press release, Taylor said: "Leaving consumer protections with existing bank regulatory agencies suggests a disregard for their failure to enforce the laws in the first place."[51] When he pressed Frank on his decision, Taylor heard what he considered "tortured reasoning." Frank told Taylor that the CFPB is about protections for individuals while the CRA is about protections for communities. Taylor's response was, "Barney, you need to read the law. They measure CRA performance based on lending to individuals, not to communities."[52]

When it became clear that CRA enforcement would not be part of the CFPB and that AFR was not going to treat this as a make-or-break issue, the civil rights and fair lending groups in AFR could have opted to leave the coalition. Some of these groups certainly thought about it. According to AFR's executive director Heather Booth, inclusion of CRA enforcement was a prime issue for these groups, and "it was a great disappointment that it wasn't going to be in this bill. There was one point where it took them a while. They needed to decide whether they would support the overall process if this wasn't in."[53]

Nancy Zirkin, executive vice president for policy for the Leadership Conference on Civil and Human Rights, was frustrated by the exclusion of the CRA from Frank's bill, but she remained results-oriented:

> At the time, it was very important to us. CRA had been attacked as a cause of the whole mortgage crisis, which was the dumbest thing I had ever heard, so it was very important to strengthen it. But Barney told us in July . . . that he couldn't do it. If we wanted to talk with the Democrats, with the Blue Dogs, fine, but he couldn't make it happen. It was a big loss for our organization, but we still needed the housing piece and we still needed the whole consumer bureau.[54]

After some hesitation, all of the civil rights and fair lending organizations not only stayed with the coalition but devoted considerable resources to creating the CFPB and enacting financial reform legislation. According to Ed Mierzwinski, "the community groups stuck with us and they provided all their field apparatus. . . . The civil rights groups were fierce and stuck with us throughout the thing."[55]

The next compromises were primarily concessions to the centrist and conservative-leaning Democratic members of the House Financial Services Committee. In the 111th Congress, in session from January 2009–January 2011, 40 percent (17 of 42) of the House Financial Services Committee were members of either the Blue Dog or New Democratic Caucus, or both.[56] The caucuses were known for their solicitousness toward the financial industries in general, and especially to voices coming from community banks in their districts.

Since the Republican minority on the Financial Services Committee was united and disciplined in its opposition to the CFPB, Barney Frank and CFPB supporters realized that their focus needed be on the centrist Democrats. Maureen Thompson, a member of the AFR steering group and a consultant to the AARP, reported, "There were so many Blue Dogs and moderate Democrats on the committee that you really needed to bring some of them over in support of the bill if you were going to be successful."[57] If the moderates chose to oppose a measure, *en bloc*, they probably had the votes to succeed. As a result, their threats had to be taken very seriously.[58] Although House Democrats, as a group, were more progressive than the subset seated on the Financial Services Committee, the bill could easily die aborning if the Blue Dogs and New Democrats were not carefully attended to.

By mid-September, despite the efforts of the administration, including a plug for the CFPB during the president's weekly video and radio address, Barney Frank was feeling the pressure from some Democrats on his committee.[59] Walt Minnick, a first-term, Blue Dog Democratic congressman from Idaho, floated a plan that would have dispensed with a new federal agency entirely. Instead, he favored encouraging existing state and federal regulators to work together in a consumer financial protection council.[60]

Minnick's approach was not acceptable to Frank, AFR, or Elizabeth Warren because the proposed council would be populated by the same regulators who had been asleep at the switch or unwilling to act in the lead-up to the financial crisis. Nevertheless, Frank demonstrated some flexibility, circulating a memo among his Democratic colleagues on September 22, indicating his willingness to soften various provisions of the CFPB bill. The memo addressed both the agency's authority and its independence.[61]

The first option extended by Frank was to trim the list of lenders subject to regulation. Frank suggested exempting merchants, retailers, and other nonfinancial businesses from the oversight of CFPB.[62] This change would address the Chamber of Commerce's claim that butchers, bakers, and candlestick makers would be driven out of business by the CFPB. It also made it more difficult for detractors to portray the CFPB as being a pernicious new bureaucratic species that would do more to invade the cash registers of businesses than protect the wallets of consumers. In addition, the memo proposed exempting auto dealers when "acting in their traditional capacities." Car dealers suspected, however, that Frank did not view brokering or making loans as falling under this category and continued to press for a more explicit exclusion for their lending activities.[63]

Further, with respect to the CFPB's authority, Chairman Frank's memo expressed his willingness to jettison the proposal that consumers be offered a plain vanilla option for mortgages and other credit transactions.[64] The plain vanilla idea had become a political lightening rod for claims by the CFPB's critics that the agency would be a financial dictator, substituting its judgment for that of consumers.[65] Advocates, though disappointed at losing plain vanilla, held their fire. A day after Treasury Secretary Geithner announced the Obama administration's willingness to let go of the controversial provision, the nation's largest consumer organization, Consumers

Union, declared that the change shouldn't deter the agency's supporters: "There's still lots to like in this important effort toward protecting consumers from predatory and unfair practices in the financial industry."[66]

Congressman Frank was less willing to compromise when it came to two additional issues regarding the CFPB's authority. One issue, whether CFPB rules would preempt state laws, was being championed by one of the more conservative Democrats on financial issues, Melissa Bean of Illinois. The other issue, an exemption from CFPB jurisdiction for auto dealers, was being raised by a Republican, John Campbell (R-Calif.). The resolution of the preemption and exemption issues in the House Committee and the final Dodd-Frank bill are the subjects of separate chapters in this book.

Frank's memo offered an additional change that would prove to be controversial after enactment of Dodd-Frank but received virtually no attention at the time. It dealt with the CFPB's structure and hence its independence. Until this point, proposals for a new consumer financial protection agency—including the first draft of Frank's bill—had envisioned a stand-alone agency with a five-member board chaired by a director. To ensure that the new agency attended to the safety and soundness of financial institutions, one seat would be reserved for the head of an agency responsible for chartering and regulating national banks.[67] A five-person governing board was common among executive-branch regulatory agencies, including the Consumer Product Safety Commission, the Federal Trade Commission, and the Securities and Exchange Commission.

Frank's revised bill made a subtle but important change. It proposed that the new agency "will be run by a single Director, who will be advised by a Consumer Financial Protection Oversight Board, which is made up of the Federal banking agencies, NCUA, FTC and HUD and the Chairman of the State Liaison Committee of the FFIEC."[68] On the one hand, the presence of multiple prudential regulators on the oversight board could be viewed as making their voice more prominent. On the other hand, the board's role was strictly advisory, with agency decision-making resting in the hands of a single person.

The potential threat to the CFPB's independence posed by the Oversight Board caught the attention of Travis Plunkett, one of AFR's key players. Plunkett was very wary: "The upshot of this is that many, not all, but many of the agencies that dropped the ball regarding abuses and unfair credit would now have an oversight role regarding this agency. Where are the consumers on this advisory board, by the way?"[69] As a seasoned political player, Plunkett knew enough not to react in all-or-nothing terms. It would take time to fully analyze the changes, especially the implications for agency independence of having a single director rather than a five-person board.

Considering Chairman Frank's proposed changes as a whole, a press release from the National Consumer Reinvestment Coalition stated that the changes "weaken an already compromised bill."[70] Most of the consumer and community groups, however, were more tempered in their responses. Ruth Susswein, a deputy director of Consumer Action, said some of the changes in Frank's proposal "would be a concern of ours."[71] Ed Mierzwinski, one of AFR's most active members, commented, "I don't think anything here is intended to weaken or eviscerate this in any way. The agency will still have a primary role of protecting consumers."[72] Ira Rheingold, head of the National Association of Consumer Advocates, reacted: "The devil is in the details—but I think you can still have a pretty effective agency."[73] If some members of the coalition were upset by Frank's proposed changes, they kept their most incendiary comments within the coalition and cooled their jets in public.

A week after Chairman Frank circulated his proposed modifications, President Obama tried to put an end to efforts to soften the bill. Press Secretary Robert Gibbs cautioned that the president, while not drawing any lines in the sand, "would not sign any bill that he thought was too weak."[74] Gibbs's statement presumably provided support and comfort to Michael Barr, Eric Stein, and Diana Farrell, the administration's key representatives in negotiations with legislators and its dealings with AFR and its allies.[75]

After four and a half days of debate and consideration of amendments, the House Committee voted 39 to 29, largely along party lines, on October 22, 2009, to approve legislation creating the CFPB. Forty-seven amendments had been offered, about half of which had passed.[76] The Republicans on the Financial Services Committee thought all the changes merely gave a new coat of paint to an old clunker, but the majority of the centrist Democrats had voted with their chairman on the big-picture question of whether there should be a CFPB.[77]

On the most contentious issue of whether CFPB jurisdiction would preempt state-level action against national banks and thrift institutions, an amendment introduced by centrist Democrat Melissa Bean of Illinois was soundly defeated. A much more narrowly crafted substitute offered by liberal Rep. Mel Watt and his centrist counterpart, Dennis Moore, was passed on a voice vote. Bean agreed to quell her opposition, at least temporarily, at the behest of the White House and liberal members of the Democratic Caucus as well as AFR and its partners.[78] But Barney Frank acknowledged that the issue was likely to resurface in the Senate and possibly even in the House when the bill came up for a floor vote.

According to Ed Mierzwinski, a veteran of many legislative campaigns for consumer rights and the chair of AFR's consumer protection working group, getting the support of moderate and conservative Democrats was one of the signal achievements of the AFR coalition. Drawing a comparison to prior campaigns, he said:

> It was always very difficult for us to win because even with the Democrats in charge, you had Melissa Bean and the New Democrats who would always vote with the Republicans or threaten to vote with the Republicans. So instead of the Republicans having 30 or 35 votes out of the 70, they essentially had 41 out of the 70 because they had the 11 conservative Dems. And that was what the difference was here. The difference was, they couldn't get the votes for their weakening amendments.[79]

AFR's executive director Heather Booth was grateful for Chairman Frank's leadership of the House committee. Booth observed:

> We never would have gotten as effective legislation on consumer financial protection as we did if we didn't have the leadership of Barney and his staff. Overall I think they played an extraordinary role. No one else in the House or Senate could have done it. There's a very small number of people who could have both designed it, had mastery over it, and could have moved it through and who wanted as strong a bill in the main as we got. There are areas in which we think it should have been stronger, but they were also dealing with the political realities, and they saw that.[80]

On the other hand, some advocates felt strongly that Chairman Frank was often too willing to make strategic compromises before they proved absolutely necessary. One long-time consumer strategist commented:

> Did he compromise prematurely? Compromised too quickly would be a friendly way of putting it. Gave away the farm would be more accurate. What always astonished me was—and this is Negotiations 101—you give up something only if you get some votes in return. And he was giving up things repeatedly without getting any votes in return. I think that he believed that what he was doing would both get votes and was the right way to do it.[81]

Despite some disappointments, the CFPB's advocates had reason to be hopeful that Frank's bill would pass in the full House where dependence on financial industry campaign cash was weaker than in the Committee. They did not expect smooth sailing, however. Above and beyond renewed objections to the CFPB from Democrats such as Minnick and Bean, an additional challenge still loomed.[82] Frank's bill dealt only with the CFPB, but everyone knew that eventually the CFPB proposal would live or die with the broader financial reform package.

Sure enough, less than three weeks after the House Financial Services voted a bill out of Committee, Senator Dodd released a discussion draft of a comprehensive financial reform bill. The CFPB was included as Title X.[83] Soon thereafter, on December 2, Congressman Frank introduced a version of Dodd's comprehensive bill, H.R. 4173, in the House.[84] The bill was called the Financial Stability Improvement Act, and its broad approach to financial regulatory reform did not materialize out of thin air. Throughout the autumn, various House committees had been discussing the topics covered in the bill, including executive compensation, regulation of derivatives, and investor protection.

Despite the new bill's 1279-page girth, the full House was able to pass it after only a few days of deliberation. Republicans slowed down the process a bit by offering amendments, none of which dealt with the CFPB.[85] Amendments offered by Democrats were more of a threat to the new agency. A showdown on the issue of preemption was avoided when some of the changes offered by Representative Bean were wrapped into a manager's amendment offered by Barney Frank.[86] Representative Minnick again offered an amendment on the House floor that would have substituted a council of existing regulators for a new consumer financial protection agency, but his amendment was defeated on December 11 by a vote of 223 to 208.[87] All the House Republicans voted for it, but they were joined by only 32 Democrats, too few to gain approval.[88] The same day, the House, after considering several more amendments, passed the entire bill, 223–202.[89]

Reflecting on Barney Frank's leadership, Assistant Treasury Secretary Michael Barr remarked: "Perhaps I wouldn't have made exactly the same compromises as he did, but Frank is an extremely experienced legislator. He got the bill out of his committee, and we have an Act that has a lot of teeth. I guess I cut him a lot of slack for that reason."[90]

From here, the CFPB's supporters had to turn their attention to the Senate. There, the chair of the Senate Banking Committee, Chris Dodd, was not perceived by the advocates to be as predictable an ally as their champion in the House, Barney Frank.

Chapter 7

Wanted: A Few Votes in the Senate

The momentum toward a financial reform package, including a new agency for consumers, slowed in the cold winter months of early 2010. Some Republican senators, recognizing the potential popularity of an agency dedicated to helping consumers, sought to rein in its independence rather than oppose it outright. Senator Robert Bennett (R-Utah) expressed the fear that a truly independent CFPB might become another Environmental Protection Agency.[1] To an environmentalist, that might be a compliment, but to Bennett it meant an agency that could impose strict rules that were painful for businesses. Bennett was willing, however, to consider an agency that was located within, and subordinate to, an already-existing financial regulator.

Meanwhile, AFR and other supporters of the CFPB were worried about the challenges facing Senator Dodd in advancing financial reform legislation. Dodd knew, for example, that the ranking Republican member of the Senate Banking Committee, Richard Shelby (R-Ala.), was vehemently opposed to the CFPB—independently structured or not. Shelby's position, if adhered to, could be a complete deal breaker. Dodd was also exquisitely sensitive to the dwindling time remaining on the Senate clock. The time pressure was a source of strength for Republicans who had many means of slowing down the legislative process.

The CFPB's supporters were probably not entirely surprised when several media outlets broke the news in mid-January that Dodd was willing to drop the idea of a fully independent consumer protection agency if such a compromise was necessary to move the entire financial reform package forward.[2] They noted that Dodd had come in for some sharp criticism from certain conservative Democrats on the Banking Committee and reasoned that he was probably wary of moving too aggressively. Wanting to shore up their position, the advocates reacted swiftly, issuing a press release that described the CFPB as "the cornerstone of meaningful financial reform."[3] A few days later, President Obama personally braced Senator Dodd in a private meeting, indicating that the CFPB, in some form, was "non-negotiable" from the White House's perspective.[4]

Dogged by the AFR and its allies, Senator Dodd reacted by pressing for a bill that included a consumer financial protection agency. Talks between Dodd and ranking Republican Richard Shelby continued through December and January but eventually crumbled in early February.[5] For Shelby, the proposal to create a new consumer agency was one of the biggest sticking points in the much broader legislative package. Shelby said, "I fully support enhancing both consumer protection and safety and soundness regulation [but] I will not support a bill that enhances one at the expense of the other."[6]

Senator Dodd then turned to another Republican on the Senate Banking Committee, first-termer Bob Corker (R-Tenn.), as a possible interlocutor. Corker had displayed some willingness to work across the aisle on financial reform. Specifically, he had been working with Democratic senator Mark Warner of Virginia on ways to wind down large, failing financial firms.[7] While opposed to a stand-alone new agency, Corker was interested in exploring other possibilities. Initially, he and Dodd seemed to agree on creating a new regulator of federally chartered financial institutions that would contain an office of consumer protection.[8] They also discussed the possibility of locating a new consumer protection agency within an existing financial regulator, such as the Treasury Department or Federal Reserve.[9] In Corker's view, either of these alternative arrangements would minimize any threats from consumer protection to the safety and soundness of financial institutions.[10]

In the face of continuing Republican opposition and the threat of a slow-down, it wasn't just Dodd who was looking for a way out of the impasse. At the end of February, the Obama administration indicated that it was open to the possibility of a less formally independent agency if this meant quick approval of a comprehensive financial reform bill.[11] According to Michael Barr of the Treasury Department, "as long as there would be an independent budget, an independent director, independent policy making, and independent enforcement, you could put the agency on the moon and it wouldn't really matter."[12]

Receiving a green light from the president, Chairman Dodd embraced Senator Corker's idea of placing the CFPB within the Federal Reserve.[13] Barney Frank reacted by calling the idea a "bad joke."[14] Syndicated columnist Harold Meyerson wrote that "placing a weakened CFPA within the Fed could be like putting the Food and Drug Administration inside, say, Pfizer."[15]

Within the advocacy community, the idea of situating the CFPB within another government entity was not well received. Elizabeth Warren had strong words in response to what was happening in the Senate Banking Committee. She said in an interview that if Congress couldn't produce a strong agency she preferred "no agency at all and plenty of blood and teeth left on the floor."[16] Warren would later soften her position on the location of the CFPB, but her words were a sign that the CFPB's supporters were growing weary of making concessions and might walk away from an overly compromised bill.

Comic Relief

With both President Obama and Senator Dodd apparently willing to make major concessions, supporters of the CFPB needed a boost. They received one in the form of two viral videos directed by Ron Howard, the hand behind movies such as *The Da Vinci Code, Frost/Nixon, A Beautiful Mind, Apollo 13,* and *Cocoon.* The videos stemmed partially from a conversation Howard had with Elizabeth Warren. He told her, "I would try to get together with a few people who might be able to get the word out [about the CFPB]."[17] Those people turned out to be some of the most famous comedians in the United States, including Jim Carrey, Will Ferrell, and Dan Aykroyd.

In the first video, actors impersonating former U.S. presidents visit the bedroom of a putative President Obama and his wife Michelle. In a dream sequence, the former presidents tell President Obama to show some gumption and support the creation of a strong CFPB, regardless of the political consequences. The video's release on March 3 was clearly meant to influence the Senate Banking Committee negotiations: it ends with a voiceover by Ron Howard, urging people to contact their senators.

The second video, released a few days later, features Heidi Montag, a blonde bombshell of an actress known for her numerous plastic surgeries. In self-deprecating fashion, she ties the dangers of plastic surgery to that of another kind of plastic: credit cards. She says: "With hidden fees and standard interest rate increases, that $11,000 jawline could end up costing you upwards of $50,000. . . . Being in debt for elective surgery is bad enough, but when I think about the thousands of Americans whose only method of paying for food is their credit cards—it's enough to make me cry without moving my new face."[18]

The video concludes with Ms. Montag reclining seductively in a bathtub. She suggests that viewers call senators Dodd and Shelby. At that point, cardboard heads of the two senators emerge from her bath bubbles and a phone number is splashed on the screen.

The videos dovetailed with an effort by AFR to get people around the country to urge Congress to enact meaningful financial reform, including a strong CFPB.[19] The videos did not attempt to educate the public about the specifics of the horse trading that was occurring within the Senate Banking Committee. With their vague exhortations, the videos were designed only to provide a general goad to the Senate.

The videos also buoyed the CFPB's supporters. Ed Mierzwinski felt the videos showed that he and his fellow advocates were not just "Washington wonks out there with no ties to real people."[20] While numerous plastic surgeries have rendered very little of Heidi Montag "real," Mierzwinski was alluding to the fact that the CFPB was now part of popular culture, and the public was watching the debate over the agency's fate. AFR's members had to feel good; it was now cool to care about the CFPB.

Dodd Offers Concessions

Against the background of an increasingly severe time crunch in the Senate and a protracted and inconclusive negotiation with Committee Republicans led by senators Shelby and Corker, Chairman Dodd felt compelled to unfurl a comprehensive revision of the bill he had first introduced in November of 2009. On March 11, Dodd called Corker and thanked him for being "a great partner" and decided to push ahead without Republican support but retaining some of their ideas for the CFPB.[21] In addition to placing the CFPB in the Federal Reserve, Dodd's bill included a veto mechanism with respect to CFPB rules to serve as a safeguard against CFPB rules that would endanger the safety and soundness of the banking system.[22] No other regulatory agency faced this kind of constraint on its independence, and the CFPB's supporters were not happy about it.[23]

Viewed from one angle, Dodd's strategy of offering concessions with respect to the CFPB's independence was a failure. His compromise approach was unpopular with the CFPB's supporters and yet it wasn't buying him any Republican support.[24] One blogger commented: "Sen. Chris Dodd is becoming the Max Baucus of financial reform. Baucus used his powerful position to trade away one popular policy on health reform after another, allegedly in search of 'bipartisan' support. Yet when that support didn't appear, none of those compromises were withdrawn. Funny how that happens."[25]

From another point of view, however, Dodd's strategy was sheer political genius. By giving ground in an attempt to drum up bipartisan support, Dodd made it easier for centrist Democrats on his committee to support the bill. And by moving beyond the protracted and tedious private negotiations with Shelby and then Corker, Dodd forced the issues into the public domain and put the onus on the Republicans to oppose his modest proposals for a consumer agency.

An interviewee close to the action observed, "There wasn't a moderate Democrat on the Committee who wanted to have a vote on it. They don't like tough votes there. The whole culture of the Senate is one that steers away from tough votes and tries to kill things in their crib."[26] Centrist senators from Republican-leaning states—John Tester of Montana, Mark Warner of Virginia, Tim Johnson of South Dakota, and Evan Bayh of Indiana—could report to their constituents that they had reached across the aisle and supported a more modest version of the new consumer protection agency. In a sense, the louder advocates complained about Dodd's compromises, the safer they made it for any wavering Democrats to vote for the bill.[27]

On March 15, Dodd introduced his bill, The Restoring American Financial Stability Act of 2010. The bill lodged the CFPB within the Federal Reserve, an idea that emerged from his failed negotiations with Corker. To reflect the new entity's location within the Fed, its name became the Consumer Financial Protection *Bureau.*

The very same day, AFR released a public statement of appreciation for "Chairman Dodd's work" but stated, quite pointedly, that it wasn't nearly enough.[28] Heather Booth said: "We believe the best way to structure a strong and independent Consumer Financial Protection Agency is through a stand-alone agency, and we are troubled by the provisions that allow Consumer Financial Protection Agency decisions to be appealed to a council dominated by institutions that failed consumers in the past."[29] AFR also objected to proposed exemptions for particular lenders (such as auto dealers) that narrowed the CFPB's jurisdiction far too much.[30]

AFR's leaders were keen not to compromise too readily. According to Lisa Donner, AFR's assistant director, the coalition had a theory for passage of the bill:

> Our view of how to pass this bill was always that having the strongest possible bill was the best way to get votes for it. . . . To pass the bill, there was going to have to be public pressure against people who were opposing it. You do better for yourself in the end by, rather than compromising a lot, making the bill good so that people will fight for it.[31]

Ed Mierzwinski concurred. He felt that public opinion demanded that Congress pass a bill, so the advocates could afford to be tough before giving their seal of approval. He said: "We were able to communicate to Congress something that their polls were also showing them, which was that if this was a weak bill, and the public attacked the bill, then Congress would look bad. That helped us tremendously."[32]

If Dodd was expecting CFPB's supporters to come around and to accept an agency housed in the Fed, he had to know that there was a limit to their flexibility. Damon Silvers, associate general counsel for the AFL-CIO and deputy chair (to chair Elizabeth Warren) of the Congressional TARP Oversight Panel, viewed Dodd's decision *not* to negotiate further concessions as crucial. According to Silvers, who was the AFL-CIO's representative to AFR, continuing to negotiate with Republican leadership to get a bill that would be broadly acceptable would have resulted in a bill that would be toothless, not just with respect to the CFPB, but in a number of other respects. "The alternative was to toughen the bill and force the Republicans out into an open fight. The administration and Dodd chose to toughen the bill, and that was the critical moment in the passage of Dodd-Frank, not just in the passage of the CFPB."[33]

AFR's second-in-command, Lisa Donner, also credited the Obama administration with encouraging Dodd to take a strong stand on the CFPB's independence. She said, "The administration's firmness about an independent consumer agency was profoundly important to holding Dodd in place, and without that, the whole thing would have fallen apart."[34] Representatives of the administration also spoke to members of AFR about the potential benefits of making the CFPB part of the Fed.

Mike Calhoun of the Center for Responsible Lending and one of AFR's most respected members wasn't especially upset about placing the CFPB within the Fed. For Calhoun, the key issue was independence. He believed that the arrangement could work and tried to convince skeptical Democrats and members of AFR:

The Center for Responsible Lending stepped out early, and I think we had a major role in helping convince a number of particularly progressive members on the Senate and the House side that that was ultimately a workable arrangement. Travis [Plunkett] and I took the lead [in convincing other organizations that putting the CFPB in the Fed would be OK.] We brought a fair amount of credibility to the table, and I think people were willing to hear us out. And people coalesced around it pretty quickly. . . . The AFR position continued to be the call for a stand-alone agency, and particularly at the field level of the AFR organizations' membership, that's where the hardest sell was. Much more so than within the Beltway, it's a much more complicated field organizing cry to say, "Let's fight for an agency embedded within the Federal Reserve."

I think it actually helped at the end of the day to have this workable compromise because conversely the rallying cry for the Chamber of Commerce and other industry groups had been no independent agency. And so having it embedded in the Fed complicated messaging for both sides. It was much harder for them to message to say the bureau embedded in the Fed is going to be this rogue agency.[35]

One member of AFR who broke with the coalition's pattern of avoiding extreme statements was John Taylor, president of the National Community Reinvestment Coalition. Speaking of Dodd's modifications to the proposed agency's structure, Taylor said:

> If the intention was a compromise on the independence of the agency, then why do it twice over? Putting the agency at the Federal Reserve and giving the systemic risk council veto power ensures that this agency will be totally hamstrung by the very agencies that failed to prevent this crisis in the first place. Does anybody believe that the Director of the CFPA will be 'independent' with Secretary Geithner and Chairman Bernanke breathing down their neck?[36]

Taylor may well have been giving expression to anger felt by other coalition members, but the tenor of his statement did not characterize the public statements of most AFR members. The coalition served as a brake on pronouncements that might sabotage the coalition's positions. According to an interviewee who did not want to be identified, "What was successful about AFR is that Taylor's aggressive statement was a huge exception."[37]

Moving the CFPB into the Federal Reserve strengthened the rationale for an approach to funding the new entity that first appeared in the original draft of H.R. 4173 passed by the House in December, 2009—namely, having the Fed fund the CFPB.[38] The CFPB's advocates had never figured out a way to fund the CFPB that would be totally free of the political influence of the congressional appropriations process and the economic influence of a system of fees on financial institutions. Elizabeth Warren had suggested a user fee—"a nickel a year for every open credit card account that a financial institution has that has to go to this agency, a penny a year for open car loans, maybe a dime a year for open mortgages"—but the idea gained no traction.[39]

Since there was no perfect source of funding, the CFPB's advocates supported a mixture of funding sources. Travis Plunkett of the Consumer

Federation of America told the House Financial Services Committee, "Funding from a variety of sources, as well as a mix of these sources, should be considered, including congressional appropriations, user fees or industry assessments, filing fees, priced services, such as for compliance exams and transaction-based fees."[40]

If the CFPB's supporters could swallow positioning the Bureau inside the Fed, Dodd could offer them a stable funding source insulated from the legislative appropriations process. His bill proposed transferring a limited amount of nonappropriated (nontaxpayer) funds from the Federal Reserve to the new bureau. The exact amount would be based on a request from the bureau's director and could not exceed 12 percent of the Fed's annual budget.[41] Even a small percentage of a huge amount is still a huge amount; it could easily exceed $500 million per year.[42]

Maureen Thompson, an AFR principal, summed up the decision to place the CFPB within the Fed this way: "There was real genius in what appeared to be a setback at the time. . . . And whoever came up with the funding structure to have it come out of the Federal Reserve's funds and not have it subject to congressional appropriations, it was, I don't know, luck, genius, you call it whatever you want."[43]

An Unexpectedly Swift Vote

In the Senate Banking Committee, Dodd braced for the more than 300 amendments that Republicans had threatened to offer. Amazingly, Senator Shelby, the lead Republican on the committee, ultimately decided to offer none of these, thereby making it possible to move quickly to a vote. As described by journalist Jim Kuhnhenn, "Senators had been expecting a long week of votes and debate, only to find themselves voting as they were still easing into their seats."[44] On March 22, the committee passed the legislative measure on a strictly party-line basis, 13–10. A bill of over 1,300 pages had been dispatched in 21 minutes.[45] Shelby remarked that seeking changes in the committee would have been pointless and that he hoped Senator Dodd would continue to seek areas of agreement before the bill reached the Senate floor.[46]

The members of AFR were as surprised as anyone about the decision by the committee Republicans to not offer amendments. As Travis Plunkett recalls:

> I spent the whole weekend, as did my colleagues, pouring over amendments. We wrote a gigantic letter opposing many of the worst amendments. . . . Then

Shelby suddenly decided they weren't going to offer any. . . . It was shocking. So that was all part of the strategy to really not engage in the details. . . . Judging from their actions, [the Republicans] thought they could kill it. . . . They made a huge strategic error. Had they engaged in some of these awful amendments they might have ended up weakening the agency to the point that . . . we would be sitting here now with me saying, 'I'm not sure this agency is going to do much of anything.'[47]

Other AFR leaders held a similar view. Ed Mierzwinski's assessment was: "The Republican leadership in the Senate just definitely held out for too much. They probably could have cut a better deal than they did, but hey, that all worked out for the best."[48] A member of AFR who preferred not to be identified was blunter: "Shelby is a smart, canny guy [but] he screwed up in letting the bill out of committee without a markup."[49]

Michael Barr had a different explanation for Shelby's move. According to Barr, the Republicans simply did not have a coherent set of positions and tactics. "You read their amendments and they contradicted each other. I think Shelby made the right call: rather than embarrass his members and himself, he decided to let Dodd get the bill to the floor, with the idea that they would fight it there."[50]

The Battle Goes Public Again

On March 15, the day Dodd formally presented his bill, Brian Gardner, an expert on regulatory issues for a large investment company, gave the reform bill only a 40 percent chance of eventual passage by the full Congress.[51] The odds were somewhat better in the Senate Banking Committee. Only a simple majority vote was needed, and Democrats outnumbered Republicans on the committee. Moreover, Chairman Dodd had announced in January that he was not going to seek another term in the Senate.[52] His long-time Democratic colleagues on the committee were unlikely to vote against a bill that could prove to be Dodd's legacy.

The full Senate was another matter. There, the minority can force the majority to garner 60 votes to overcome a threatened or actual filibuster. During the December 2009 lame duck session of Congress, the Democrats had been able to push their health care reform bill through the Senate with exactly 60 votes, none of which came from a Republican. Since that time, however, Republican Scott Brown had taken the Massachusetts senatorial seat of the late Democratic stalwart, Ted Kennedy of Massachusetts (with Democrat Paul Kirk Jr. serving temporarily in the interim). Hence, the

Democrats would need at least one Republican vote to enact financial reform and more if any Democrat defected.

After the March 22 vote in the Senate Banking Committee, both supporters and opponents of comprehensive financial reform mobilized fully for the Senate floor vote, often focusing on the CFPB. The U.S. Chamber of Commerce launched a renewed campaign against creating a new agency in any form. In a March 26 press release, the Chamber called for "an alternative approach to strengthen consumer protection without creating an agency with unchecked powers and massive authority over the economy."[53] The Chamber's message, self-described as "part of a multi-million dollar nationwide grassroots campaign," included outreach via television, radio, and online advertising.[54] As of late March, the Chamber had already spent $3 million on advertisements critical of financial reform proposals and planned to spend at least that much on future ads.[55]

As with the Chamber's autumn advertising campaign against the CFPB, this one painted the agency as a threat to small businesses. The main television ad showed a man unable to sleep. He checks his alarm clock and sees that it is 2:48 A.M. As dawn approaches, he decides to get up and head to work. The ad's complete narration is as follows: "Americans are losing sleep over this economy, especially small business owners worrying about payroll and mounting bills. Now Washington wants to make it worse, with the CFPA, a massive new federal agency that will create more layers of regulation and bureaucracy. The CFPA will make it harder for small businesses to access credit. Small businesses work too hard to suffer further. Urge Congress to stop the CFPA. Go to StopTheCFPA.com."[56]

The "no sleep" ad eventually won a Reed Award for excellence in campaign management, political consulting, and political design.[57] Not everyone was impressed, though. Speaking with Bill Moyer, Gretchen Morgenstern, a leading business columnist of *The New York Times,* assessed it this way:

> What's interesting about that ad, Bill, is that it takes two completely separate things and melds them together. There is a problem for small businesses right now. They can't get money from the banks who will not lend to them, okay? So, I have sympathy for the small business owner. And small business drives America and drives employment in this country. So, yes, they are beleaguered. But they are not beleaguered because of a consumer protection finance agency. They are beleaguered because the banks took too many risks and are now withdrawing from the market and will not lend to them. So, it's very clever. It's very sophisticated. It's cynical. To talk about the poor beleaguered small business owner who exists and then to make them feel like this thing, this consumer finance agency is going to add to their burden. It's ludicrous.[58]

Of course, the beauty of being the U.S. Chamber of Commerce is having local chambers of commerce throughout the country. Members of these local bodies were encouraged to employ the entire political toolkit: write to the members of the Senate Banking Committee, submit op-ed pieces to their local newspapers, host an event to discuss the CFPB, and link their local website to the national website, stopthecfpa.com.[59]

Three of AFR's most financially powerful members—AARP, Americans United for Change, and MoveOn.org's political action committee—tried countering with their own mass media ad campaigns. The AARP ad debuted on April 19 and took the form of a country music sing-along. It played on resentment of bailouts of big banks and mortgage lenders, and it concluded: "Stop the fat cats from putting your money at risk. Tell your senators to pass financial reform now."[60]

Americans United for Change ran an ad on national cable television that portrayed the heads of Wall Street firms as criminals, calling them "the most dangerous men in America."[61] The men were accused of wiping out more than 8 million American jobs and attempting to kill legislation that would hold financial institutions accountable. Viewers were supposed to call their senators if they saw these dangerous men. The Moveon.org ad portrayed Senate Minority Leader Mitch McConnell as being in the pocket of Wall Street interests and as unfit to lead any financial reform effort.[62] The ads carried a strong populist message but, unlike those of the Chamber of Commerce, made no mention of the CFPB.

In addition to a limited advertising campaign, the CFPB's supporters expanded their advocacy toolkit to embrace "people power." Throughout the month of April, AFR worked with National People's Action to organize "showdowns" in a variety of locations. The showdowns were modeled after the Showdown in Chicago, held in October 2009.[63] Led by the SEIU, Jobs with Justice, and National People's Action, an estimated 5,000 protestors had made life uncomfortable for the attendees of the American Bankers Association annual meeting in The Windy City.[64]

The Chicago protesters had a diverse agenda, but creating a new agency to protect consumers was high on it. During a speech to the protesters, Illinois senator Dick Durbin asked bankers to stop opposing the CFPB.[65] FDIC chairman Sheila Bair delivered the same message.[66] At another venue, a call and response involving 700 people was heard. One person yelled: "Tell me what you want, what you really want." Hundreds of voices shouted back, "Our homes back!" Then again: "Tell me what you need, what you really need." The crowd answered back: "CFPA!"[67]

The Showdown in Chicago and its successor demonstrations in 2010 were an opportunity for "everyday people—retirees, farmers, workers, homeowners, renters, students, clergy, and small business owners from across the United States . . . [to ask] Congress to stand with the people and enact financial reform to hold banks accountable and strengthen the American economy."[68] During April 2010, showdowns took place in Illinois, Massachusetts, Missouri, New York, and North Carolina.[69] The largest, not surprisingly, was on Wall Street and drew somewhere between 4,000 and 8,000 protesters, according to police estimates.[70]

George Goehl, executive director of National People's Action and an active member of AFR from the time of its launch, viewed consistent public displays of frustration and anger with the financial crisis as essential to the campaign for financial reform . . . and beyond:

> We decided we needed to engage in the policy fight while also trying to build a movement that could advance more transformative change. We put some of our eggs in the legislative basket but also put many in the movement-building basket. As promising as the moment was for financial reform, it still meant playing within a set of margins that were quite narrow compared to what was and still is needed in terms of reform. It was clear to us that engaging in a direct lobbying campaign, while obviously critical, was in and of itself not going to shift the broader narrative.[71]

Getting to 60 Votes: Cloture and Floor Vote in the Senate

Attempts to cross the partisan divide on the financial reform bill ended in mid-April. According to Senate Minority Leader Mitch McConnell, fault for the end of negotiations lay—as it always did in his view—with President Obama. McConnell claimed that the White House had told Senate Democrats to cease their effort to find a bipartisan solution. "I naively thought we were heading in that direction until the strings were pulled on the Democratic leaders," McConnell said.[72] Senate Majority Leader Harry Reid saw the situation differently, describing McConnell's claim of a lock-out as "a figment of his imagination."[73]

On April 15, Senator Dodd officially submitted the bill that had been passed four weeks earlier by the Senate Banking Committee. The legislation would be Senate Bill 3217, the Restoring American Financial Stability Act of 2010. Given that the substance of the bill had been available for a month, a vote was anticipated within a matter of days.

It was time for AFR and its allies to make their final push for a favorable Senate vote. In addition to the showdowns in various cities and efforts to get people to call or write to their senators, AFR sent its own letter to senators Reid and McConnell on April 23. The letter asked for an up-or-down vote on financial reform.[74] While this might sound innocuous, it was an attempt to overcome a likely Republican-led filibuster. Given the Democratic majority in the Senate, the request was tantamount to asking the Republicans to give in. To back up the demand for a vote, AFR helped organize a massive letter-writing campaign as well as fly-in visits to legislators in Washington, D.C. by state-level activists.[75]

On the heels of a speech by President Obama urging quick action on financial reform, Senate Majority Leader Harry Reid filed for a cloture vote.[76] If passed, discussion of the financial reform bill would end, the threat of a filibuster would be overcome, and a vote would be taken. Republicans asked for more time to reach a deal, but Reid responded: "I'm not going to waste any more time of the American people while they come up with some agreement. The games of stalling are over."[77]

Reid announced his intentions on Friday, April 23. On Monday, Reid lost his cloture vote.[78] The same thing happened on Tuesday and Wednesday.[79] Finally, a few opponents of cloture started to waver.[80] A Tuesday hearing held by the Senate committee investigating the causes of the financial crisis had increased the political cost of siding with the big financial companies and prolonging debate. During the investigative hearing, Sen. Carl Levin (D-Mich.) skewered Goldman Sachs for the heavy sale of securities to its investors that Goldman's own analysts described as "a shitty deal."[81] Repeating the scatological phrase, Levin reduced Goldman, the proud, highly acclaimed, and ultra-successful financial colossus, to the level of a snake oil salesman.

Rather than lose a close vote, the Republicans relented. By unanimous consent, the Senate approved a motion to launch debate.[82] Senator Shelby referred to unspecified compromises as the reason for backing down, but he hastened to point out his continued opposition to the CFPB.[83]

During the next few weeks, there were numerous efforts to amend the Senate version of the financial reform legislation. A few amendments were submitted by Democrats to strengthen the bill, but most of the amendments were offered by Republicans to weaken various provisions. With respect to the CFPB, the most far-reaching amendments were submitted by Senator Shelby. He was still determined to prevent the CFPB from being an independent agency, even one located in the Fed.

On May 5, Shelby offered Amendment #3826 to Dodd's bill. Shelby's proposal was to make the new agency a division within the Federal Deposit Insurance Corporation. That in itself wasn't patently unacceptable to the CFPB's supporters given the pro-consumer sympathies of the FDIC's leader, Sheila Bair, but the amendment also specified that the new agency would not be able to finalize any rules without the FDIC's approval. Moreover, the new agency's funding mechanism would be changed. Instead of having a dedicated portion of the Federal Reserve's budget, the agency's funding would come from assessments on regulated financial institutions and could only be used to cover supervisory and rule-making activities, not rule enforcement.[84]

Clearly, the Shelby amendment would have greatly weakened the CFPB. During Senate debate the following day, Sen. Jeff Merkeley (D-Ore.) described the amendment this way: "The Shelby amendment No. 3826 carves the heart out of this bill. This dog don't hunt. In fact, this dog doesn't bite. I don't even think this dog barks. For that matter, I am not so sure it is a dog. That is how bad the Shelby amendment is."[85] The Senate promptly rejected the amendment by a largely party-line vote of 61–38.[86]

After dealing with a variety of other amendments, including one by Sen. John Thune (R-S.Dak.) that would have terminated the CFPB after four years, the next step for Senate Majority Leader Harry Reid was to cut off debate and get a vote on the comprehensive bill.[87] This proved more difficult than Reid expected because two Democratic senators, Maria Cantwell of Washington and Russ Feingold of Wisconsin, wouldn't vote for cloture. Their argument in opposition was that the bill was too weak in areas unrelated to the CFPB, such as the regulation of derivatives.[88] On the positive side, however, Republican senators Susan Collins and Olympia Snowe of Maine indicated a readiness to vote with Democrats in favor of ending debate.

Collins and Snowe, two moderate Republicans, had crossed the aisle before, most notably in early 2009 to support President Obama's stimulus package.[89] Reid would need their votes plus one or two more unless Cantwell and Feingold came around, and they were being intransigent.

The next day, May 20, Reid found the two votes needed to enact cloture. The easy one came from Sen. Arlen Specter (D-Pa.) who had been absent for the previous day's vote. The critical vote then was cast by Republican senator Scott Brown, making the vote 60–40.[90] Brown's vote was part of a strategy that unfolded over the next two months to extract key concessions for big financial companies based in his state.[91] The maneuvers would probably have impressed the prior occupant of his Senate seat, Ted Kennedy, who was no stranger to late night Senate conversions himself. Later that day, with only a simple majority needed to pass the bill, Brown and Republican senator Charles Grassley of Iowa voted with the 53 Democrats, two Independents (Joe Lieberman and Bernie Sanders), and Republicans Collins and Snowe on the bill itself. The final vote was 59–39.[92]

The day before voting for the reform bill, Grassley had voted against closure, citing his concerns about the so-called Volcker Rule—a proposal that would have limited the kinds of speculative investments in which financial institutions could engage.[93] Grassley said he ultimately voted for the bill, despite its flaws, because "a message needs to be sent to Wall Street that business-as-usual is over."[94]

Senator Brown's motivations were more specific. In a press release issued the day after voting for cloture, Brown said: "I supported moving the financial bill forward today because I received assurances from Senator Reid and his leadership team that the issues related to Massachusetts in the financial reform bill will be fixed before it is signed into law. We are still working to ensure these commitments are fulfilled prior to a final vote."[95] Essentially, Brown wanted to cut a deal that would benefit Boston-based financial giants, such as Fidelity Investments and State Street Corporation, and the final bill testified to his success in this regard.[96]

Conference Committee

When the financial reform bill passed the Senate, the drama wasn't over. The bills passed by the House and Senate had many differences, and these needed to be reconciled by a Senate-House conference committee before a final piece of legislation could emerge. Barney Frank, as chair of the conference committee, could be expected to fight for a strong bill, but overall, the composition of the committee was not auspicious. A report by Public Citizen and the Center for Responsive Politics found that 56 current lobbyists for financial sector firms had previously been staffers for the 43 members of the committee.[97] The opportunities for industry influence on the final complexion of the bill were therefore legion.

Some of the differences in need of reconciliation did not involve the CFPB directly. An amendment offered by Sen. Dick Durbin and approved in the Senate was especially controversial. The amendment required the Federal Reserve to reduce the fees paid to banks by retailers when their customers use debit cards. As expected, the amendment "created a lobbying donnybrook between banks and retailers."[98]

At least four issues regarding the CFPB and its independence faced the conferees. Most important, the House version of the bill envisioned the CFPB as a free-standing agency whereas the Senate bill housed the CFPB inside the Federal Reserve. The Senate version prevailed.

Second, the House version had essentially no institutional checks on the CFPB's rule-making authority. The Senate bill, in contrast, allowed CFPB rules to be overturned by a two-thirds majority vote by a Financial Stability Oversight Council (FSOC).[99] Again, the Senate version was adopted by the conference committee.

Third, there was the question of the CFPB's leadership structure: would it be led by a single director (with an advisory board) or by a five-person board? The Senate version called for a single director with a five-year term, but there was a difference of opinion between Barney Frank and Henry Waxman, an equally powerful Democrat. Whereas Frank wanted a single director, Waxman wanted a board of commissioners.[100] Waxman argued that a board of commissioners with staggered terms would reduce political influences on the agency. It would also put the new body in line with existing agencies such as the Federal Trade Commission and the Federal Communications Commission.

When Waxman inserted his proposed structure for the CFPB in the version of the bill approved by the House Energy and Commerce Committee the previous autumn, Representative Frank was not pleased. Frank released a statement saying: "Going from a single executive able to act promptly and efficiently to a five-member commission with staggered terms will weaken the capacity of the agency to provide consumer protection."[101] During the House Floor vote in December 2009, Frank outmaneuvered Waxman by using the oldest negotiating trick in the book: "Give me what I want now, and I will give you what you want later." The CFPB would initially be led by a director. Then, two years later, on the "agency conversion date," when the functions of various agencies would be transferred to the new agency, the governing structure would change. The single director would be replaced by five commissioners with staggered terms.

The members of AFR took no strong position on the leadership structure debate. Travis Plunkett, of the Consumer Federation of America and one of AFR's leading legislative tacticians, wasn't sure at the time where to stand on the single director vs. five-person board debate. He said, "It wasn't clear cut. The main reason I fell into the single director camp was because the start-up process during the first couple of years would be so significant and so important. Having a linear hierarchy is much more efficient and potentially successful."[102]

The Senate version of the bill aligned with Frank's preferred leadership structure for the CFPB—a director with a five-year term and no reference to a multiperson board. In the reconciliation of the House and Senate versions, Waxman's idea of an eventual changeover in structure disappeared.

Finally, the House version envisioned the CFPB being funded by fees levied on financial institutions. The Senate bill had the CFPB receiving its funding from the Federal Reserve in an amount equal to 10–12 percent of the Fed's total operating expenses each year.[103] The difference was again resolved in favor of the Senate's version.

The final round of conference committee deliberations went on without reprieve, and AFR stalwarts like Travis Plunkett and Ed Mierzwinski pulled an all-nighter. On the morning of June 25, the Conference Committee concluded its work. With respect to the CFPB, the conferees went with the Senate version on all of the issues pertaining to CFPB independence. The CFPB received a strong funding source and a single director, but it would not be a stand-alone agency, and its rule-making would be subject to a potential veto from the FSOC. The Senate's ambivalent position was likely due to the fragility of the 60-vote coalition required for passage.

The House approved the reconciled version on June 30; it was now up to the Senate. The Senate's vote retained some drama since it was unknown whether the four Republicans who voted for the bill in May would do so again. Indeed, Senator Grassley abandoned the bill, but Republicans Collins, Snowe, and Brown stood their ground, and Democrat Maria Cantwell finally came around and voted for the bill.[104] Brown received a nudge when representatives of Americans for Financial Reform and its member organization MASSPIRG pretended to give Brown a luxury BMW. The idea behind the media-covered event was to show the contrast between Brown's pickup-truck/common-man image and the company he would be keeping if he voted with Wall Street fat cats.[105] On July 15, with only a simple majority needed, the bill passed the Senate by a margin of 60 to 39.[106] President Obama speedily signed the Dodd-Frank Wall Street Reform and Consumer Protection Act on July 21.[107] The White House press release regarding the signing ceremony listed Elizabeth Warren and most of AFR's leaders—Heather Booth, Ed Mierzwinski, Travis Plunkett, Michael Calhoun, Nancy Zirkin, Pam Banks, and Heather McGhee—as expected attendees.[108]

An Agency Is Born

The CFPB was only a piece of the Dodd-Frank Act, and the entire Act showed the signs of compromise. Nancy Zirkin, executive vice president of the Leadership Conference on Civil and Human Rights and one of AFR's most pragmatic voices, said: "This is not a great bill. This is not the end of the world bill. It's 26 percent cooked and the rest is in the regulations [that are still to come]."[109] Still, it could have been much worse for the bill's advocates. The many compromises that were deemed necessary to get a bill passed could have split the AFR coalition, and they nearly did so at several points. But the coalition, led by a skillful Heather Booth and aided by its allies in Congress and the Obama administration, held.[110] The fact that AFR and its partners were unified, disciplined, and remote from the dramatic interludes that commonly mark coalition lobbying efforts was recognized as a tremendous achievement and source of strength by insiders involved in the entire Dodd-Frank legislative process.[111]

With respect to the CFPB, an agency had been created with a workable structure and a solid funding source. Superimposed on the agency, however, was an unprecedented set of controls designed to balance independence and accountability. Most notably, CFPB rules could be overturned if they were determined to be in conflict with the safety and soundness of the U.S. financial or banking system.[112] In principle, this mechanism sounds prudent and reasonable, but it leaves a lot of room to determine when a conflict is sufficient to justify intervention. Beyond agency independence, there were many other wins, losses, and compromises, including fights over which industries would be covered by the CFPB and which would not.[113] Still, the CFPB had gone from pipedream to reality in the remarkably short period of three years.

Chapter 8

Auto Dealers Drive for an Exemption

Congressman John Campbell (R-Calif.), a self-described fiscal conservative, resides in the Shady Canyon section of Irvine, California, an affluent community in the heart of Southern California's Orange County. Before taking his seat in the House of Representatives in December 2005, Campbell spent 25 years in the auto business. At various times he owned or advised 13 car dealerships representing both foreign and domestic automakers including Saab, Ford, Mazda, and Saturn.[1]

By the time he arrived in D.C., Campbell had disgorged his financial interests in the dealerships but retained a substantial business connection with the automobile industry.[2] Congressional financial disclosure reports are imprecise, but during 2008–2010 Campbell netted rental income somewhere in the range of $3–22 million from real estate leased to auto-related corporations (dealers and other entities).[3] In addition to rental income, Campbell was a top beneficiary of auto industry campaign largesse. In the 2010 congressional funding cycle, he was elevated to the number two slot on the automotive industry gift list for the House of Representatives, immediately behind fellow car dealer Scott Rigell (R-Va.).[4]

Campbell is especially well remembered in the auto industry for his amendment to Chairman Barney Frank's September 2009 discussion draft of the financial reform bill. At the time, Frank's draft was circulating in the House Financial Services Committee as part of the markup phase. The Campbell amendment, cosponsored by Rep. Bill Posey (R-Fla.), was vigorously opposed by Frank.[5] It was written to create a special interest exemption for auto dealers from the newly proposed Consumer Financial Protection Bureau. Critics believed the loophole would block one of the bill's major policy objectives: across-the-board consumer safeguards regardless of lender or product designation.

Consumer Problems with Auto Loans

Loans are a huge and profitable part of the business for car dealers and for lenders. Of the 50 million car buyers in 2009, 94 percent financed their purchases by loan. The average new car loan approached $25,000.[6] According to a study published by the Center for Responsible Lending, the average dealer markup on each loan in 2009 was $714.[7] The markup represents the amount the dealer keeps as compensation for brokering a loan to a bank or some other lender, such as GMAC or Ford Credit.[8] The markup has frequently been derided as a "kickback." Whatever term is used, however, there is no denying that it represents a lucrative element of the dealer business—generating an estimated $25.8 billion a year.[9]

As Raj Date and Brian Reed, both veterans of the financial services industry, reported in a widely cited paper on the topic, the size of the auto finance loan and leasing business was approximately $850 billion in 2009.[10] In dollar terms, the auto loan and leasing business is even bigger than credit cards.

The auto financing sector is made up of two channels. The *direct* channel is the smaller of the two. In the direct channel, the purchaser obtains financing right from a lender, such as a credit union, with the dealer having no financial involvement in the transaction. The direct channel represents about 20 percent of the business. The second, so-called *indirect* channel is about 80 percent of the business. In the indirect channel, the dealer is situated between the purchaser and the lender. The dealership receives compensation for a number of intermediary services it performs.

For dealers, the financing part of their business generates more than half of their profits—outpacing markups earned from the sale of vehicles. According to Date,

> Not only are dealers a giant part of auto lending, but auto lending is a giant part of dealer economics. Over the past ten years, gross profit per new car has plummeted by a third. That would seem catastrophic in what was, even a decade ago, the brutally thin-margin business of selling cars. But dealers, somehow, still were profitable in 2008. The main reason: Over this same period, dealers were able to double their amount of higher-margin finance and insurance income.[11]

Since auto dealers have no financial interest in transactions flowing through the direct channel, the CFPB would have no role to play there of concern to dealers. In the indirect channel, however, dealers perform a variety of crucial hands-on functions. They originate loans, negotiate lending terms and conditions with customers (including the size of markups), and they broker and sell loans to permanent lenders. Payments for these services are bundled into the final cost of the purchase transaction. Until then, borrowers have no way of knowing and comparing total costs.

The crucial question posed by the Campbell amendment was whether dealer operations in the indirect channel should be exempt from the CFPB's oversight responsibility. The dealers put forward two broad claims to support an exemption. The first was a policy argument and the second more of a political-emotional appeal. Their policy argument was that dealers functioned as middlemen, not as lenders. Since dealer financial assistance activities posed no systemic risk to the economy, CFPB regulation was unwarranted. As part of this first argument, dealers claimed that CFPB oversight would ultimately raise consumer costs.[12] The second prong of the dealers' case was that car dealerships were small, community-based (and community-supporting) businesses which were reeling from the recent meltdown of the whole auto industry and particularly from the termination of many franchise agreements by manufacturers. In a sense, this was the "too small to succeed" counterpart to the more familiar "too big to fail" argument made by big banks.

Opponents of the exemption, including AFR coalition members, challenged the legal proposition that dealers were simply intermediaries, not lenders, and they produced loan documents to prove it.[13] They also argued that dealer-assisted financing had long been a backwater of consumer protection practice and buttressed the point with complaint statistics compiled by Better Business Bureaus and state and local consumer agencies.[14] In the view of AFR's members, exempting dealer-assisted financing from CFPB oversight would be tantamount to awarding an Academy Award for abusive behavior. Among the many practices documented by AFR and others were bait and switch tactics, packing loans with hidden charges, price-gouging, racial discrimination, loan steering, falsification, and other predatory acts. Further, AFR and members of the coalition argued that exemption of such a significant share of consumer credit—autos being the second largest consumer expenditure—would inevitably undermine the overall impact of the consumer protection reform package.[15]

Frank Outgunned

On June 24, 2009, almost immediately after receiving the administration's White Paper on financial and regulatory restructuring, the House Financial

Services Committee held its first hearing.[16] Representatives of the auto dealer industry did not testify or submit comments for the record of the hearing. At the very beginning of the session Chairman Barney Frank announced that he intended to begin marking up a bill in July and voting it out of committee before the House began its August recess. As if to emphasize this brisk time schedule, Frank cautioned members to "pay close attention."[17]

The Chairman moved very quickly and introduced H.R. 3126 on July 8. The bill dealt exclusively with the consumer financial protection elements of the Obama administration's plan for financial reform. Despite Frank's wish to report H.R. 3126 out of committee within the month, the House began its August recess before the bill could be marked up. Returning from recess after Labor Day, Frank introduced on September 25 a "discussion draft" for committee consideration.[18] In an apparent reaction to flak from the auto dealers, the draft included a new provision that exempted a limited subset of car dealers from CFPB oversight.[19] The committee did not hold any public hearings on the discussion draft, and auto dealer lobbyists appear to have been too preoccupied with other matters such as the "cash for clunkers" program and the cutback of dealer franchises to have mustered an all-out attack on the congressional citadel.[20]

As soon as the industry focused, seriously, on the discussion draft, the National Automobile Dealers Association (NADA) mobilized its lobbying arm and took aim at Frank, accusing him of backtracking on a written commitment to the Democratic members of his committee. The NADA letter threatened to oppose the bill with its narrowly written exemption unless a revised version was introduced with a "clear exclusion from CFPA regulation for auto dealers acting in their traditional capacities."[21] The committee was simultaneously lacerated by the brand-new AFR coalition in a letter strongly opposing the carve-out provision.[22]

On October 15, a week after the NADA letter was sent to the chairman, Representative Campbell, a member of the House Committee on Financial Services, submitted an amendment which did precisely what the industry had demanded. The Campbell amendment provided a broad exemption from the CFPB for the vast majority of new car dealers—those who brokered financing instead of providing it directly to customers.[23] NADA mobilized a brief call-in action to counteract opposition to the amendment mounted by its traditional lending rivals in the community banking industry.[24] Then on Thursday, October 22, the Campbell amendment was passed in Committee on a recorded vote of 47–21. On the final tally, 19 Democrats joined all the Republican members in voting for the amendment.[25] Some of the Democrats initially braved industry displeasure by voting against the provision. Then, observing that the amendment would pass in any event, they switched their votes, thereby earning the thinly veiled disapprobation of Chairman Frank (delivered with his patented scowl).[26]

Ironically, Frank Luntz, a noted pollster and political strategist, was at that moment on the brink of advising Republican legislators that special interest loopholes were toxic to public thinking about financial reform. Luntz advised that loopholes should be illuminated and attacked whenever they arose.[27] Getting Democrats to cross-over and vote in favor of the auto dealer loophole was, therefore, a master stroke. It provided just the cover Republicans needed to diffuse the spotlight and make the claim that the carve-out (loophole) was a bipartisan measure.

Blogging at *Firedoglake*, David Dayen described the auto dealer exemption as "probably the worst amendment in the entire Financial Services Committee markup on regulatory reform."[28] Later, on the same day that the column appeared, the House Financial Services Committee passed an amended version of H.R. 3126 with the carve-out provision intact.

Less than two months later (on December 11, 2009), the identical dealer carve-out provision was folded into and adopted by the full House of Representatives as part of the omnibus Wall Street Reform and Consumer Protection bill, H.R. 4173. The House allotted a total of three hours of debate to the entire 1,700-page measure. About 10 minutes of that debate was reserved for a colloquy between Representatives Campbell and Mel Watt (D-N.C.) on the auto exemption. The specific purpose of the colloquy was to explain why it had been impossible to work out perfecting language for the carve-out. Apparently, Watt and Campbell had been named by Frank as the interlocutors in this matter. They were well on their way to resolving the language issues via cell phone from their respective homes in North Carolina and California when Campbell interrupted the negotiations to ask for a time-out to catch the USC football game on TV. Watt was only too happy to accede so he could watch a Carolina Panthers game. (Both teams lost.) Unable to find a convenient time to finalize the negotiation, they decided to leave well enough alone and accept a manager's amendment.[29]

Senate Consideration

If the House set a grueling pace for itself on the bill to create a new consumer agency, the generally more deliberative Senate operated at warp speed. From start to finish, the House took 171 days to vote out the bill while over to the Senate side, action was completed in 119 days. The course of action in the House was reasonably linear. Chairman Frank had a game plan, and while there were periodic perturbations arising from amendments (such as Representative Campbell's), consideration moved fairly predictably from one milepost to the next. To be sure, Frank was constantly vigilant, taking the temperature of his members and calculating the level of committee support issue-by-issue.

In part, the flow on the House side reflected the time that was required for groups on all sides of the complex matter to get up to speed. This was especially the case for the brand-new AFR coalition which faced the immense task of organizing itself while simultaneously trying to cope with every aspect of the House bill and other emerging bills on financial reform. By the time action shifted to the Senate side, the groups had mastered a good deal of the material and were better prepared to enter the fray. This increased the likelihood of more fireworks erupting in the Senate.

When the Senate Banking Committee first began its work on a financial regulatory reform bill, it did not make any provision for an auto dealer carve-out. Even without an explicit provision, however, the climate appeared to be reasonably favorable for eventually providing a carve-out on the Senate side. For one thing, Senate Banking Committee chairman Chris Dodd (D-Conn.) was committed to working across the aisle with Ranking Member Richard Shelby (R-Ala.). If a bipartisan relationship could produce results on divisive cornerstone issues such as the independent status of a consumer financing agency, then the way might be smoothed for the introduction of a Republican-sponsored amendment somewhere down the line. But legislative politics is notoriously fickle, and car dealers wanted a more secure foundation.

Auto dealers had that foundation and its name was "Main Street." According to Census Bureau statistics, there were over 18,000 new car dealerships spread throughout the United States in 2009. They employed approximately 900,000 people, an average of 50 per dealership. Annual revenue per dealer was slightly in excess of $26 million.[30] This profile fit comfortably into the general picture of the country's small business economy.

Dealers profited from their well-burnished image as small, community-based businesses, stalwarts of Main Street, and dependable supporters of Little League Baseball and Rotary. As James Surowiecki observed in *The New Yorker*, "it seemed like every communiqué from the dealers' association included the phrase 'Main Street auto dealers.' This was a disingenuous argument—something like seventy per cent of auto loans are securitized or financed by Wall Street—but rhetorically effective. Auto dealers may collectively make up a huge industry, but most of them are small businessmen, just the kind of regular Americans that congressmen like to be seen as standing up for."[31]

On top of that, the dealers had a sophisticated and financially generous network of metro, state, and federal trade associations that were quite capable of mobilizing their members to call, visit, and contribute.[32]

By the time the Senate began to work on its bill, the Frank Luntz memo to Republican members on political messaging had begun to circulate. A theme Luntz repeated over and again was that small business ownership and small businesses in general were part of the American Dream. That being the case, financial reform legislation could be effectively framed by its industry and political critics as an existential threat to small, community-based businesses in every state and congressional district. As if to feed on that theme, NADA sponsored a rather self-serving poll purporting to show that a majority of Americans would reject the CFPB when they learned that it would drive up their borrowing costs and "dictate to auto dealers how they pay their employees."[33] Luntz's prescription was to portray regulation not merely as a drag on small business but as a feckless, bloated bureaucracy—incapable of achieving what it set out to accomplish.

Celinda Lake, a Democratic political communications consultant who did some polling for the AFR coalition, commented on the Luntz memo soon after its release.[34] In her response, she, too, made note of the crucial symbolic importance of small business in relation to financial reform. Her advice, however, was precisely the opposite of Luntz's. Instead of sending a message picturing financial reform as a mortal threat to small business, the frame that Lake recommended was to characterize financial reform as the way to safeguard small business from the unfairness and abuses of big banks, Wall Street, credit card companies, and CEOs. The messaging differences could not have been more starkly defined: government as the enemy of small business versus government as its friend.

Carve-Out Opponents

Since the House had sent over an omnibus bill that incorporated an auto dealer exemption, the Senate knew it would have to deal with the issue one way or the other. Either it would have to enact a measure of its own design, whether a copycat or some different approach, or it would have to deal with the House version—accepting or rejecting it—when the two bills eventually went to a Conference Committee to work out legislative differences. In any event, opponents as well as backers of the carve-out were on notice and thus began to lobby the Senate early in the process.

NADA and other carve-out activists could not have been too surprised to find consumer, civil rights, and military groups on full alert in the Senate corridors. The newly formed AFR Coalition chose Cora Ganzglass, an attorney and legislative director of the National Association of Consumer Advocates, and Susan Weinstock, head of the Consumer Federation of America's Financial Reform Campaign, to co-lead its auto dealer advocacy. Both Ganzglass and Weinstock were well steeped in the predatory lending practices of the industry and were in contact with state and local consumer agencies and consumer attorneys who were current on developments in the field and could relate to legislators throughout the country.[35]

Civil rights groups, including the NAACP, the Urban League, the National Council of La Raza, and the Leadership Conference on Civil and Human Rights, emphasized a particular slice of the auto dealer financing problem. These groups came armed with statistics showing that black, brown, and yellow-skinned car buyers routinely paid far more for new and used car credit than equivalent white borrowers and that they suffered other forms of racial discrimination in automotive lending.[36] Among the studies cited was one by the National Consumer Law Center, a member of the AFR coalition. The Center published state-specific data from lawsuits it had settled with car lenders during the period 2003–2007. Those data reported racial disparities (African Americans compared with whites) in dealer markups for Ford, GMAC, and Honda. The markups represented the amount the dealer charged over and above the "buy rate" quoted by the lender that took the borrower's credit status into account. Nationally, the race differentials averaged 154 percent for Honda, 181 percent for Ford and 270 percent for GMAC, but in some states they far exceeded 400 percent.[37]

The military was represented by a number of organizations. An umbrella group, the Military Coalition, had more than 30 organizations representing 5.5 million active duty, military reserve, retired vets, and their families. The Coalition was actively engaged in the carve-out issue. Retired rear admiral Jan Gaudio and his organization, the Navy-Marine Corps Relief Society, were among the most active military spokesmen on the issue. Gaudio had earlier shared with members of Congress his reasons for opposing the Campbell amendment on the House side. The Marine Corps had long been concerned with the financial difficulties experienced by troops and their families and had identified auto purchases as one of the most common problems encountered. After an initial survey, the Corps had commissioned an academic study led by Professor Karen Varcoe at the University of California at Riverside. As far back as 2003, Varcoe and her colleagues reported:

Buying a new car as soon as possible after reaching the first duty station is number one on the typical young Marine's list, and also numbered first on the list of top financial problems by participants at many of the state-side installations. Car dealers and lending institutions seem to be in unintentional collusion to encourage Marines to buy new cars instead of more affordable used ones. The car dealers entice the Marine to buy on credit with little or no down payment and the lending institutions, as one staff NCO explained, are unwilling to give loans for used cars except over the long term at high rates of interest, 'and the guy's going to be leaving before that. Or they can't afford the short-term loans the banks and credit unions will give them for used cars.' A great many young Marines begin their careers by shouldering thousands of dollars' worth of debt in this way.[38]

No one could legitimately accuse Gaudio of being an ideologically driven opponent of the auto dealer industry, and that fact undoubtedly increased his credibility on Capitol Hill. The admiral, a retired combat pilot, made frequent visits to the House and Senate from his office in Ballston, Virginia, a D.C. suburb, in order to alert congressional offices to the tricks some car dealers played on service members and their families. With him, he brought a trove of case files containing first-hand reports of scams targeting service members as well as their family members left at home during Iraq/Afghanistan rotations.

One of Admiral Gaudio's lobbying advantages was that he could go beyond generic PowerPoint presentations and could deliver place-specific information to various congressional offices. As Gaudio explained it, "If we were talking to a local congressman from Virginia, we could talk specifically to Virginia or Hampton Roads; same thing for California. Wherever Navy and Marine Corps had a presence, we could talk to how that's impacting your people in your districts."[39]

Michael Archer, a retired marine judge advocate, offered a good example of local intelligence on abusive practices in auto financing. After leaving active duty in 2003, Archer served as a supervisory attorney at Camp Lejeune, North Carolina, where he frequently dealt with matters arising out of car financing. In November 2009, Archer prepared and circulated to consumer groups a five-page summary of dealer financing abuses in the Lejeune area.[40] While it looked a bit like a formal legal indictment, the content captured the bleak and seedy feel of everyday business practice in some parts of the industry. A couple of examples provide the flavor.

Summary. Marine private first class is urged to, and does, sign sales / purchase agreement to buy a vehicle for $17,900. He drives away with no financing.

When he returns, he is surprised (based on earlier conversation with the dealer) to learn that he will be financed at 15%, and that additional fees hike up the price of the car up another $2K.

Summary. Wife of deployed lance corporal goes to Wilmington to purchase a vehicle. She gives them a $1,000 down payment and drives the vehicle off the lot, with the understanding that if the dealer can't get her financing and she returns the vehicle without 'excessive mileage' the contract will be rescinded. The dealer is unable to obtain a loan and directs her to return the car, which she does. The dealer refuses to return the deposit and sticks her with additional fees, including auto insurance.

Although opposition from consumer and civil rights groups was predictable, what might have caught carve-out supporters on the wrong foot was forceful opposition expressed by the country's top defense department and military service leadership. There was some precedent for this unusual pairing in an earlier fight against payday lending.

While military organizations never joined AFR, the wildcard collaboration forged between members of the military community and the AFR coalition was potentially formidable. It added an extra dimension to the list of congressional office doors that might open to opponents of the carve-out. If the auto dealers played the Main Street or small business card, opponents could match it with some pretty good cards of their own.

Seeking Bipartisanship

By early winter, negotiations in the Banking Committee between Dodd and Shelby—tempestuous in the best of times—had soured yet again, slowing progress toward reaching a bipartisan agreement and marking up a bill for Senate consideration.[41] "We were stuck. I just feel like we weren't getting anywhere," said Dodd in an interview.[42] Dodd reluctantly threatened to direct his staff to draft a Democratic proposal but stayed his hand at the last moment. Instead of giving up on a consensus approach and inviting the near-certain loss of the Republican support Democrats would eventually need on the Senate floor, Dodd invited a first term Republican, Jim Corker of Tennessee, to become his negotiating partner. As discussed in the previous chapter, that strategy was chancy for both men: it put Corker in the position of having to go over the head of the far more senior and experienced negotiator, Shelby, and it exposed Dodd to the risk of lengthening debate in the event Republican members failed to give Corker their support.

The Dodd-Corker negotiations were far more congenial and productive than earlier discussions with Shelby had been. On one of the toughest issues, the structure of the agency, Corker and Dodd apparently agreed to float the idea of lodging the CFPB within the Fed. The proposal was roundly condemned. It was contrary to the president's original call for an independent agency; it met strong opposition from Barney Frank; the banks hated it; and Robert Weissman at Public Citizen characterized the idea of consumer protection at the Fed as an "oxymoron."[43]

Travis Plunkett, the legislative director of the Consumer Federation of America, claims that Dodd was never going to compromise the independence of the CFPB. When Corker realized he had been "outnegotiated" by Dodd, he "abandoned ship."[44] Shelby, who had never fully lost track of the negotiations, reinserted himself in the talks at the beginning of March only to balk on the crucial issue of the location and independence of the CFPB.[45] On March 11, with an appreciative bow in Corker's direction, Dodd concluded that he had little option other than to bail out on the bipartisan effort and to move a Democratic bill in the committee to a vote. On April 15, the Banking Committee reported a bill to the Senate (S. 3217—Restoring American Financial Stability Act of 2010), but protracted negotiations, interspersed with threats of filibuster, awaited the bill on the Senate floor.

Ten days before the committee bill was reported to the full Senate, on April 5, 2010, the auto dealers' shoe dropped. Senator Sam Brownback (R-Kans.) announced that he would soon introduce an amendment to exempt a majority of auto dealers from the CFPB. There was some concern among advocates of the CFPB that Jon Tester (D-Mont.), too, might introduce a dealer-exemption bill. When he did not, it was viewed by the advocacy community as a "big victory."[46] Eileen Toback, AFR's director of field operations, opined, "He was, I think, particularly moved by the military."[47] The Brownback amendment, a companion to the Campbell provision passed by the House, was formally submitted on May 4.[48] The strategic delay gave Brownback room to maneuver and to leverage his influence on the course of the full bill going forward.[49]

The announcement of the Brownback amendment in early April triggered a barrage of reaction from all sides. As it had in the case of payday lending to servicemen, the Defense Department made the argument that financial stress undermined military readiness—a heavy and unusual claim to make in view of the situation in Iraq and Afghanistan. In February, Undersecretary Clifford Stanley had gone on record as opposing a CFPB exemption for "unscrupulous automobile sales and financing practices."[50] In a letter to Assistant Treasury Secretary Michael Barr, one of the administration's lead strategists and negotiators on financial reform, Stanley reported that 72 percent of the military's financial counselors who responded to a recent Department of Defense survey reported having counseled service personnel about auto financing abuses in the past six-month period.[51] Soon after Brownback's announcement, the Military Coalition addressed a letter to Chairman Dodd and Ranking Member Shelby referring to the Stanley data and opposing any carve-out.[52]

Although the survey's lack of scientific rigor was questioned by Brownback and the auto dealers and may have lessened its impact to some degree, the fact that the Pentagon was so vigorous and public in its stand against predatory auto lending practices created a clear rallying point for carve-out opponents.[53] Holly Petraeus, the director of the Better Business Bureau's Military Line Program and wife of Gen. David Petraeus, the American commander in Afghanistan, joined the debate. In a media briefing with senators Durbin and Reed, she echoed Secretary Stanley's concerns, remarking that as a military spouse and daughter she could speak as something of a subject matter specialist on the military family and its financial travails.[54] Similarly, retired rear admiral Jan Gaudio of the Navy and Marine Corps Relief Society reported that the Stanley letter, followed by letters from service secretaries, resonated with him and encouraged his organization to pursue the issue on Capitol Hill.[55]

These interventions were followed on May 12 by a special statement issued by President Obama. The message, laden with references to "special interests," "loopholes and exemptions," and "misleading sales tactics," was highly unusual. Indeed, it was the only one issued directly by the president over the course of the entire legislative debate on financial restructuring and consumer protection. The president said:

> Throughout the debate on Wall Street reform, I have urged members of the Senate to fight the efforts of special interests and their lobbyists to weaken consumer protections. An amendment that the Senate will soon consider would do exactly that, undermining strong consumer protections with a special loophole for auto dealer-lenders. This amendment would carve out a special exemption for these lenders that would allow them to inflate rates, insert hidden fees into the fine print of paperwork, and include expensive add-ons that catch purchasers by surprise. This amendment guts provisions that empower consumers with clear information that allows them to make the financial decisions that work best for them and simply encourages misleading sales tactics that hurt American consumers. . . . We simply cannot let lobbyist-inspired loopholes and special carve-outs weaken real reform that will empower American families.[56]

In a statement issued the same day by Ed Tonkin, chairman of NADA and himself an auto dealer from Portland, Oregon, the industry promptly struck back. It matched the president tit for tat with its own coded phrases—Main Street, not lenders but "facilitators," and subject to double regulation.

> Sadly, the White House is continuing to issue misleading statements in its efforts to get auto dealers wrongly included in Wall Street reform legislation. Much of what's included in its latest statement is pure fiction. . . . These dealers are not banks. They are facilitators. And dealer-assisted financing is already heavily regulated—and should not be subject to double regulation. . . . For the President, in the statement attributed to him, to malign an entire industry made up of Main Street businesses run by dedicated men and women and their employees is shocking.[57]

In collaborative visits to Senate offices with Susan Weinstock of the Consumer Federation of America and Cora Ganzglass of the National Association of Consumer Advocates, Gaudio paid particular attention to the military liaison to the various members. The military aides understood the problem in a way that the financial specialists and legislative staff might not. Typically, these aides were not the most senior staffers on the issue, but they could be helpful as firsthand resources and sounding boards.

NADA calculated that approximately a dozen Senate votes on both sides of the aisle were in play on the carve-out issue.[58] It is probable that AFR's vote count was similar. Some of the earliest office calls initiated by Gaudio, Ganzglass, and Weinstock were to the offices of senators McCain, Tester, Landrieu, Ben Nelson, Collins, and Snowe.

The AFR coalition's overall strategy was to frame the exemption as representing a clear struggle between the local dealers, on one side, and the military, racial minorities, small banks, and everyday auto buyers on the other. AFR's task, in turn, was to make sure each senator understood that there were two clear and competing sides to the issue. As Susan Weinstock put it in a *Washington Post* op-ed column, "So . . . whose side are you on—the auto dealers or our troops, small banks, credit unions, civil rights organizations and consumer groups? Seems like an obvious choice."[59]

Even within AFR and the Military Coalition, however, the perspective of polarization was not accepted uniformly. Admiral Gaudio reacted adversely to a *Washington Post* story that characterized the dispute as being "an uncomfortable choice between the interests of the military and car dealers, who run one of the most influential and deep-pocketed political action committees in Washington and tend to be intimately involved in politics in lawmakers' home districts."[60] "I didn't agree with that framing. . . . I didn't agree that it was the military versus the auto dealers," said Gaudio.[61] Within AFR, Pam Banks, senior policy counsel for Consumers Union, recalled that she took some flak for her organization's stand against the exemption. She recalled receiving "calls from members who expressed disagreement with the organization's position against the car dealers."[62]

Nancy Zirkin of the Leadership Conference on Civil and Human Rights led AFR's overall lobbying campaign on the bill. Zirkin, a respected and veteran Hill lobbyist, worked with lobbyists on her own staff as well as those, such as Graciella Aponte of The National Council of La Raza, who were seconded by AFR member organizations. Zirkin offered a somewhat different perspective on the Main Street narrative. Through her Hill-oriented prism, the Main Street–small business frame gave uncommitted senators a chance to argue, with some logic, that a vote against autos and for consumers would be politically untenable in their particular states. Referring to a Democratic moderate from the South, Zirkin recalled him arguing that auto dealers in his area were typically small, self-funding businesses with no ties to Wall Street. In addition, they were politically powerful in his state. Zirkin countered that it was the huge lenders like GMAC who are the real parties at interest and are "being fronted for by the dealers," but the congressman "didn't understand what the hell we were talking about."[63]

The industry played the Main Street–small business theme very skillfully. NADA, in conjunction with its state and metro affiliates, organized a succession of scheduled dealer call-in days, action alerts, and Washington fly-in visits. On April 26, 100 local dealers descended on the Senate to help build support for the Brownback measure announced earlier that month. Three weeks later, another 200 dealers went up to the Hill to lobby for the full Senate's support on the amendment going to the Conference Committee.[64]

In a very strange turn of events during the legislative endgame, Senator Brownback withdrew his amendment to avoid having the unrelated (and to him, undesirable) Merkley-Levin measure concerning proprietary trading by banks from being tacked onto it. In its stead, Brownback introduced a "sense of the Senate" measure that would instruct Senate conferees to accept the House-passed Campbell amendment that provided the exclusion he had sought.

On May 24, the Senate voted in favor of Brownback's Sense of the Senate proposal by a 2-to-1 margin (60–30), with 29 Democrats crossing party lines. Ironically, 10 of the 18 charter members of the Senate Military Families Caucus (set up in August 2010) voted for the Brownback measure and against the recommendation of the president, the military, and AFR.[65] This vote, possibly more than any other, reflected the sheer power of the Main Street/Small Business frame, melded with the organizational prowess of

18,000 car dealers in every congressional district, to trump other highly attractive messages in the political environment. In retrospect, Caren Benjamin, one of AFR's experts in political communication, concluded regretfully, "It ended up very badly. . . . We lost."[66] Cora Ganzglass of the National Association of Consumer Advocates took a bit of solace in the fact that Dodd-Frank granted expedited rulemaking authority to the Federal Trade Commission to define unfair and deceptive practices of auto dealers.[67] Ganzglass said, perhaps with a touch of rationalization, "Now our take is . . . that the auto dealers are going to rue the day they were exempted."[68]

Chapter 9

Preemption: The Role of State Reformers

At first blush, the words "federal preemption" may sound a bit wonky and abstract. In practice, however, they have an extraordinarily practical edge to them. On one public issue after another, from environmental protection to privacy, from immigration to financial services, federal preemption has been the key to how laws and regulations are actually enforced.

The Meaning and Importance of Preemption

Preemption is a legal doctrine used to determine which of multiple levels of government has the right to rule on a particular issue.[1] In 1996, the U.S. Office of Thrift Supervision promulgated a sweeping preemption rule stating that federally chartered savings associations did not have to observe state lending laws; in 2004, the Office of the Comptroller of the Currency followed suit with a rule prohibiting states from enforcing their laws against national banks and their subsidiaries.[2] In consideration of the Dodd-Frank Act, the preemption question triggered tendentious disputes between the states and the federal government over responsibility for enforcing federal laws against predatory lending and other consumer financial abuses. The basic controversy turned on the proposition that federal laws should automatically preempt state consumer financial protection statutes when it came to policing federally chartered lending institutions and their subsidiaries.[3] The notion was that the higher level of government should routinely supersede the lower one, irrespective of the quality of enforcement or the strictness of the rules applied.

AFR and the advocacy community were heavily opposed to federal preemption. Their most compelling arguments were that federal bank regulators had by and large failed in their enforcement mission and that borrowers living in states with strong consumer laws were demonstrably better off than their peers residing in states subject to weaker federal or state rules.

The issue was so acute that Heather Booth regarded the legislative proposals for federal preemption as the single biggest threat to the Consumer Financial Protection Bureau of any that arose during the entire debate.[4] Understandably, the idea that in a comprehensive financial reform bill, the very same federal agencies that had demonstrated clear indifference (or hostility) to the protection of borrowers would now be permitted to hamstring stricter state consumer protections was totally anathema to the advocates.

In March 2009, Illinois attorney general Lisa Madigan testified in the House Financial Services Committee that Illinois' efforts to stop deceptive lending had been inhibited by federal preemption policies and by rules that allowed lenders to select their own regulators—obviously with a bias toward the most business-friendly amongst them.[5] Four months later, at the very beginning of the congressional debate, Travis Plunkett of the Consumer Federation of America made the advocates' argument forcefully and at length in his testimony before the Senate Banking Committee. Plunkett, a veteran of many legislative battles dealing with consumer issues in housing and credit markets, testified that:

> Combining safety and soundness supervision—with its focus on bank profitability—in the same institution as consumer protection magnified an ideological predisposition or anti-regulatory bias by federal officials that led to unwillingness to rein in abusive lending before it triggered the housing and economic crises. Though we now know that consumer protection leads to effective safety and soundness, structural flaws in the federal regulatory system compromised the independence of banking regulators, encouraged them to overlook, ignore and minimize their mission to protect consumers.[6]

In 2000, well before Dodd-Frank and the CFPB had ever been contemplated, Ed Mierzwinski, the consumer program director of U.S. PIRG, testified before the House Banking and Financial Services Committee against federal preemption of state laws dealing with abusive ATM surcharges and other banking practices. And in 2003, a coalition of civil rights, fair lending and consumer groups emphatically criticized the Office of the Comptroller of the Currency for trying to preempt state enforcement of antipredatory lending laws against national banks and their subsidiaries.[7] Thus, federal preemption of state lending laws, particularly those dealing with enforcement of antipredatory and abusive practices, was not a stranger to members of the House Financial Services Committee considering the proposal to create a new consumer financial protection agency.

Preemption was especially important to the battle against consumer lending abuses because a number of states had taken the lead on predatory lending and had a history of enforcing strong and innovative consumer financial protections in their respective jurisdictions. North Carolina acted first (in 1999) to restrict certain abusive practices on all mortgage loans and to impose additional restrictions on high-cost loans.[8] The state of Georgia passed a similar antipredatory lending law in 2002. After that, the Massachusetts attorney general obtained injunctive relief against a state chartered bank, pursuing the innovative claim that its adjustable-rate mortgage products and underwriting practices were "presumptively unfair" under Massachusetts law.[9]

Former state attorney general Eliot Spitzer, speaking for New York and other states, had, in 2008, excoriated the administration of George W. Bush for its apathetic posture toward consumer protections and made the argument that the states could respond more swiftly than their federal counterparts to changing business practices.

> Predatory lending was widely understood to present a looming national crisis. This threat was so clear that as New York attorney general, I joined with colleagues in the other 49 states in attempting to fill the void left by the federal government. Individually, and together, state attorneys general of both parties brought litigation or entered into settlements with many subprime lenders that were engaged in predatory lending practices. Several state legislatures, including New York's, enacted laws aimed at curbing such practices.
>
> ... Not only did the Bush administration do nothing to protect consumers, it embarked on an aggressive and unprecedented campaign to prevent states from protecting their residents from the very problems to which the federal government was turning a blind eye. ... The administration accomplished this feat through an obscure federal agency called the Office of the Comptroller of the Currency (OCC).[10]

While in one sense, the preemption debate reflected fundamental disputes about the constitutional issue of federalism, in another, it posed very practical concerns for lenders and borrowers, alike. For borrowers, the dispute was about the latitude states would have to: monitor and aggressively challenge abusive practices in the field; respond, promptly, to novel problems that arose; and fill perceived gaps in federal law and regulations.[11] The core idea held by preemption's foes was that the federal law should set a floor for borrower protections, leaving individual states with the discretion to regulate more strictly. In some ways, the consumer position against preemption could also be understood as a response to uncertainty: who was to know how effectively a brand-new federal consumer financial protection agency, the CFPB, would actually function?

For lenders, on the other hand, the preemption debate spoke to significant business issues such as the feasibility and cost of complying with multiple regulatory requirements instead of a single national standard.[12] The big national banks with business across the country hated the idea of having to comply with the ever-changing consumer protection regimes of many states. And the debate also embodied potential competitive implications inasmuch as some lenders historically had been exempt from state regulation while others had been obliged to comply.

Throughout the Dodd-Frank congressional debate, the interests of lenders and others who favored a weaker consumer protection agency (and thus wanted federal CFPB statutes to trump state-level laws) were pitted against those of the AFR and its partners (state attorneys general and others) who fought zealously for enactment of the strongest possible consumer protection laws. Although no one ever carried a hand-painted sign reading "Stop Preemption Now" during the congressional campaign, the outcome of the preemption debate had important ramifications for consumer protection.

Mr. President, Please Help the States Deal with the Financial Crisis

After eight years of the Bush administration's hostility toward states' concerns about preemption, one of the first things all 50 attorneys general did after Barack Obama's inauguration was to send a letter urging him to reconsider the federal government's position on preemption and asking the Department of Justice to file a brief in support of New York attorney general Andrew Cuomo's pending Supreme Court challenge to the preemptive powers of the OCC. The letter from the AGs concluded:

> As you have stated, our country needs to start anew, putting the people's interests ahead of special interests. Unfair and deceptive practices in mortgage lending contributed to the current financial crisis. This conduct flourished under the misguided application of preemption that constitutes the current OCC position. We ask that your administration reject the OCC's aggressive preemption position in the upcoming briefing and argument of the *Cuomo* case in the Supreme Court.[13]

The position of the state AGs on preemption was backed by a cross section of leading consumer, civil rights, and fair lending advocates. When given the microphone at congressional hearings in 2009, these advocates made the case that preemption was a leading cause of the mortgage crisis and that ending it might help prevent another. Nancy Zirkin of the Leadership Conference on Civil and Human Rights expressed doubts that federal regulators could ever properly protect consumers as long as they were "financially dependent on the institutions they are tasked with policing."[14] Travis Plunkett of the Consumer Federation of America stressed the need for any new federal agency to set the floor but not the ceiling for national consumer protection standards.[15] If there was going to be any preemption, Ed Mierzwinski of U.S. PIRG testified, it should be CFPB preemption of any state consumer protection standards that are weaker than those of the new agency.[16]

The Obama administration was listening. First, in its White Paper on Regulatory Reform and again in the Treasury Department's draft legislation to create the CFPB, the administration came down on the side of the states and the advocates opposed to preemption. The White Paper asserted that the rules of a new consumer protection agency should "serve as a floor, not a ceiling. The states should have the ability to adopt and enforce stricter laws for institutions of all types, regardless of charter."[17]

The Opposition Speaks

Initially, the CFPB's most adamant opponents did not trouble themselves with the issue of preemption because they did not want to see a new agency at all. Those opponents who did allow for the possibility that some type of new agency might be created came out in strong support of preemption. If there were to be new rules, they should be uniform across states, not some crazy patchwork quilt of regulations. Testifying before the House Committee on Financial Services, Steve Bartlett, head of the Financial Services Roundtable, was repelled by the idea of a financial services company having to comply with different state laws: "This is like saying that different truck safety features can be mandated by each state, and the trucking company must change its equipment at state borders to travel across state lines. Such a system would not be good for American commerce, and the imposition of different state requirements on identical or similar financial products would likewise have a negative impact on consumers."[18]

Other members of the financial services community articulated the "level playing field" argument: if there were to be any CFPB rules, they should apply equally across all states and across all types of lending institutions. While traditional bank lenders were used to government regulation, they could not abide more favorable treatment being given to their competitors. The banks hurled brickbats at nonbanks such as Countrywide Finance, New Century, American Home Mortgage, and Ameriquest for the excesses that brought on the mortgage meltdown. If the banks were going to face new rules, so should their competitors. R. Michael Menzies, speaking to the House Financial Services Committee on behalf of the 5,000-member Independent Community Bankers Association, made the point that it "is critical to extend supervision and oversight to those nonbank entities that contributed to the current financial crisis largely because they did not fall under any agency's regulatory umbrella."[19] In that respect at least, the CFPB's main proponents and opponents saw eye to eye.

The Bean Amendment

The bill introduced in July 2009 by House Financial Services Committee chairman Barney Frank, H.R. 3126, envisioned a new consumer financial protection agency that would allow the states to enforce their own consumer protection laws against federally chartered lending institutions to the extent they were stricter than the CFPB's. This was also the position preferred by AFR and its partners.

The burden of changing the bill to reclaim federal preemptive rights fell to the lending industry and its supporters. The main proponents of preemption were the big national banks that typically operated across state lines. The smaller community banks, whose political champions were mainly their local congressmen, were less affected by preemption and did not weigh in heavily on the issue.[20] Ultimately, the best chance for lenders during the House debate lay within the House Financial Services Committee, which was heavily populated by centrist Democrats with strong ties to the financial industry.

This centrist faction's leader on the committee was Melissa Bean, a third termer from Illinois' 8th District, a northwest suburb of Chicago. Decennial (2010) Census data show that her district was predominantly white, well educated, and financially better off than the national average.[21] Bean, 47 years old in 2009, was vice chair of the Congressional New Democrat Caucus and a member of the Blue Dog Coalition. Her political profile meshed comfortably with that of her constituents: fiscally conservative (she voted for the Bush tax cut and had an 82% approval rating from the Chamber of Commerce in 2008) but socially liberal with a 100 percent approval rating from the prochoice group NARAL and 80 percent from the Human Rights Campaign.[22] Her leading contributors in 2008 reflected this mix. The progressive women's lobby, Emily's List, was her single biggest contributor, but the finance-insurance-real estate sector gave Bean nearly a million dollars, far more than any other sector.[23]

From July until the latter part of September 2009, the House Committee on Financial Services was fully immersed in introductory hearings on all aspects of the CFPB bill. This activity temporarily held the industry's pitch for federal preemption in abeyance. Toward the end of September, with hearings winding up, Barney Frank began to take soundings within his committee. It was clear from the start that the Republican members of the House Committee could be counted upon to solidly oppose Frank's leadership on the issue. Thus, it was not worth devoting much time to seeking out compromise with the ranking Republican on the committee, Spencer Bachus (R-Ala.), and his troops. The focus of Frank's attention was the bloc of Blue Dog and New Democrat members on his committee, led by Melissa Bean. Frank looked to AFR and other advocates for assistance with Representative Bean and her industry-supported attempts to weaken the impact of state laws and enforcement efforts.

Frank's late-September assessment led to a decision to scale back his original proposal and to offer some concessions to the crucial Democratic centrist bloc. It was at that juncture that certain reform proposals dropped out. One victim was the mandated plain vanilla mortgage—a favorite of both Assistant Treasury Secretary Michael Barr, one of the administration's top strategists, and Elizabeth Warren, an ardent proponent of financial simplification.[24]

Frank's concessions triggered a reaction from proponents of federal preemption. Journalist Pat Garofalo reported, "The financial services industry now sees an opening, and is turning up the pressure on moderate Democrats on the panel to push for more concessions."[25] As Frank's bill moved toward markup and a vote in his committee, Melissa Bean stepped forward as the centrist Democrats' lead negotiator on the issue of federal preemption. In late September, Bean told the magazine *Politico*: "The whole point of the CFPA is to have robust consumer protections that are universally enforced. [The proposed legislation] moves us back to sort of this inconsistency of not knowing what set of rules to follow for nationally chartered organizations. And that doesn't equally protect consumers. It creates inconsistency; it adds additional cost for consumers."[26]

Given that Chairman Frank was implacably opposed to her preemption position, Bean decided that promoting an amendment in committee was probably her strongest card. Beginning in late September, the media was full of reports that Bean was "expected" to offer an amendment, was "preparing" the amendment, and "was poised" to offer it.[27]

The impending Bean amendment, in turn, precipitated a very strong reaction from AFR and its allies. In a letter to members of the House in December 2009, the AFR summarized its main objections: the amendment would expand the authority of federal bank regulators to exempt national banks from state laws and regulations; it would enlarge the scope of federal preemption to areas not already covered and would undo longstanding policies dealing with equal credit opportunity, debt collection and others; and it would restrict the ability of the courts to provide necessary checks and balances over bank regulators.[28]

In an unforeseen way, the emergence of Congresswoman Bean as leader of the federal preemption bid was extremely fortuitous for AFR and its allies. The basic strategy adopted by AFR was to isolate Bean in her Illinois congressional district; to spank her as publicly as possible in the area news media, town hall meetings, street demonstrations and targeted e-blasts; and to lean on her to withdraw her amendment.

AFR's Bean-centric approach turned out to be very savvy, strategically. It conserved the group's scarce resources because it did not draw other members of the Blue Dogs and New Dems into the vortex of the dispute. In addition, it capitalized on important Chicago-area ties, including Heather Booth's deep connections to the Chicago activist and progressive political community and, at least implicitly, the street-cred of several other local players—Barack Obama and Rahm Emanuel. Had the advocates actively shopped for home field advantage, they could hardly have found a more sympathetic venue.

Moving into the campaign, arguably, the advocates' most crucial antipreemption ally was Illinois' democratic attorney general, Lisa Madigan. Madigan was elected Illinois' first female attorney general in 2002 and was reelected in 2006. Her father, Michael Madigan, had been speaker of the Illinois House of Representatives for many years, so the younger Madigan knew a little something about political street fighting. In December 2008, she had been unafraid to file a motion with the Illinois Supreme Court to temporarily remove Gov. Rod Blagojevich from office.[29] Although that motion was turned down, Blagojevich was indicted shortly thereafter and later convicted.

Madigan, a longtime colleague of PIRG consumer leader Ed Mierzwinski and others in the AFR family, rallied to the antipreemption call despite the inevitable friction she was likely to create among elected Illinois Democrats.

Madigan's longstanding opposition to federal preemption, based on its adverse impact on Illinois citizens, together with her high voter approval ratings, made her a formidable opponent for Bean. Madigan's access to socially liberal voters in Bean's district and elsewhere in the state could be expected to jeopardize Bean's ability to retain her favored status with progressive social lobbies such as Emily's List because those groups would presumably look askance at Bean's posture in favor of bankers against borrowers and the middle class.

In early October, after Madigan and Bean had chatted about the CFPB, the polite Madigan wrote Bean a thank you note. Madigan began by appealing to their common role: "We, as elected officials, are charged with protecting the consumers of Illinois."[30] Madigan then argued that the best way to do this would be giving states the ability to enforce any rules issued by the CFPB and allowing states to enact tougher laws if they saw fit. The letter concluded: "The CFPA Act, as proposed by President Obama, respects the vital role of states in safeguarding our consumers and markets from abusive lending practices. The people of Illinois deserve a final bill that retains that respect and, thus, offers the strongest possible protection for consumers."[31]

Madigan employed additional efforts to pressure Bean. According to Ed Mierzwinski, AFR's main liaison to the attorneys general, "General Madigan activated her political apparatus. So if you were on her 'Friends of Lisa Madigan' list, you were getting emails from her urging you to contact Melissa Bean and tell her to do the right thing."[32] AFR's director of field operations, Eileen Toback, raved about Madigan's efforts: "Lisa Madigan was like a rock star there. . . . She had town halls. They were doing radio interviews. There were letters to the editor."[33]

Madigan was certainly not working alone in trying to win over Representative Bean. On October 14, in the midst of the committee markup of H.R. 3126, she joined in a press event with a number of AFR partner organizations, some of which were staffed by alumni of Booth's Midwest Academy. Alongside her were representatives of several Chicago-area groups—Illinois Citizen Action, AARP, the Spanish Coalition for Housing, the Woodstock Institute, the Neighborhood Housing Services of Chicago, Business and Professional People for the Public Interest, and Loyola University of Chicago. Together, they urged the members of the Illinois congressional delegation to support Barney Frank's bill to create the CFPB.[34] At other times Madigan participated in joint press conferences and similar media events with Elizabeth Warren, Heather Booth, Ed Mierzwinski, and other CFPB advocates.

Ben Clark of the National Fair Housing Alliance was impressed that grassroots organizations had become involved in the preemption fight. To him, "preemption had very clear and obvious civil rights implications," but he recognized that the issue could appear arcane.[35] Clark said, "It's funny because [preemption] is a very technical issue for a lot of people. I don't think it's something that would ordinarily be accessible to the public."[36]

Inside the House Financial Services Committee, Chairman Frank, unwavering in his opposition to federal preemption, was seeking to defuse a showdown that would openly divide Committee Democrats on the issue. Apparently, Frank and Bean reached an agreement that would involve a little kabuki theater. The two would engage in a colloquy in which Bean would first offer her amendment and lay out her concerns. Frank would respond by promising to consider her views as the bill moved to the House floor. Bean would then withdraw her amendment, retaining the right to reintroduce it when the bill came to the House floor for a vote.[37] The planned colloquy inadvertently fell apart when Bean's family came down with swine flu and she was too contagious to travel to Washington to take part in the committee debate.[38] No one else in the centrist bloc stood up as her understudy.

In a further effort to heal the divide among the Committee's Democrats, Rep. Mel Watt (D-N.C.), a leader of the progressive bloc, partnered with Rep. Dennis Moore (D-Kans.), a centrist member of the Blue Dog Caucus, on an amendment that was approved by voice vote. It permitted the Office of the Comptroller of the Currency or the Office of Thrift Supervision to intervene and preempt state laws—but only under a much more restricted set of conditions. The Watt-Moore amendment limited OCC and OTS preemption to those cases where state law discriminates against nationally chartered institutions or "significantly interferes with" a national bank's ability to engage in banking.[39] For all practical purposes, though, Chairman Frank had won the round when, on October 22, the committee discharged the bill and sent it on its way to the full House without ever voting on the Bean amendment.

On the House Floor

When the full House took up the CFPB, Representative Bean opted to relitigate the preemption issue, following through on the warning she had given Barney Frank while the amendment was still in committee. She insisted that her preemption amendment be placed before the full House for a vote. The implied threat was that, without such a vote, she and her supporters would block the procedural rule that was required to bring the entire bill to the floor for consideration.[40]

By then, however, the stakes had been elevated. The narrowly defined House Financial Services Committee version of the bill had been merged into a more comprehensive Senate bill at the beginning of December. On the House side, the bill focused exclusively on CFPB, whereas in the Senate it blanketed all aspects of Wall Street and consumer protection reform. Thus, if push came to shove, and if the Blue Dog-New Dem threat was successfully exercised, it could potentially bring down the entire reform package—not just the CFPB provisions. Blogger Mike Elk was irate, writing: "Here [Bean] goes again: Wall Street's favorite Democrat, Rep. Melissa Bean, D-Ill., is once again shilling for the banks."[41]

Counting the votes, AFR and its allies had to take the threat posed by Bean's floor amendment very seriously—and they did. Forty of the nation's attorneys general reiterated their opposition to preemption in a letter to Congress in early November.[42] AFR sent its own letter of opposition to the House of Representatives on December 9. The letter made reference to a study recently conducted by the Center for Community Capital at the University of North Carolina that found that states with stronger antipredatory lending laws fared better during the foreclosure crisis than states with weaker laws.[43] In concluding, the AFR letter pointed to the compromise that had already been struck in the House Financial Services Committee under which state laws could be preempted if they truly interfered with the business of banking.[44]

Although Barney Frank, now acting as the bill's manager on the House floor, was outwardly dismissive of Bean's threat, he made sure not to slam the door entirely on the centrist-conservative bloc. Strangely enough, House minority leader John Boehner was equally skeptical about Bean's ploy. No stranger to legislative artifice himself, Boehner quipped that if Bean had the votes to "bring down the procedural rule," she would have called for a vote, not taken a recess.[45]

Given the stakes involved, Barney Frank decided to placate Bean and the moderate Democratic bloc by agreeing to integrate, into the so-called Manager's Amendment, some concessionary preemption language worked out in Speaker Nancy Pelosi's office in concert with the vehemently anti-preemption Treasury Department led by Deputy Secretary Neal Wolin and Assistant Secretary Michael Barr.[46] This pragmatic decision made it possible for Frank to bring the bill to the House floor for a vote without further delay from Democratic centrists. On December 11, the bill passed in the House by a margin of 223–211.

Frank's decision also meant that the Bean amendment would never face a formal vote in the House—either in committee or on the floor. That helped him preserve some room for maneuver and shielded him from extreme pressure from the AFR and the advocates, on the one side, and the New Dems, Blue Dogs and business interests, on the other.

The task of finding a compromise position on preemption was complicated by the issue's extreme importance to both sides. Little more than two months earlier, Mike Calhoun, the president of the Center for Responsible Lending and a key AFR partner, had testified in Frank's committee, citing a litany of problems brought about as a result of federal preemption. In a subsequent interview, Calhoun said: "We were upfront with everyone and said if [the bill] is preemptive we are full out opposed to it. For example, if it was preemptive you could have someone come in and set a very industry-friendly payday lending set of regulations that would have the impact of authorizing payday lending throughout the country and overriding state protection. . . . For us, that risk was not worth the gain."[47]

Joining Calhoun at the House hearing at the end of September, Edward Yingling, president and CEO of the American Bankers Association, made it abundantly clear that from the perspective of the big national banks, tampering with federal preemption would reduce the availability of credit and undercut the CFPB's objective of simplification and clarification of consumer information. Instead of a one-page disclosure form, weakening federal preemption, Yingling argued, would result in "page after page of disclaimers and disclosures about all the differing state and local laws applicable."[48]

Although the language incorporated in the Manager's Amendment ostensibly narrowed some preexisting preemption provisions found in federal court decisions and agency rules, it was seen as having broadened others. According to Lauren Saunders, a preemption expert at the National Consumer Law Center, the split decision was at least neutral and possibly marginally helpful in terms of limiting the authority of the OCC to preempt state laws governing national banks. Furthermore, it codified state authority to pursue nonpreempted claims against national banks in court—a victory for Saunders and the antipreemption forces.[49]

Preemption Moves Over to the Senate

After all was said and done in the House, attention shifted to the Senate where the durability of the House-passed preemption language remained a big question mark. Would the Senate accept the House accommodation or address federal preemption on its own terms? In either case, the problem of holding everything together was now in the hands of Sen. Christopher Dodd.

As the action moved to the Senate side, the political dynamics of the preemption issue promised to be even more complicated than they had been in the House. On the House side, Barney Frank had been a strong, albeit pragmatic, opponent of federal preemption. As a result, the advocates were secure, knowing they had a steadfast ally, even if their day-to-day interactions with Chairman Frank were sometimes tetchy. On the Senate side, Banking Committee chairman Chris Dodd had a more conciliatory style that some advocates felt was not as well-suited to attacking controversial issues head-on.

Part of the difference between the two committee chairmen could well have reflected the culture of their legislative bodies. The House is more confrontational. In the Senate, a quiet word to one's colleague can take care of a problem and avoid a lot of drama. In any event, whether it was personal style or differences in the institutional environment of the two chambers, some advocates were manifestly anxious about Dodd's leadership.[50] Even though some experienced advocates considered Dodd's initial proposal to have been the single best draft bill from their perspective, many were apprehensive about his commitment to go to war to preserve the particular provisions of greatest importance to them, including preemption.[51]

Dodd's task, and that of AFR and its allies, became significantly more complicated when two preemption amendments were dropped in the Senate hopper during floor debate in mid-May 2010. The first amendment was submitted by Dodd's sometime Republican negotiating partner, Bob Corker; the other was introduced by his moderate Democratic colleague, Tom Carper, an ex-governor of Delaware and successor to the seat vacated by Vice President Joe Biden. Carper, a moderate Democrat with 100 percent recent approval ratings from NARAL, the League of Conservation Voters and the AFL-CIO, 45 percent from Public Citizen's Congress Watch, 27 percent from the U.S. Chamber of Commerce, and 12 percent from the National Taxpayers Union, was joined by three Democratic cosponsors on the Banking Committee: senators Evan Bayh, John Warner and Tim Johnson.[52]

The Corker Amendment was by far the more extreme of the two. The most important change from the perspective of the advocates was that the amendment did not allow the states to enforce their own laws pertaining to national banks if these laws were stricter than corresponding federal statutes. This limitation defeated one of the cardinal objectives of AFR and its partners. It also barred states from examining national banks and their subsidiaries—examination being a quintessential function of state regulators—and restricted the scope of the states' enforcement of nonpreempted state laws.

Senator Corker argued that, absent his amendment, financial institutions could be subject to 50 different state standards and legal interpretations. That result, in his view, would be onerous and expensive for the institutions and would lead to unnecessary complexity as well as increased costs and less product choice for consumers.

In many respects, the Carper amendment was less extreme than Corker's. Carper allowed state officials to apply federal CFPB rules governing national banks under the Supreme Court's 1996 Barnett standard. That standard meant that the OCC could preempt state laws on a case-by-case basis if they interfered, substantially, with the business of banking, but not on an across-the-board basis as had been its practice following the agency's 2004 rulemaking. But the Carper amendment circumscribed the states' authority to enforce rules stricter than those issued by the CFPB. It also permitted the OCC to preempt state actions against federally chartered financial institutions and prohibited states from bringing class action suits against national banks.

While AFR, with strong support from Michael Barr at Treasury and Diana Farrell in the White House's National Economic Council, tried mightily to defeat the Carper Amendment and retain state-initiated consumer safeguards, they faced several challenges that ultimately undermined their efforts. Most important, the Corker amendment provided a foil that allowed all but three Democrats (Evan Bayh, Ben Nelson, and Robert Byrd) to vote against the extreme version of preemption, while leaving space to support a more modest, compromise proposal.

Paradoxically, opposition from AFR and its allies to the Carper proposal may have only strengthened the chances of its success. Democrats interested in reaching a compromise, including liberal-leaning members such as senators Lautenberg, Klobuchar, Kerry, and Menendez and leadership heavies like Chuck Schumer, could well have capitalized on the pushback from advocates to score a twofer. First, they could offer a meaningful accommodation to the lending community as a gesture of goodwill and, second, they could claim their independence and nonideological stance on the matter. Toward this end, Carper provided his colleagues one helpful talking point, namely that strengthening state enforcement too much could unwittingly wind up reducing some of the pressure on the CFPB to be the tough cop on the beat.

As it became increasingly obvious that a large fraction of the Democrats, including many in the leadership, wanted to vote in favor of the Carper amendment, Senator Dodd, with the support of the Treasury (a stalwart in the antipreemption camp), and members of the Democratic leadership sat down to iron out a compromise with Tom Carper. Their compromise position led to a landslide bipartisan vote (80–18) in favor of the amendment on May 18.[53] On the same day, the Corker amendment went down to defeat by a solid margin of 55–43, almost entirely along party lines.

Immediately after the vote on the Carper amendment, Lauren Saunders, manager of the National Consumer Law Center's Washington, D.C. office, released an assessment of the Dodd-Carper agreement. Writing on behalf of the AFR, she observed:

> Senator Dodd and Senator Carper have reached a deal to modify Senator Carper's amendment #3949 on the role of states in protecting consumers under the Wall Street reform bill. The deal compromises a bill further that is already full of concessions to the banks and the bank regulators who failed us, but it does not give in to the bank demands to remove the states entirely from their responsibility to protect their residents. . . . The bill continues to give bank regulators too much authority to immunize banks from state law, and the deal makes it easier for bank regulators to preempt state law even if there is no federal protection in place. But it does curb the preemption excesses of the last ten years, when bank regulators wiped out consumer protection laws governing mortgages, credit cards and other products, without even looking at whether particular laws that address gaps in federal protection impose a significant burden on banking.[54]

At the conclusion of the Senate vote on the Carper Amendment, Elizabeth Warren weighed in as well: "The big banks and their army of lobbyists have fought aggressively to block states from being able to pass and enforce laws to protect their own citizens. No other industry gets the special exception from state law that the big banks demand. The compromise today is disappointing, but it does not cut out the states entirely and it ensures that the big banks will face some scrutiny from state officials."[55] In response to Warren's summation, the left-leaning blogger David Dayen commented, "Sounds like she's talking herself into being OK with it."[56]

Now, as the respective chambers concluded their action on the issue of federal preemption and headed into the legislative conference committee, the main differences between the two had been narrowed substantially. A good indication of the converging positions was the fact that federal preemption did not even appear on AFR's top 10 Conference Priorities List, a document circulated to conferees on June 15, 2010.[57] What had started out as, according to Heather Booth, potentially the key roadblock to adoption of a satisfactory consumer protection program had been reduced to a short list of manageable and mostly technical differences.

The Conference Committee

Going into the conference to hammer out discrepancies between the two chambers, differences certainly existed between the House and Senate approaches. Nevertheless, both versions would help rein-in the federal financial regulators' overzealous application of preemption as a means of neutralizing state consumer protection laws affecting national banks.[58] That achieved one of the advocates' top priorities.

AFR nonetheless continued to press conferees to adopt a House provision that would require that federal preemptive statutes be supported by a specific standard before they could replace state laws. To make their case, advocates referred to instances where a perfectly sound state consumer protection law had been replaced by absolutely "nothing."[59] And they preferred the House proposal which allowed state attorneys general to enforce any applicable federal law and any nonpreempted state law against national banks over the Senate provision which limited AG enforcement to CFPB regulations.

After a month of off-and-on wrangling in the conference committee, much of it broadcast live on C-Span, conferees approved the 2,319-page omnibus Dodd-Frank bill, a product 75 times as monumental in length as the original Federal Reserve Act of 1913. Lauren Saunders of the National Consumer Law Center highlighted what she saw as the ultimate outcome on the issue of preemption. First and foremost, she observed, Dodd-Frank represented a direct attack on the OCC and Office of Thrift Supervision regulations and should effectively repeal their preemptive regulations.[60] That would mean that the overreaching OCC and OTS regulations, which had asserted the right to preempt entire fields of state consumer protection in one fell swoop, would now be limited to case-by-case preemptions and then, only in situations where the regulator has substantial evidence that *specific* state consumer laws discriminate against, prevent, or significantly interfere with a national bank's powers (under the Supreme Court's *Barnett Bank* standard).

Second, Dodd-Frank did not explicitly address whether the same restriction relating to OCC and OTS preemption applied as well to *general* state consumer laws governing unfair or deceptive practices, contracts, and other common laws. Saunders argued that "this silence should be interpreted as a rule against preemption of general state laws."[61] And third, the Act reversed regulations that exempted the subsidiaries of national banks from the effect of state consumer laws.[62]

At the end of the day, advocates could legitimately claim a significant incremental improvement in consumer financial protections—if not the home run some had initially hoped for. Saunders remarked, "We feel pretty good about it. I mean, at least we feel it's as good as we could have gotten. How it will work in the end is very much an open question. But it turned out better than we expected, and that wasn't just us."[63]

At the End

While Barney Frank, perhaps slightly more than Chris Dodd, was genuinely committed to strong state consumer enforcement, it was always going to be very tough to make preemption into a do-or-die issue on the Hill. Even with Frank's legislative artisanship in committee and on the floor, aiming for a kill shot—the complete defeat of preemption—was simply beyond reach. On its face, preemption was not a big money matter; it was hard to paint it as a question of lender greed in the typical sound-bite mode. In terms of selling the issue's importance to the mainstream media, the blogosphere, and the public, it was a struggle to alter the perception that preemption was a battle of control between state and federal bureaucrats and not much more than that.

It was only slightly less difficult to attract preemption champions than to turn the underlying problem into a sexy policy issue. Very few states had attorneys general eager to become avid, antipreemption warriors. Most state AG's (regardless of political affiliation) could be counted on to oppose federal preemption for institutional reasons but not to immerse themselves deeply in the law and politics of Dodd-Frank. Lisa Madigan's willingness to jump into the dispute with both feet was unusual, and her alliance with AFR and other state and local advocates was decisive as a strategy for outflanking Melissa Bean in the House. Had the mainstream Democrats on Frank's committee introduced a less sweeping amendment than Bean's (along the lines of Tom Carper's in the Senate) or had Frank allowed Bean's proposal to come to a vote, there is no way of knowing what the outcome would have been. As it turned out, AFR's efforts in the House to defeat weakening amendments and to focus its heaviest guns on Representative Bean's proposal certainly helped deliver the political message Chairman Frank was looking for to negotiate a reasonably good agreement with the centrist bloc on his committee and in the House.

Unlike the House where AFR had the tools and willingness to use them to challenge obstructive proposals pushed by centrist Democrats, the situation facing them in the Senate was far more complicated. In the Senate, advocates were forced to recognize that many basically consumer-friendly Democrats were prepared to give them some assistance but not everything they wanted. Senators like Schumer, Lautenberg, Kerry, and Klobuchar had important financial services constituents whom they were going to displease on other Dodd-Frank issues, so they were keen to find some matters on which they could side with these powerful industries. Preemption via the Carper option was one. Plus, the support of these senators would be vital on other aspects of the financial reform bill, so it would be unproductive to press too hard on an issue without public appeal and an obvious Senate champion. The key, then, was to help Chairman Dodd negotiate the most favorable terms possible with his progressive Democratic colleagues.

The Treasury Department and the White House stood firm but finally joined members of the Democratic leadership in moving Dodd to a compromise with Carper. AFR and its partners continued to provide support in the form of legislative language and policy arguments. But mostly, they kept up the pressure through Hill lobbying, communications with grassroots organizations, a readiness to seek strategic compromises, and a unity of support, irrespective of the positions asserted individually by some of their partners.

In all, the advocates could legitimately claim an incremental victory and certainly the avoidance of any major setback on federal preemption. Nevertheless, on this matter as with so many other aspects of Dodd-Frank, those most closely involved with the legislative struggle would have to wait for CFPB actions and court interpretations to know the outcome of their labors.

Chapter 10

What Did the Advocates Accomplish and How?

In 2009, a newly formed consortium of progressive-leaning advocacy groups and individual activists in the United States responded to the global economic collapse by mobilizing an unprecedented legislative campaign for financial reform.[1] Members of the embryonic alliance crossed traditional demographic and socioeconomic lines, social movement categories, and geographic boundaries.

One of the campaign's cardinal objectives was to tame the unscrupulous and abusive lending practices adopted by bank and nonbank institutions active in the consumer financial marketplace. With strong support from the incoming Obama administration, the alliance worked with key congressional leaders to help pass the Dodd-Frank Act. The Consumer Financial Protection Bureau, a key component of the Dodd-Frank Act, embodied many of the preventive and remedial measures campaigners had worked hard to achieve.

While time alone will tell whether the CFPB fulfills its mission as an effective public watchdog on behalf of consumers, it is not too early to identify some of the positive contributions that Professor Warren's *policy entrepreneurship* and the AFR's *organizational leadership and advocacy methods* made to the success of the CFPB campaign and to think about applications to future people's campaigns.[2]

Contributions of the Advocates

When President Obama signed the Dodd-Frank Act on July 21, 2010, what had the CFPB's advocates achieved? It certainly felt like a major victory to the coalition's leaders. Ed Mierzwinski described the bill as "the strongest consumer financial reform since deposit insurance."[3] Travis Plunkett drew the lesson that "moneyed interests don't always win in Washington."[4] The campaign confirmed what Heather Booth believed all along: "If we organize, we can win."[5] Meanwhile, Edward Yingling, head of the American Bankers Association and a leader of the forces opposed to the CFPB, resigned after 25 years with the ABA.[6]

Harvard law professor Elizabeth Warren has been justly celebrated for her entrepreneurial role in masterminding the CFPB. She came up with the original idea for a single-purpose consumer financial protection agency to address the deteriorating economic conditions of working and middle class borrowers; she rounded up definitive commitments for legislative action from the 2008 Democratic presidential candidates even before the financial maelstrom had fully developed; while serving as chair of the Congressional Oversight Panel for the Troubled Asset Relief Program she developed a comprehensive set of regulatory reform principals that became the core of the Dodd-Frank legislation; and she ultimately served as a familiar and trusted public face for the new agency as the legislative process took shape.

The coalition Americans for Financial Reform, the other stalwart of the legislative effort, was perhaps less visible to the general public but no less important to the campaign's overall success. AFR served as an adept inside player, pulling together and skillfully managing a broad and diverse alliance of Washington-based and state and local citizens' organizations. It won respect for its expertise on the full complement of complex financial and consumer protection issues that made up the legislative package. And it was strategically adroit, matching political opportunities with the capabilities and resources at its disposal.

Indeed, the coalition's credibility—stemming from its size and diversity along racial, ethnic, economic and regional lines—demanded and received attention from politicians, industry, and the media. Without AFR's work, educating and focusing the public's attention on the harmful effects of abusive lending, the campaign could not have prevailed.

During the campaign, AFR and Professor Warren engaged in different but synergistic activities. AFR successfully played two important and overlapping roles. It stood up as the tangible representative of aggrieved middle- and working-class consumers (Main Street) and brought personal stories from all over the country to the public's attention. By so doing, it served to popularize and legitimize Elizabeth Warren's original call for financial protection, and it deflected criticism that Warren was nothing more than a self-appointed Harvard promoter pushing an elitist cause. Second, AFR represented and provided leadership to citizen groups before Congress, the Obama administration, the media, and members of the lending and business communities.

At the same time, but on a parallel track, Professor Warren was leading a highly visible public classroom, teaching consumers and politicians to understand how "tricks and traps" embedded in typical mortgage and credit card agreements worked to undermine the fairness of the marketplace. As an unabashed advocate of capitalism, Warren was affronted by the phenomenon she referred to in unvarnished terms as contracts larded with "bullshit promises."[7]

Any reference to AFR as Elizabeth Warren's posse should not be construed as suggesting that the interplay between the coalition and Warren was a one-way street. Far from it. Warren's charisma and universally acknowledged adherence to cause were inspirational to AFR activists. They embraced her persona and message as a means of energizing their own membership. AFR sought her active participation in jointly sponsored events, press and bloggers' conferences, and strategy sessions. Having her on-board enhanced the coalition's own access and credibility within the political and media communities. Although Professor Warren was not a member of the coalition *per se* and didn't formally coordinate her strategy and tactics with AFR, the two were well aware of their respective positions. Little daylight came between them on any important issue. This tended to solidify the image of a broad-based, unified, interactive movement.

Policy Entrepreneur

By 2007, when Warren proposed a new agency in her article "Unsafe at Any Rate" in *Democracy*, the problems of unfair lending she was writing about were hardly new: they were simply intractable. They represented the icing on a very lucrative business model that looked as if it would persist forever. For years, advocates had attacked the problem by dramatizing the negative impact of unfair and deceptive lending on individuals and then proposing piecemeal solutions for each issue. With a few exceptions, this approach was nugatory and the status quo persisted.[8]

A turning point in Warren's argument for a new agency came when she began to put the problem of unsafe and unscrupulous lending in a larger frame. Practices she viewed as legally impermissible and morally corrupt were not only injurious to borrowers; they also functioned as triggers for a powerful financial crisis that would topple housing and credit markets throughout the world.[9] By broadening the issue from individual harm to global calamity, she was able to dislodge a problem that had long been stuck in place.

Political scientist John Kingdon and a subsequent generation of public policy scholars define people who function like Warren as "policy entrepreneurs."[10] According to Kingdon, policy entrepreneurs are specialized public actors, in and out of government, who are acutely aware of seemingly insoluble problems and who become especially alert to attention-focusing events that have the capacity to shock the system and precipitate change. Warren reframed the old issue of unfair lending in light of a major external shock to the policy environment, a technique by which less powerful interests have sometimes overcome barriers to their political agenda put in place by entrenched stakeholders.[11]

Policy entrepreneurs are masters of political timing. Attentive to the most propitious moment to act, the policy entrepreneur is alive to critical shifts in political power (say, a change in the control of Congress or the White House or a shift in the leadership of a crucial legislative committee). As a window of opportunity opens, policy entrepreneurs couple their definition of the problem with a vision of substantial policy reform.[12] The policy entrepreneur then seizes the moment to close the deal by convincing new political management and other stakeholders in the relevant policy network to initiate the proposed change as a means of responding to the external shock.

While in many ways Professor Warren's approach to policy change in the case of the CFPB was consistent with Kingdom's classic model of policy entrepreneurship, her strategy for winning adequate support to reconstruct regulation of the formidable consumer lending sector was more methodically planned and proactive than the theory and reported cases would suggest.[13] The scholarly literature describes a sustained pause in the action during which time the policy entrepreneur scans the environment, waiting for precisely the right external shock or fortuitous political event to happen. The policy entrepreneur's special skill involves sensing *the magic moment* during which policy change is most likely to take place.

Professor Warren, in contrast, was far more actively involved; indeed, she helped create the conditions and mobilized the resources needed to precipitate change.[14] Remarkably, it took but three years from publication of her initial call-to-action to final enactment of Dodd-Frank. During that time she mobilized top-level political commitments for regulatory reform, was intimately involved in the creation of AFR (a cross-movement, national people's coalition), developed a comprehensive outline of an omnibus reform bill that set the pattern for the Obama administration and the Congress, and introduced both the issue and the reform solution to the people, the media, and relevant stakeholders. Given these accomplishments, Elizabeth Warren should be regarded, more correctly, as an *activist policy entrepreneur.*

Defending Main Street

Elizabeth Warren's goals throughout were to ensure that financial services would be safe and sound for all Americans and to equalize credit opportunities by eliminating racial and class-related discriminatory practices. To emphasize the ubiquity of unsafe and abusive credit practices, Professor Warren opted to frame the problem, inclusively, in terms of the "middle class." As used by Warren, "middle class" was never meant to be a coded term for dividing the middle class from any other segment of American society, nor was it understood as such by advocates of working or low-income Americans. To the extent there was ever any tension between AFR's members and Professor Warren, it tended to be constructive. As Janis Bowdler of the National Council of La Raza observed, "We remind her frequently that our [Latino] community still has an agenda here and demands. There is still a healthy exchange to remind her of our perspective and our priorities and to point out they're important and shouldn't get lost in the conversation."[15]

In practice, Professor Warren's frame of reference resonated with a broad swath of working and middle-class Americans, not simply a particular segment. It included those who financed their homes with mortgage loans, bought consumer durables on credit, went to school on student loans, used credit cards for everyday purchases and emergencies, and were exposed to a multiplicity of other credit products and vendors.

This inclusive perspective was deeply ingrained in Warren as a result of her extensive research program at Harvard Law School dealing with the causes and effects of bankruptcy. There, she reached the conclusion that the majority of American families were just a quick step away from financial collapse. For a typical middle-class, two-wage-earner family, an illness or any other serious, unforeseen contingency could break its back financially. Too often, the family's only recourse would be to hit the credit cards or seek emergency financing of some sort. At that particularly vulnerable moment, unscrupulous and abusive—but not unusual—lending practices could trigger a downward spiral of borrowing and overindebtedness.

This inclusive perspective had strong moral as well as strategic implications—the latter because it vastly increased and diversified the base of support for the campaign's objectives. It also strengthened the political voice that the overall community of borrowers projected inasmuch as low income and minority consumers would have been more easily ignored had they been speaking, exclusively, on behalf of their own interests.[16]

Pressuring for Policy Change

In economist Albert Hirschman's classic formulation, *voice* refers to a strategy for seeking change through the expression of popular dissatisfaction with the perceived performance of business or government.[17] Voice has many dimensions, including the direct request for change, petitioning a higher authority to mandate change in others (as in lobbying for legislation), and mobilizing public opinion. In short, voice is the effort to accomplish change from within a system. This definition aptly describes AFR's involvement with Dodd-Frank.

AFR's path to political influence began with skilled leadership and the willingness of its member groups to subordinate their individual organizational priorities to the goal of enacting a good—if not perfect—financial reform and consumer protection bill. Operationally, this required consistency and discipline so that AFR could speak coherently and be viewed as representing a unified position. The important payoff was that AFR and its partner groups did not dissipate their persuasive power through internally clashing voices and dissonant messaging.

AFR's impact on the legislative process had several additional sources. In most prior citizens' campaigns, the voice of advocates was effectively suppressed by virtue of resource starvation. AFR was extremely efficient in spending its own, very limited financial resources and was able to obtain a certain amount of additional resources—dollars and people—from its member organizations and external donors. Further, AFR was able to develop a field presence to complement its lobbying within the Washington Beltway. Its underlying strategy was to mobilize the field as a vehicle for keeping the drumbeat of financial reform perpetually thrumming before national and local audiences and to raise the cost of political opposition by focusing media attention on key adversaries. Tying together all of these attributes of AFR was a basic pragmatism, rooted in the dictum "do not let a serious crisis go to waste." This pragmatism was especially evident in AFR's work with the Congress and the Obama administration.

Leadership and Cohesion

In our interviews, no one was bold enough to take full credit for being the first to have nominated Heather Booth to lead AFR, but recruiting her was a stroke of genius. Booth brought the organizing and cross-movement co-alition management experience, sophisticated professionalism, discipline, and sheer doggedness necessary for a campaign with such ambitious goals and formidable opposition. In turn, she had the vision and connections to recruit key AFR staffers, especially Lisa Donner and Eileen Toback. While the two had less experience than Booth in the intricacies of Washington lobbying, they had considerable familiarity with organizing at the grass-roots and grasstops levels. AFR also had extremely efficient steering and executive committees. Despite representing more than 250 organizations, some of which were networks of organizations themselves, these commit-tees were able to respond rapidly when key decisions needed to be made in very short order.

One of AFR's original strategic objectives was to organize a unified, disciplined, and well managed cross-movement coalition with sufficient capacity to make a significant difference in the Dodd-Frank debate. Many coalitions are fraught with internal policy disputes or battles over access to fame and glory. Others find it impossible to make decisions and to re-spond to external challenges on a timely and united basis. Cross-movement coalitions face the added challenges of diverse priorities and limited famil-iarity with unrelated groups. In this case, the external challenges brought about by the demands of many overlapping legislative mini-processes (particularly, the various titles of the Dodd-Frank bill, two houses of Con-gress, and a multiplicity of committees) demanded extraordinary skill and agility.

Two comments—both from senior partners in the coalition process—exemplify the high level of achievement by AFR's leaders in crafting a smoothly functioning coalition. One remark was that the typical Washing-ton legislative coalition takes far more from its contributors than it ever re-turns. This campaign tipped the standard calculus on its head.[18] The other was more personal. It came from a veteran of many decades of organiza-tional and coalition leadership who said he'd learned so much about how to motivate and lead that he was utterly humbled.

Maintaining long-term cohesion and coherence within such a diverse coalition in the face of potentially powerful centrifugal forces of political and organizational competition stood out as a hallmark achievement for AFR. Had the coalition split at any time or lost any of its key members, this weakness would have been recognized and probably exploited by opponents. Similarly, had any of the partner organizations gone seriously off-message or, in the heat of the moment, had they antagonized any of the key legislative players, they could have jeopardized the entire enterprise.

AFR employed an effective and unusual strategy for remaining unified during the Dodd-Frank campaign. In one of its initial decisions, organizers committed themselves to piecing together a large coalition of groups, recognizing as they did so that the central interests of the various members would probably not converge perfectly. Broadening the base of the alliance had obvious appeal. A common thread was that each group could identify one or more sections of the omnibus legislation that represented a key element of its particular agenda. By pairing some groups worried about derivatives, for example, with others more concerned about consumer protections, AFR was able to multiply its total base of members and to tap into their political networks and resources. The interests of each group would thereby be strengthened by the collegial support of the others.

At the same time, the strategy of broadening was not without its risks.[19] If individual groups grew suspicious that their special priorities were receiving less attention than their campaign partners' issues, the approach could be a source of friction. AFR addressed this potential downside in two ways. First, it decided *not* to tradeoff one priority against another. This meant that no group needed to be concerned that, after working on a long and arduous campaign, its top issue could eventually succumb to others in endgame negotiations. And next, the coalition adopted rules of the game that called for each member to cover its colleagues' backs. Thus, those worried about structural safety and soundness issues, for instance, were on-call to backstop the consumer protection groups—and vice versa. This created a force-multiplier effect.

A key requirement for functioning as an effective coalition is speaking with a single voice. In communicating with their members, AFR's organizations pounded out several simple messages. One was the idea that consumers needed a new "cop on the beat." Another was the clear disjunction between the interests of Wall Street and those of Main Street. Policy makers needed to answer the question: Which side are you on? Are you for the big bankers or the everyday borrowers? AFR's leaders were also unified by Elizabeth Warren's toaster image. For example, Bill Ragen of the Service Employees International Union said that the message that "You can't sell toasters that burst into flames, so how can you sell mortgages that do the same thing?" resonated really well with his members.[20]

Maximizing Resources and Building a Field Operation

AFR was never a well-funded organization, but it was capable of doing what it had to do. At most, it raised 2 million dollars from foundations. To supplement this funding, AFR was forced to rely on the willingness of its member-organizations to contribute money and in-kind personnel and services—resources that typically had to be taken away from other campaigns. AFR also managed to get some vital polling and communications consulting on a reduced fee or pro bono basis.

Given AFR's modest base of resources, it was critical that it deploy them shrewdly. In the campaign for the Consumer Financial Protection Bureau, AFR defined two of its primary missions as: shoring up leadership commitment (mainly in the Senate) for a strong and independent agency plus defeating weakening amendments, delays, and other procedural strategies designed to bog down action on Dodd-Frank. A key to the effectiveness of AFR's strategy was how adroitly it blended situational needs and opportunities within the frank limitations of its own resources and capabilities. It may have stretched, but it never promised much more than it could deliver.

With respect to both missions, AFR's ability to focus its limited resources on the most critical problems to which it could constructively contribute, without squandering its energy on unproductive distractions, was particularly impressive. This often meant that AFR was obliged to observe from the sidelines as the House or Senate chair worked out problems with committee members. Although the coalition would almost certainly have preferred to be more frequently and proactively involved in the internal deal-making process, it was sufficiently disciplined to respect the limitations imposed by its resources and roles as advisor and advocate.

To accomplish its concrete legislative objectives, AFR also needed to build a grassroots presence. Its field operations had to show lawmakers—whether through phone calls to their offices, visits, emails, media advertising, op-ed pieces or street demonstrations—that voters actually cared about financial reform and would hold legislators accountable for their positions.

Because the resources AFR had for fieldwork were quite constrained, it placed a premium on strategic focusing. Its field operation was based largely on small-dollar-amount contracts with organizations in numerous states. The main job of the contractors was to educate and mobilize local leaders and members of the public. In support of these goals, contractors were expected to seek media coverage (e.g., by placing op-eds and letters to the editor, setting up meetings with editorial boards, and making themselves available for radio interviews). The other major prong of the field strategy was earning media attention—primarily through direct actions, such as the Showdown in Chicago. AFR's field contractors and member organizations were in regular communication with Lisa Donner and Eileen Toback, AFR's primary points of contact. While the work of each contractor reflected local conditions, AFR provided consistency through common materials and training.

Although AFR had contractors in 29 states, the intensity of AFR's field work reflected its legislative priorities. AFR concentrated its resources on districts of the moderate Democrats whose votes were uncertain or who might be tempted to support weakening amendments. To a lesser extent, AFR's field activities focused on representatives or senators who opposed financial reform. AFR's message was that these members of Congress had chosen Wall Street over Main Street and would be held accountable.

Dealing with Rep. Melissa Bean's federal preemption amendment provides an instructive illustration of how AFR was able to make a difference on the ground. Several factors contributed to AFR's largely successful effort to defeat Bean's weakening amendment. A key was that a number of members of the coalition enjoyed good, long-term, working relationships with Chairman Barney Frank and Rep. Mel Watt (D-N.C.)—the two committee leaders most able to support AFR on the preemption issue and whose states, Massachusetts and North Carolina, had already been ahead of the curve on curbing predatory lending practices.

AFR and its member-organizations also encouraged attorneys general to pressure other members of Congress for expanded state enforcement flexibility. One of these attorneys general was Lisa Madigan, who was based conveniently in Melissa Bean's home state of Illinois. Coordinating her efforts with AFR, Madigan was an indefatigable advocate for strong state enforcement and was willing to lend her professional prestige as well as her email contact list to the project, notwithstanding the political risk to herself of upsetting some Democrats at home.

Finally, AFR, itself, mobilized people power and field organization in Bean's home district. Her suburban Chicago district was virtually next door to one of AFR's strongholds. Given Heather Booth's deep connections to Chicago-area organizations and politics, the area was a hospitable venue for AFR advocacy. Had Melissa Bean been a representative from, say, South Carolina—or most other states—AFR's home-field advantage clearly would have been attenuated.

Insistently and Consistently Pragmatic

The U.S. legislative process functions to beat back any efforts at dramatic change, even in the aftermath of a crisis. If enacting federal legislation was AFR's goal, a rigorously pragmatic approach was the only realistic option. This was not going to be a slam dunk for the coalition—some of whose member-organizations were more habituated to incremental change than others. Deciding what claims to make, how hard to push, and ultimately what outcomes to accept or reject was a significant challenge for AFR. Despite the combination of a Democratic president and a Democrat-controlled Congress—and the national revulsion against the excesses that brought about the financial meltdown—there were no guarantees of success on all the issues.

The message about pragmatism was delivered most effectively by AFR's House legislative champion, Barney Frank. Frank had put the consumer movement on alert in the spring of 2008 that he could only push the ball so far without a grassroots movement behind him.[21] Subsequently, in a May 2009 commencement address, delivered at American University, Frank announced: "Idealism without pragmatism is just a way to flatter your ego."[22]

The coalition was soon tested by Chairman Frank himself. Some members of AFR, especially those representing the fair housing, community development and civil rights communities, were avidly in favor of shifting oversight of the Community Reinvestment Act from the existing federal bank regulators to the CFPB as a means of strengthening enforcement. Frank took soundings and concluded that this shift would not work in the context of Dodd-Frank but could be revisited later. Although this was crushing news for many coalition members, they decided to accept it and to pursue other objectives. There were clearly other moments, too, when members of the coalition may have grumbled and wanted to walk away, but the campaign's most experienced players brought them back into the fold.

Another critical demonstration of pragmatism came in March 2010 when Senator Dodd went public with his plan to locate the CFPB inside the Federal Reserve. Initially the advocates reacted heatedly to the idea. After further study, however, they measured the proposal against its ability to produce an effective agency—not its correspondence to some rigid, ideological notion of what the new agency should look like.

Being so deeply enmeshed in the legislative process was difficult for those members of AFR who had traditionally preferred taking strong positions that politicians viewed as "unrealistic." For other coalition members, moving beyond a reliance on Capitol Hill lobbying was the test of their willingness to engage in new activities for the sake of a political victory. In the past, these organizations had thought it possible to succeed without generating district-level voter support for one of their own bills. They viewed their strengths as being policy and analysis, rather than Hill lobbying. Frank's unmistakable message meant that to play, you've got to pay—with political currency. This message resonated with Heather Booth's longstanding organizing philosophy, so she was a very willing adherent. The unions and civil rights organization were also experienced political players and had the infrastructure to activate call lists and action alerts. For some of the other AFR member groups, it was a stretch—but one they knew they had to make.

Where Was AFR Most Severely Challenged?

With respect to the CFPB, Elizabeth Warren, the members of AFR, and the other supporters of a new agency got far more than half a loaf. Still, there were several forces they could not fully overcome. One was the desire of moderates—and even some liberal Democrats—to provide finance industry constituents and backers a tangible benefit to offset losses elsewhere in the Dodd-Frank Act. This problem is best exemplified by the Carper preemption amendment, which partially limited the power of state laws and regulations. Second, while to a very great extent Elizabeth Warren and AFR succeeded in making the benefits of a consumer agency to middle class Americans the touchstone of the CFPB campaign, there were certain cases in which another compelling political force—small businesses—trumped the agency's supporters. A paradigm case was the power of local auto dealers—found in virtually every legislative district—to successfully lobby for important exemptions from the regulatory power of the CFPB. Third, the CFPB's advocates were never able to fully mobilize and channel the public rage that they fervently believed lay ready to be tapped.

The issue of weakening the states' role in consumer financial protection represented the most troublesome Democrat-initiated challenge to the authority of the CFPB. AFR and many of its allies were dead set against federal preemptive language, the net effect of which would be to deprive pro-consumer states the ability to implement laws and rules *stronger* than those adopted by the federal government.

Senator Tom Carper, successor to Vice President Joe Biden's Delaware seat, introduced a moderate, pro-preemption amendment on the Senate floor that offered Democrats an opportunity to cast an industry-friendly vote and to avoid being tarred as antibusiness activists. Carper and

37 other Democrats—including such liberals as John Kerry, Carl Levin, Maria Cantwell, Barbara Mikulski, Patty Murray, Charles Schumer, and even Chris Dodd—voted overwhelmingly, along with all 41 Republicans (and Independent Joe Lieberman), to restrict the ability of states to bring actions against federally chartered lenders.[23] The crucial factor that gave these Democrats the political cover they needed to support the Carper amendment was that it was far less objectionable than one offered by Republican Bob Corker. Under the circumstances, AFR was helpless to stop it.

Car dealers have long been the butt of irreverent gibes, but on the important issue of auto loan exemptions, they are politically well organized and are generally regarded as civic-minded members of the Main Street community. Despite the fact that large players like GM Finance are likely to be the primary beneficiaries of the CFPB carve-out, members of Congress came under extreme pressure from their local dealerships to take care of small businesses back home. Not even AFR's innovative alliance with members of the Military Coalition on behalf of active duty and veteran service members/families, plus the direct intervention of President Obama and some top Defense Department officials, could overcome the small business argument that the CFPB should focus on Wall Street but stay well clear of Main Street. Again, the auto dealer exemption presented legislators with an irresistible opportunity to side with Main Street small business and simultaneously give their financial backers a favorable vote.

A third way in which the CFPB's supporters fell short of their aspirations was their inability to fully channel the suffering that people were feeling as workers, mortgage holders, and consumers as well as their outrage against lender abuse. The member organizations of AFR had hoped to convert this pain and anger into political demands for strong regulatory reform from both their progressive-leaning base and the public in general.

Advocates worked hard to create messages that would make the public aware of the proposed new consumer protection agency and to persuade people that the agency would help them. The CFPB's supporters were innovative in their use of grassroots and grasstops communication, e-alerts, social networking, video, and other media. Their message was that the CFPB was going to be a new type of government agency, one firmly on the side of consumers. They repeatedly described the CFPB as the consumer's "cop on the beat," associating the proposed agency with one of the most essential and tangible aspects of government.

Opinion polls gave advocates of financial reform hope that members of the public would take some type of political action, whether it be writing a letter to a congresswoman or participating in a street demonstration. In multiple surveys, supporters of financial reform outnumbered opponents by a margin of 2 to 1. Yet facts on the ground plainly showed that AFR had difficulty getting key elements of its base to act on these beliefs. Bill Ragen of the SEIU lamented the lack of more worker participation in grassroots demonstrations: "I don't think we really cracked the code in terms of getting to the level we'd hoped to get."[24]

The same general point applies to members of the Millennial Generation composed of people through their twenties and thirties. Members of this generation had reason to be upset by high indebtedness and onerous loan terms—with student loans, auto financing, and credit card bills as prominent components.[25] In addition, they faced increased difficulty in obtaining a decent salary from which to pay down their debts. But they, too, failed to respond to this squeeze by calling for strong public regulation. Heather McGhee of the progressive think tank (and AFR member group) DEMOS offered her own explanation of the disconnect between public pain and the demand for government action. She lamented that one of "the most pernicious effects of the Reagan Revolution" was pushing public policy solutions "off the radar entirely" for younger citizens.[26]

While the AFR coalition correctly identified the depth of public antagonism toward Wall Street's greed and abusive consumer lending practices and built its campaign around the overwhelming popular desire for pro-consumer change, it may have underestimated the prevailing distrust in government as a deterrent. Political scientists William Galston and Elaine Kamarck tried to make this point to the incoming Obama administration in November, 2008. Galston and Kamarck wrote: "[T]rust shapes the limits of political possibilities. When trust is high, policy-makers may reasonably hope to enact and implement federal solutions to our most pressing problems. When trust is low, as it is today and has been for much of the past few decades, policy-makers face more constraints."[27]

In the instance of the CFPB, a cynical public was being asked to buy the proposition that government would have the guts and power—or even the competence—needed to overturn the fundamental rules of the game. Indeed, Frank Luntz's 2010 strategy memo for the opponents of financial reform saw public cynicism as a key asset:

Now, more than ever, the American people question the government's ability to effectively address the issue. Billions in handouts to Wall Street. A stimulus bill that isn't creating jobs. Cash for Clunkers. Health Care. A "Credit Card Bill of Rights" that increases fees and interest rates on consumers. The

American people believe Washington has gone wrong, and these legislative initiatives have become symbols of Washington's inability to do anything right. . . . This is your critical advantage. Washington's incompetence is the common ground on which you can build support.[28]

In an odd convergence, Democratic pollster and strategist Stan Greenberg almost channeled Luntz' diagnosis:

Oddly, many voters prefer the policies of Democrats to the policies of Republicans. They just don't trust the Democrats to carry out those promises. . . . They thought Democrats were more likely to champion the middle class. . . . But in smaller, more probing focus groups, voters show they are fairly cynical about Democratic politicians' stands. They tune out the politicians' fine speeches and plans and express sentiments like these: 'It's just words.' 'There's just such a control of government by the wealthy that whatever happens, it's not working for all the people; it's working for a few of the people. '[29]

At the end of the day, it is not known whether, and to what extent, the advocates did more than pierce the veil of popular skepticism toward government. Perhaps the most balanced conclusion that can be drawn is that the advocates did not have enough juice to fully energize popular faith in the efficacy of public solutions; nonetheless they were able to neutralize antagonism sufficiently to assure that the vast store of popular outrage and the accompanying fear of global recession pushed wavering policymakers to take remedial action.

Progressive Advocates: Contributions, Successes, and Lessons from Dodd-Frank

The campaign for financial reform was a response to a colossal, economic disaster for ordinary working- and middle-class families. Elizabeth Warren and AFR were at the forefront of the effort to clear the wreckage and deter future disasters.

The people in the campaign to enact financial reform did many things right. They coalesced quickly, dropping any hostility toward working in an elective political framework. They mobilized a critical mass of progressive organizations in Washington and across the country and created a structure for integrating the field with D.C. operations. They thought big, pursuing a comprehensive legislative package rather than squandering their energy on smaller, piecemeal issues. They assembled a cross-movement coalition broad enough to fight on multiple fronts, synergistic enough to multiply the power of their individual contributions, and resourced well enough to make their voices heard and take the sort of political actions their congressional compatriots needed to win key votes. Their agenda included elements that were meaningful to each group. The passage of any single element was viewed as being less likely to the extent that the coalition suffered any attrition.

Operationally, the coalition entrusted leadership and management to a skilled community organizer who was also a very experienced manager and a prominent political insider. The result was a culture of trust and hard work that was functional, day-to-day, despite a tense and highly polarized political environment. It was a culture and style that supplanted the more common but counterproductive characteristics of ego and organizational competition. The team assembled was deep, diverse, and sophisticated in terms of training and skill sets. They communicated effectively, framing their cause as a middle-class issue and their solution as putting a new cop on the beat for consumers. Conversely, they steered clear of narrowing their appeals to race- or class-based interests. And they compromised wisely, maintaining steadfastness on goals but flexibility on means. All this may seem pretty straightforward, but the fact is these elements have eluded the vast majority of public interest campaigners.

Despite having successfully mounted a strong public advocacy campaign, one whose urgency was brought home by plummeting economic conditions, the cold reality was that a difference of just one or two votes in the U.S. Senate could have doomed passage of the Dodd-Frank bill. While we can safely conclude that David largely prevailed against Goliath in this case, it was clearly a very close call. Was this success a one-off phenomenon arising out of the unique exigencies of the moment and the particular players involved? Or, is it possible that strategic and tactical lessons learned from this episode may seed other campaigns still on the distant horizon?

The question of the Dodd-Frank campaign's relevance is especially important now that citizen lobbying seems to have swung back in the direction of economic issues such as growing disparities in income and wealth, structural unemployment, and the deterioration of social mobility. One sign of the resurgence of bread-and-butter campaigning is the agenda that has been pursued by some of the prominent members of the new, less-institutionalized insurgent groups such as Occupy Wall Street, Justice for Janitors, and the anti–World Trade Organization campaigners.

While the Dodd-Frank campaigners and some of the new generation of progressive activists share common concerns, their immediate goals and strategic approaches are quite different. A critical question, therefore, is the extent to which the nuggets of strategic and tactical experience gained by advocates in the Dodd-Frank campaign will be relevant and exportable to groups operating in a less institutionalized framework of direct democracy. Although the question is far from being settled, there are some encouraging indications of bridges being built between traditional groups and newer entities (including significant union endorsement of the Occupy movement) that instill hope that lessons learned will not be squandered.[30]

In distilling actionable implications of the Dodd-Frank campaign for future activism, the underlying narrative is important to keep in mind. As a first example, it is noteworthy that advocates for consumer financial reform could point to more than a devastating economic crisis as the rationale for accepting their regulatory solutions. Their script also had identifiable, clearly defined villains whose misdeeds had brought the global economy to the edge of collapse: Wall Street bankers and other reckless lenders. At least temporarily, these enormously powerful interests were forced on the defensive. Even their Republican allies had to admit publicly that "something" had to be done to prevent another financial meltdown; they just didn't want to support anything specific.

A readily-identifiable villain may not always be available, but sometimes it is a matter of making one apparent. Consider the fight for a higher and automatically indexed minimum wage. Opponents typically claim that raising the minimum wage would disproportionately hurt small businesses and force them to lay off workers. No one wants to see that come about. What would happen to the debate, however, if it were more widely known that "the majority [66 percent] of low-wage workers are not employed by small businesses, but rather by large corporations with over 100 employees," most of which have recovered from the Great Recession?[31] One lesson of the financial reform campaign is the importance of attributing responsibility for a problem to an entity that does not immediately evoke public sympathy for its own pain. A related lesson is that making a very clear causal link between individual pain (unsafe and deceptive lending for consumers, subsustainable wages for workers) and broader, unacceptable social and economic outcomes (demand-led recession, global market collapse) makes a campaign more likely to garner support from conservatives as well as progressives.

A second key feature of the Dodd-Frank narrative was the constant and convincing theme of the victims as members of the middle class. The credit for framing the issue this way begins with Elizabeth Warren who learned about the precariousness of many middle-class householders through her extensive studies of bankruptcy.

A major, recent study of legislative campaigns supports the overall conclusion that legislative struggles aiming to benefit lower classes or racial minorities have been less successful than those oriented toward middle-class concerns.[32] Some of this differential in political success can be attributed to variations in resources and participation. In general, however, embedding issues of race and income within a more comprehensive campaign can broaden the base and promote a more auspicious outcome. This was certainly the case in the Dodd-Frank campaign where the pros and cons of a "big tent" strategy for minorities and low-income groups were openly and thoroughly aired.

While there is a legitimate danger that the emphasis and focus on the middle class could drown out concerns more particular to less advantaged citizens, the AFR campaign showed that this risk can be averted, at least to a large degree. It demonstrated the possibility and mutual advantage of working across class, race, and other dividing lines for the group as a whole and for its component parts.

In the Dodd-Frank campaign, organizations representing working-class and minority groups were willing to jump on board and trust Elizabeth Warren and the leaders of AFR that their distinctive interests would not be ignored. The campaign largely delivered on its promises to represent these needs. In addition to addressing serious problems in the subprime mortgage market, among payday lenders, and in other nonbank sectors disproportionately utilized by low-income and minority borrowers, the coalition fought successfully to establish special offices within the CFPB for minorities and service members—two groups with a long history of financial exploitation. Thinking about lessons distilled for future cross-movement, economic justice campaigns, it appears that constructing the biggest tent possible retains its appeal and value. But extraordinary care will be needed to deliver significant benefits for those people whose membership in the middle class is little more than an aspiration.

A third issue relates to the thorny question of the solutions to be sought. Astute observers as diverse as David Brooks in the libertarian camp and Michael McCann on the left have pointed out that progressives face a huge problem. They can and do make a compelling case for any number of social, economic, and political ills, but too often they hit the disconnect button when it comes to selling their preferred solution: government.[33] As a reflection, popular attachment and commitment to progressive policy proposals have been shallower than might otherwise be expected. Ask progressive-leaning people how they feel about abusive lending and onerous Wall Street banking practices and their responses are off the chart. Then ask how they feel about some form of public solution—even if it's easily recognized as being consumer-friendly—and their reactions are far more modulated.

In the campaign for Dodd-Frank and the CFPB, the depth and ubiquity of the problem combined with the ability of advocates to attribute it to those "greedy and unscrupulous" lenders and their Wall Street enablers successfully neutralized the more fundamental distrust in government regulation as a solution—at least to a certain degree. But the inability to channel public suffering into protest left Dodd-Frank advocates scratching their heads, wondering if more effort, greater resources, and additional time would have worked to change attitudes toward regulatory reform. Maybe yes, maybe no. Either way, the Dodd-Frank campaigners were fortunate to have sidestepped the ultimate problem of popular faith in effective government. The lesson is that this elision may not be possible in subsequent progressive campaigns.

Finding solutions to deep societal ills seems all the more formidable when one views the situation as, in the words of former labor secretary Robert Reich, "a rigged game—an economy that won't respond, a democracy that won't listen, and a financial sector that holds all the cards."[34] Did the Dodd-Frank advocates change the deep and enduring rules of the game? Did their work successfully alter the fundamental power relations that pervade our politics and govern our economic life? Perhaps not to the full extent activists had aspired and worked so hard to achieve. But was their effort worthy of the term "success" as they defined it? We believe the verdict must be "yes."

The Dodd-Frank campaign clearly demonstrated that given an opening for change and working with the strategies and resources reasonably available to them, a broad-based people's alliance could successfully challenge the financially strongest, most entrenched of interests and deliver significant benefits to average people. As Heather Booth had counseled community organizers many thousands of times: "Win change for people with measurable results" and, by giving them power, "transform them so they deepen their commitment."[35]

Backward and Forward with Elizabeth Warren

Norman I. Silber[1]

The rich story Larry Kirsch and Robert Mayer tell in these pages about the development of the idea of a Consumer Financial Protection organization in the federal government is based on their extensive documentary research and their interviews with many key participants. Elizabeth Warren was one such participant, and she plays a central part in their story. During the spring of 2012, and in the midst of her competition in the race to become the next senator from Massachusetts, I asked Professor Warren to correspond with me and with the authors about CFPB's genesis; about her concerns when launching the new Bureau; and about its future. This *Afterword* incorporates her responses.

Looking Backward

The original idea for a new government agency that Warren and Oren Bar-Gill floated was not predestined to succeed. It emerged as one of several promising systemic proposals for helping consumers to address predatory lending and other consumer debt problems. Originally theirs was an approach with no greater likelihood for success than several others. Even after the financial meltdown in 2008, and the growth of support in scholarly and advocacy communities, the idea of a safety commission devoted to financial products still seemed aspirational rather than feasible.

Warren recalled that at the beginning of her attempt to get Congress to authorize an independent financial consumer protection agency, she too subscribed to the common view: that "the odds of success were too low for any optimism." "Let's face it," she said, "an army of lobbyists had lined up against the new agency. Almost no one in Washington thought it had a chance to become law."

As earlier chapters reveal, Democratic congressional leaders themselves responded pessimistically. As Warren recalls it, Barney Frank let her know that money and power were stacked up so high against the CFPB, in his words, that "getting any movement on a consumer agency wouldn't even qualify *as a pipe dream*." Unwilling to relent, however, Warren looked to more experienced Washington advocates for advice. On a train from New York to Washington she spoke with Damon Silvers, the experienced policy advisor in the office of the general counsel at the AFL-CIO. Silvers told her that the only way she would successfully win an agency would be "to get organized—I mean really organized." Kirsch and Mayer describe the formation, soon thereafter, of "Americans for Financial Reform."

AFR set to work urging the reform of the banking system, including as a central goal the creation of the consumer agency. Warren, in a manner largely consistent with the evaluation of Larry Kirsch and Rob Mayer in this book, noted the skill with which Heather Booth and later Lisa Donner engaged consumer groups, labor unions, civil rights organizations, and other advocates. More than 200 large and small organizations were shaped into an alliance with AFR at its center. Warren chose to emphasize the much larger circle of determined activists who became engaged in support for an independent agency after receiving encouragement from these organizations:

> [AFR nurtured the interest of] thousands of other Americans from around the country. Some were in loose groups; others were bloggers, letter-to-the-editor writers, people who spoke up at town hall meetings and who signed petitions, and those who wrote their Members of Congress.

From Warren's point of view, it was this amorphous constellation, composed of groups with public interest, civil rights, labor and consumer roots—nurtured but not directed by AFR—which coalesced into a public interest fighting force of its own and faced the "army of industry lobbyists." These organizations successfully held Congress to the job of reforming regulation of the financial sector. The various groups, Warren recalled, pursued similar objectives without the need for—or ability of—AFR to issue marching orders or to exert forceful control. Individuals and organizations brought their own perspective to the fight, she recalled, "but we were all motivated by the same fundamental idea: [that] consumers deserved a voice and a watch dog in Washington to level the playing field."

Warren remembered most clearly one near-death experience for her project. It occurred during the winter of 2010, at the moment at which the bill which eventually became Dodd-Frank, including the consumer agency, had been passed in the House of Representatives, which was then under the solid control of Democrats. The bill waited for consideration in committee in the more evenly divided Senate, where it was widely understood that the harder fight would be waged. Under Senate rules, "a smaller number of people could kill any new proposal, and the bill stalled there."

Newspapers and television broadcasts were reporting that the consumer agency, "according to sources," had died in committee. "It appeared as though the financial reform bill would be reported out of committee without a consumer agency—which meant it would die without a vote." Preventing that outcome—and getting an up-or-down vote on the agency—would require turning around the committee members.

The culture and procedures of the Senate made it all too easy for senators "to leave no fingerprints when and if they wanted to kill a proposal in the darkness." Warren, along with others, wanted to establish a sense of individual accountability for the fate of the agency in every member of the Senate Committee. Activists would need to try to insist on transparency and "to compensate for the industry's money and lobbying muscle with free media and volunteer work." Warren remembered reacting to "doubling down" on the "level playing field" arguments that the AFR organizations previously had been making:

> We spent a lot of timing saying as loudly and clearly as we could that there must be a vote—a simple, up or down vote, where each senator would have to declare whether they stood with the banks or stood with families. We made phone calls, wrote blogs, and went on every television, radio and podcast that we could.

Their intensified efforts did the trick.

Elizabeth Warren's perspective about the enactment of what is the first major consumer agency created in the 21st century is in most respects consistent with the account that Kirsch and Mayer have presented. It also corresponds with the accounts given by progressive historians of the conditions that have been necessary for the creation of the major 20th-century agencies charged with consumer protection, including the Food and Drug Administration, the Consumer Product Safety Commission, and the Securities and Exchange Commission. Heightened public interest in the successful enactment of a consumer agency translated into the congressional perception of a political reality favorable to reform. Advocacy groups, pro-consumer politicians, and news organizations sustained public interest.

Nonetheless, Warren's perspective emphasizes the triumph and vindication of the system for educating citizens in a participatory democracy, rather than the triumph of clever organizing tactics: "when the day came to kill the consumer agency in the U.S. Senate," she told us, "the agency survived *only because too many people across the country said 'this matters to me—and I want to see how Congress votes.'*" Refreshed by the Congress's receptiveness to moderate reform, Warren took great comfort in the working democracy. "Ultimately," she pointed out, "we got a vote, and the American people got the good, strong agency they deserved. This time around, David beat Goliath."

The CFPB Start-Up

As Benjamin Franklin walked out of the Constitutional Convention of 1787, an onlooker asked him what sort of government the delegates were creating. "A republic, madam, if you can keep it," Franklin famously replied. Onlookers today want to know what sort of consumer protection agency Congress created. "An independent agency, if we can keep it," Warren might well respond. From the day it was created, questions about the long-term durability and effectiveness of the CFPB have been raised. Is it independent enough to resist industry lobbying efforts over a long period? Will it die before receiving the chance to prove itself? If it does survive, what can it accomplish?

Elizabeth Warren did not become the Bureau's first director—as many people believe she should have. But instead, as President Obama's advisor, she played an outsized role in structuring, staffing, and institutionalizing public spiritedness at the CFPB. In this role she tried to make sure the right people occupied the right jobs at the new agency: she wanted civil servants who truly believed "that government can work for the people." "Every single day we tried to think about who we were there to serve, what tools we'd been given to get the job done, and how we could make the agency work for families."

How could an agency so excoriated by political and economic opponents hope to survive? The CFPB's new staff recognized that the agency was "born in a tough fight and that the fight would continue." The staff knew that it had "a chance to do some real good for American families and for the U.S. economy" and that "chances like this don't come along very often, [so] every single person at the agency wants to make the most of this moment."

Looking Forward

Going forward, the biggest challenges to CFPB are existential. The agency from the moment of its creation came under blistering fire from predictable quarters. Elizabeth observes that big banks and their lobbyists are not giving up their efforts at destroying its effectiveness:

> The lobbyists and their allies claim that the changes [they have proposed] are about making the agency more accountable, but that's nonsense. The proposed changes are backdoor attempts to give the lobbyists more influence over the agency—and to weaken consumer protection.

Threats to the CFPB persist long after its authorization: these are byproducts of the partisan divide at the moment of its birth, the bitterly divided political environment, and the continuing power of financial institutions. As Kirsch and Mayer have described, even after Democrats won the battle to legislate the creation of the Bureau, Republican lawmakers tried to block the appointment of any CFPB director without a modification in the accountability structure of the agency. President Obama's recess appointment of Richard Cordray elicited a constitutional challenge to the president's ability to evade the Senate's "advise and consent" power. A continuing hostility to the agency emanates from the Republican Party and the financial services industry, which tries to scuttle rules or regulations that offer meaningful restrictions on business practices that generate profit.

If court challenges to the constitutionality of the appointment are rejected; if the next president does not make dismantling the CFPB a priority; and if, despite industry pressure, Congress does not repeal or dramatically alter the CFPB's authorizing legislation, then an even more enduring problem will remain. The hardest remaining problem will be the need to prevent the agency from being captured by the financial services industry.

Consumer-oriented activists inside the agency thought hard about the problem of capture as they conceptualized and then built CFPB. Warren and the staff "identified the problem of capture and repeatedly talked about what we could do to deal with it," understanding that "many agencies begin with good intentions but eventually get captured by the industries they are supposed to regulate." It was the concern about capture that had motivated Warren and AFR to insist on independent budget authority, structural independence, and autonomy of the director in the final bill. "We [all] knew that structure matters," she said.

After the Bureau's phase-in began, Warren and her colleagues developed structural and programmatic elements to help to prevent undue influence by lobbyists from any quarter. One strategy was to foster trust and prevent secret influence by using technology to promote transparency. The decision "to put all our goals in plain sight" by posting them on the Bureau's website served this purpose. In its projects, the staff of the Bureau "identified as clearly as we could what we were trying to accomplish. We thought this would help people all across the country hold the agency accountable, both for the objectives it set and whether it ultimately achieved those objectives."

At a broader level, Warren recalled believing that the odds of capture or legislative evisceration could be reduced by adhering closely to—perhaps by defining overly narrowly—the Bureau's mission: to restore competitiveness in consumer financial markets. "The agency is built on optimism," she contended:

> the belief that markets can work, providing great value for customers and great opportunities for honest competitors. . . . CFPB is based on the idea that prices should be clear, risks should be clear, and consumers should be able to compare three or four credit cards or three or four mortgages straight up before making a final decision. . . . In order to accomplish some of these goals, the agency must, as the title of Dodd-Frank suggests, protect consumers from abusive financial services practices.

Warren declared great frustration with the central attack being made by the opposition, namely the claim that CFPB would interfere with free markets. She said that this critique "bugged" her because its mission was actually to *preserve* free markets:

> The lobbyists for the big banks said some variation of this about a million times: a new agency will crush innovation. Nothing could be further from the truth. An unregulated market meant that the competitors who were willing to take the biggest risks, tell the biggest lies, or cut the most corners, could drag down millions of consumers—and take the whole market with it. A properly functioning market is a well-regulated market, one that creates transparency and makes sure there's a cop on the beat to keep all the actors honest.

Thus was the decades-old fissure among consumer protection policymakers—the division between those who believe government regulation is a net gain, or a net loss, to competitiveness—refought between Democrats and Republicans today in the modern rhetoric of economic competition.

Elizabeth Warren's expression of liberal faith in regulated free markets rings authentically; and it is held also by most of the large active organizations who worked within the umbrella of AFR—including the AFL-CIO, the Civil Rights Leadership Council, Consumers Union, U.S. PIRG, SEIU, and others. None of them adhered to a genuinely radical view of government control. Warren's focus on restoring the middle class through a combination of efforts to promote competitiveness and various forms of safety net assistance further cemented her and the agency she championed squarely inside the moderate political tradition. It was only a great *collateral benefit* of this moderate approach to market reform, Warren indicated, that identifying the mission of CFPB with promoting competition helps to protect it against efforts to kill the Bureau or to diminish its authority.

Onward

"Seeing the CFPB go from an idea to a fully functional agency is terrific," Warren said, "but it's really just an extension of what I've worked on for years. I've studied changes in both the economy and the law that have hammered American families." Her larger political ambitions appear to herself and many others as the natural outgrowth of her long-term interest in promoting consumer welfare. Her view of what the American middle class needs to survive in the years ahead transcends what a single consumer agency might accomplish. "The very foundations of America's middle class are starting to tremble, and I've tried to think of every possible way that we can to reverse that trend before it is too late. The consumer agency is part of that—but only a part."

The destiny of the CFPB itself depends on the quality of decision making within its office; it also depends on political and judicial developments that are outside of its control. Warren's counsel to the agency strikes two correspondingly different chords—one emphasizing focus, and one emphasizing combat:

> The best thing the agency can do is avoid getting distracted. The agency should continue doing what it does best: protecting consumers and making the markets work well. But outside the agency, it would be a major error to become complacent. The fight isn't over; it's just moved to quieter, darker

alleys. We need to remain willing to fight against efforts to roll back the CFPB.

How will the story of CFPB ultimately be regarded? Nobody has a crystal ball. When asked about CFPB 10 years from now, however, her answer conveys guarded optimism. "Me?" she asked. "I'm feeling pretty good about this agency."

Notes

Chapter 1

1. "California Home Prices 50 Percent Off March 2007 Peak—Why California Home Prices Will Be Impacted by Multi-Year State Budget Deficits, Higher Interest Rates, and a Backlog of Distressed Properties," *Dr. Housing Bubble* (blog), March 27, 2011, http://www.doctorhousingbubble.com/california-home-prices-50-percent-off-march-2007-peak-why-california-home-prices-will-be-impacted-by-multi-year-state-budget-deficits/; Moxley Real Estate Team, "Looking Back to The Peak of the California Housing Market," *Pleasanton Home* (blog), February 3, 2010, http://www.moxleyteam.com/pleasanton/pleasanton-homes/looking-back-to-the-peak-of-the-california-housing-market/; Michael Goodman and Robert Nakosteen, "Diverging Destinies: The Commonwealth's Relatively Robust but Imbalanced Economic Recovery," *MassBenchmarks: The Journal of the Massachusetts Economy* 9, (2011), accessed August 11, 2012, http://www.massbenchmarks.org/publications/bulletin/09_bulletin_071411/currents.pdf.

2. Jeremy W. Peters, "Fed Chief Suggests US Interest Rates Will Hold Steady," *New York Times,* February 14, 2007, http://www.nytimes.com/2007/02/14/business/worldbusiness/14iht-Fed.4596377.html.

3. *Economic Outlook: Hearing Before the Joint Economic Committee,* U.S. Congress, 110th Cong. (2007) (statement of Ben Bernanke, Chair Board of Governors, Federal Reserve System). http://www.federalreserve.gov/newsevents/testimony/bernanke20070328a.htm.

4. "Treasury's Paulson—Subprime's Woes Largely Contained," *UK.Reuters.com,* April 20, 2007, http://uk.reuters.com/article/2007/04/20/usa-subprime-paulson-idUKWBT00686520070420.

5. Elizabeth Warren, "A Fair Deal for Families: The Need for a Financial Products Safety Commission" (presentation, May 2007 Risk Working Group Meeting of the Tobin Project, Harvard University, Cambridge, Massachusetts, May 6, 2007). http://www.tobinproject.org/news-article/may-2007-risk-working-group-meeting.

6. The article was published with the title, "Unsafe at any Rate," *Democracy* 5 (Summer 2007).

7. Jacob Hacker, et al., "Economic Insecurity and the Great Recession: Findings from the Economic Security Index," (November 2011). http://econo micsecurityindex.org/assets/ESI%20Full%20Report%202011.pdf. The index computed by Hacker shows that 20 percent of Americans experienced declining income availability in each of the years 2008–2010 compared with 15 percent in a single year, 1986.

8. Annamaria Lusardi, Daniel Schneider, and Peter Tufano, "Financially Fragile Households: Evidence and Implications," *Brookings Papers on Economic Activity* (Spring 2011): 83–134. Those surveyed reported a perceived inability to raise $2,000 within 30 days. http://www.brookings.edu/~/media/projects/bpea/spring%202011/2011a_bpea_lusardi.

9. Lesley Alderman, "Demystifying and Maybe Decreasing, the Emergency Room Bill," *New York Times,* sec. B, p. 5, August 6, 2010.

10. Transformative research is the Tobin Project's own description of its agenda. http://www.tobinproject.org/home.

11. Abby Goodnough, "Barney Frank, a Top Liberal, Won't Seek Re-election," *New York Times,* sec. A, p. 16, November 28, 2011; The Tobin Group, " May 2007: Risk Working Group Meeting," http://www.tobinproject.org/news-article/may-2007-risk-working-group-meeting.

12. The Ganz piece was not related in any way to the Tobin Workshop.

13. Heather Booth, "Can We Win for Progressive Change?," *TPM Blog,* March 25, 2007, http://tpmcafe.talkingpointsmemo.com/2007/03/25-week/.

14. In addition to better organization, Booth cited what she called the "fracturing" of the right wing hegemony in American politics and the worsening of objective economic conditions as being two factors supportive of progressive political change. Ibid. Writing in 2007, Booth was prescient about the timing of the economic collapse that would come about as a result of the lancing of the housing bubble in 2008.

15. A similar point has been made, more recently, by Naomi Klein, in the context of the Occupy Movement. " ... when people drop out and just try to build their utopia and don't engage with the systems of power, that's when they become irrelevant and also when they are extremely vulnerable to state power and will often get smashed." Naomi Klein and Yotam Marom, "Why Now? What's Next? Naomi Klein and Yotam Marom in Conversation about Occupy Wall Street," *The Nation,* January 9, 2012.

16. "Barney Frank Explains His Criticism of the National Equality March," *Towleroad* (blog), October 15, 2009, http://www.towleroad.com/2009/10/barney-frank-explains-his-criticism-of-the-national-equality-march.html#ixzz1szzjCjJ3.

17. Shahien Nasiripour, "Elizabeth Warren's Farewell Note: 'I Leave This Agency, But Not This Fight,'" *HuffPo Business,* September 28, 2011, http://www.huffingtonpost.com/2011/07/29/elizabeth-warren-farewell-note_n_913425.html.

18. Some of the best treatments are: Kathleen Engle and Patricia A. McCoy, *The Subprime Virus* (New York: Oxford University Press, 2011); Dan Immergluck, *Foreclosed* (Ithaca: Cornell University Press, 2009); Bethaney McLean and Joe Nocera, *All the Devils are Here* (New York: Portfolio/Penguin, 2010); Gretchen Morgenson

and Joshua Rosner, *Reckless Endangerment* (New York: Times Books, 2011); Paul Muolo and Mathew Padilla, *Chain of Blame* (Hoboken, NJ: John Wiley & Sons, 2008); Mark Zandi, *Financial Shock* (Upper Saddle River, NJ: FT Press, 2008).

19. About a third of all mortgages originated in 2006 were Option ARMs. Congress authorized Adjustable Rate Mortgages in 1982 (Title VII of the Garn–St. Germain Depository Institutions Act). For a non-technical definition of an Adjustable Rate Mortgage, see, Board of Governors of the Federal Reserve System, "Consumer Handbook on Adjustable-Rate Mortgages" (unpublished, 2011), http://www.federalreserve.gov/pubs/arms/arms_english.htm. Emanuel Moench, James Vickery, and Diego Aragon, "Why Is the Market Share of Adjustable-Rate Mortgages So Low?" *Federal Reserve Bank of New York Current Issues in Economics and Finance* 16 (2010):1–11, accessed July 17, 2011, http://www.newyorkfed.org/research/current_issues/ci16-8.html.

20. "Nightmare Mortgages," *BloombergBusinessweek Magazine,* September 10, 2006, http://www.businessweek.com/magazine/content/06_37/b4000001.htm.

21. *Armando Plascencia and Others v. Lending 1st Mortgage, Lending 1st Mortgage, LLC, EMC Mortgage Corp. and DOES 1–10,* U.S. District Court, (N.D. Cal.) Case No. C-07-4485—CW, Third Amended Complaint, July 1, 2008.

22. Edmund Andrews, "Fed Shrugged as Subprime Crisis Spread," *New York Times,* December 18, 2007, http://www.nytimes.com/2007/12/18/business/18subprime.html?pagewanted=all. Subsequently, the commission of inquiry organized to investigate the causes of the financial and economic crisis received testimony from Sabeth Siddique, the assistant director for credit risk in the Division of Banking Regulation and Supervision of the Federal Reserve Board, indicating that as early as 2005 Fed examiners had found widespread deterioration in the quality of underwriting and lending standards that was "very alarming." Siddique briefed the Board of Governors and regional directors but according to one attendee, Governor Susan Bies, "[s]ome people on the board and regional presidents . . . just wanted to come to a different answer. So they did ignore it, or the full thrust of it." Financial Crisis Inquiry Commission, *Final Report of the National Commission on the Causes of the Financial and Economic Crisis in the United States* (Washington, D.C.: Government Printing Office, 2011), 49.

23. For an interesting discussion of the definition and use of the term "predatory lending," see, Elenore Longobardi, "How 'Subprime' Crushed 'Predatory,'" *Columbia Journalism Review* 48, no.3 (2009): 45.

24. Michael Calhoun, Transcript of the Federal Reserve System Consumer Advisory Council Meeting, March 6, 2008. http://www.federalreserve.gov/about thefed/cac/cac_20080306.htm.

25. Sarah Ludwig, Transcript of the Federal Reserve System Consumer Advisory Council Meeting, March 6, 2008. http://www.federalreserve.gov/aboutthefed/cac/cac_20080306.htm.

26. The Plascencias' legal complaint included the prepayment penalty provision of their loan.

27. Transcript of the Federal Reserve System Consumer Advisory Council Meeting of March 6, 2008, http://www.federalreserve.gov/aboutthefed/cac/cac_

20080306.htm, pp. 20–24. As Lisa Rice of the National Fair Housing Alliance described it, a central goal of the Civil Rights and Fair Lending Community has been to bring about "reforms that would bring the entire market on a level playing field and eliminate this two-tiered system that traps borrowers of color into the residual market that is more high cost, that is not regulated, and that has more abusive products and practices." Among these practices were "the qualified mortgage standards, the anti-steering provision, the provisions against yield spread premiums, abusive prepayment penalties." Lisa Rice, interview by authors, February 18, 2011.

28. Ben Bernanke, "Monetary Policy and the Housing Bubble" (presentation, Annual Meeting of the American Economic Association, Atlanta, Georgia, January 3, 2010), http://www.federalreserve.gov/newsevents/speech/bernanke20100103a.htm.

29. Richard Eskow, "18 Former Fed Consumer Advisory Council Members Want an Independent CFPA (Campaign for America's Future)," Woodstock Institute, unpublished press release (March 16, 2010), http://www.woodstockinst. org/press-clips/federal-banking-regulatory-reform/18-former-fed-consumer-advisory-council-members-want-an-independent-cfpa-%28campaign-for-america%27s-future%29/.

Chapter 2

1. James Surowiecki, "Video: Elizabeth Warren," *New Yorker,* November 16, 2009; Elizabeth Warren, "Remarks" (presentation, Joanne Alter Women in Government Lecture, Chicago, Illinois, February 23, 2011), http://www.consumerfinance. gov/speech/joanne-alter-women-in-government-lecture/.

2. Jason Zengerle, "A Saint with Sharp Elbows," *New York Magazine,* November 13, 2011, http://nymag.com/news/politics/elizabeth-warren-2011-11/.

3. Katie Porter, "Secrets about Elizabeth Warren Revealed," *Credit Slips* (blog), July 22, 2010, http://www.creditslips.org/creditslips/2010/07/secrets-about-elizabeth-warren.html.

4. Her brother, David Herring, recalls her being "tougher than a snake." Dennis Brady, "Elizabeth Warren, Likely to Head New Consumer Agency, Provokes Strong Feelings," *Washington Post,* August 13, 2010, http://www.washingtonpost. com/wp-dyn/content/article/2010/08/12/AR2010081206356.html.

5. Another would be her preference for light touch/principle-based regulation in lieu of command-and-control or rule-based regulation. Ben Protess, "Warren Courts Her Top Critics," *New York Times,* March 30, 2011, http://dealbook. nytimes.com/2011/03/30/warren-courts-her-top-critics/.

Ward Rathke, a cofounder of ACORN, points out that Warren took a very public position in favor of school vouchers in outright opposition to the position of the liberal teachers' unions. Wade Rathke, "Elizabeth Warren's Two-Income Trap," *Chief Organizer* (blog), January 18, 2011, http://chieforganizer.org/2011/01/18/ elizabeth-warren%E2%80%99s-two-income-trap.

6. Jodi Kantor, "Behind Consumer Agency Idea, A Tireless Advocate," *New York Times,* March 24, 2010, http://www.nytimes.com/2010/03/25/business/25warren. html. As pictured in Time Magazine (online), she's brought JP Morgan boss

Jamie Diamond to tears. Stephen Gandel, "Why Jamie Dimon is Afraid of Elizabeth Warren," *Curious Capitalist* (blog), May 4, 2010, http://curiouscapitalist.blogs.time.com/2010/05/04/why-jamie-dimon-is-afraid-of-elizabeth-warren/.

7. Tim Fernholz, "Present at the Re-Creation," *The American Prospect*, September 14, 2009, http://prospect.org/article/present-re-creation-0.

8. Anya Kamenetz, "It's Banks vs. Families, Who Will Come Out on Top? Q&A with Elizabeth Warren," *Fast Company*, March 11, 2010.

Elizabeth Warren, "Remarks" (presentation, Joanne Alter Women in Government Lecture, Chicago, Illinois, February 23, 2011), http://www.consumerfinance.gov/speech/joanne-alter-women-in-government-lecture/.

9. Elizabeth Warren, "Unsafe at any Rate".

10. Anya Kamenetz, "It's Banks vs. Families, Who Will Come Out on Top? Q&A with Elizabeth Warren," *Fast Company*, March 11, 2010. http://www.fastcompany.com/1578370/elizabeth-warren-its-banks-vs-families)

11. Elizabeth Warren, "Unsafe at any Rate".

12. Teresa Sullivan, Elizabeth Warren and Jay L. Westbrook, *As We Forgive Our Debtors: Consumer Credit and Bankruptcy in America* (New York: Oxford University Press, 1989); Elizabeth Warren, Teresa A. Sullivan and Jay Lawrence Westbrook, *The Fragile Middle Class: Americans in Debt* (New Haven: Yale University Press, 2000); Elizabeth Warren, "Congress and the Credit Industry: More Bad News for Families," in *Law and Class in America: Trends Since the Cold War*, ed. Paul Carrington and Trina Jones (New York: New York University Press, 2006); Elizabeth Warren, "The Vanishing Middle Class," in *Ending Poverty in America: How to Restore the American Dream*, ed. John Edwards, Marion Crain, and Arne Kalleberg (New York: The New Press, 2007).

13. The root cause was Congress's elimination of the usury ceilings in the late 1970s. *Marquette National Bank v. First Omaha Service Corp.*, 439 U.S. 299 (1978); Tamara Draut, Credit Card Industry Practices: In Brief, DEMOS, June 6, 2004, http://archive.demos.org/pubs/IndustryPractices_WEB.pdf.

14. Bradford Plumer, "The Two Income Trap," *Mother Jones*, November 8, 2004; *Medical Bankruptcy: Middle Class Families at Risk: Hearing Before the Judiciary Committee*, U.S. House of Representatives, 110th Cong. (2007) (statement of Elizabeth Warren). http://www.judiciary.house.gov/hearings/July2007/Warren070717.pdf; Robert Lawless, "Symposium: Consumer Bankruptcy and Credit in The Wake of the 2005 Act: the Paradox of Consumer Credit," *University of Illinois Law Review* (2007): 347–74.

15. Rebecca Johnson, "Elizabeth Warren Held to Account," *Vogue*, December 20, 2010, http://www.vogue.com/magazine/article/elizabeth-warren-held-to-account/.

16. Elizabeth Warren, "Feminomics: Women and Bankruptcy," *Huffington Post*, December 17, 2009, http://www.huffingtonpost.com/elizabeth-warren/feminomics-women-and-bank_b_395667.html.

17. Tamara Draut, et al., "The Plastic Safety Net: The Reality behind Debt in America," DEMOS and the Center for Responsible Lending, October 2005, http://www.responsiblelending.org/credit-cards/research-analysis/DEMOS-101205.pdf.

18. *Examining the Billing, Marketing, and Disclosure Practices of the Credit Card Industry and Their Impact on Consumers: Hearing Before the Committee on Banking, Housing and Urban Affairs,* U.S. Senate, 110th Cong. (2007) (statement of Elizabeth Warren). http://banking.senate.gov/public/index.cfm?FuseAction=Files. View&FileStore_id=d4fcda94-c9d7-4df7-bf10-dd69ad008c0f.

19. Ibid.

20. *The Effect of Current Credit Card Industry Practices on Consumers: Hearing before the Committee on Banking, Housing and Urban Affairs,* U.S. Senate, 110th Cong. (2007) (statement of Travis Plunkett). http://banking.senate.gov/public/index. cfm?FuseAction=Files.View&FileStore_id=766faff0250143ac-ae39791b0d883585.

21. *Watters v. Wachovia Bank,* 550 U.S. 1 (2007).

22. Elizabeth Warren, "Unsafe at any Rate."

23. Elizabeth Warren, "The Broken Consumer Credit Market," in *Make Markets Be Markets,* ed. Robert Johnson and Erica Payne, (New York: Roosevelt Institute, 2009), http://makemarketsbemarkets.org/report/MakeMarketsBeMar kets.pdf.

24. Elizabeth Warren, "Wall Street's Race to the Bottom," *Wall Street Journal,* February 8, 2010, http://online.wsj.com/article/SB100014240527487036304045 75053514188773400.html.

25. Perhaps the strongest incentive was that regulated lenders funded the budgets of their designated regulators through fees.

26. "Elizabeth Warren," *The Colbert Report,* Comedy Central, May 3, 2010, http://www.colbertnation.com/the-colbert-report-videos/308723/may-03-2010/ elizabeth-warren.

27. Warren also recognized that consumer protection would have a spillover benefit in terms of reduced lending risk.

28. Elizabeth Warren, "Unsafe at any Rate."

29. Warren, "Three Myths about the Consumer Financial Product Agency," *The Baseline Scenario* (blog), July 21, 2009, http://baselinescenario.com/2009/07/21/ three-myths-about-the-consumer-financial-product-agency/. Under certain circumstances, however, transparency is not enough—in which case more robust actions such as the prohibition of practices most susceptible to abuse may be necessary. James Surowiecki, "Caveat Mortgagor," *New Yorker,* July 6, 2009, http://www. newyorker.com/talk/financial/2009/07/06/090706ta_talk_surowiecki. But John Weinberg, an economist and vice president for research of the Federal Reserve Bank of Richmond, recently argued that the "regulatory prohibition of lending practices should be viewed very cautiously" because some borrowers might be worse off as a consequence of the prohibition, for example, by facing more limited product choices. John Weinberg, "Borrowing by U.S. Households," *Federal Reserve Bank of Richmond Economic Quarterly* 92, (2006): 177–94, accessed June 5, 2012, http://www.richmondfed.org/publications/research/economic_quarterly/2006/ summer/pdf/weinberg.pdf.

30. Michael Barr, Sendhil Mullainathan, and Eldar Shafir, "Behaviorally Informed Financial Services Regulation," New America Foundation, October 2008, accessed May 17, 2010, http://www.newamerica.net/files/naf_behavioral_v5.pdf.

31. Richard H. Thaler and Cass R. Sunstein, *Nudge: Improving Decisions About Health, Wealth, and Happiness* (New Haven: Yale University Press, 2008).

32. In the end, although lenders believed themselves to be shoved by product nudges and induced Barney Frank to drop the proposal as being too subjective and not worth the fight, an alternative approach, the so-called qualified mortgage, was passed. Some observers believe that the plain vanilla–like ingredients of the qualified mortgage category will ultimately dominate because secondary market lenders (not consumers) will insist on them.

33. Erik Gerding, "The Subprime Crisis and the Link between Consumer Financial Protection and Systemic Risk," *FIU Law Review* (forthcoming), accessed July 22, 2012, http://works.bepress.com/erik_gerding/4.

34. *Improving Federal Consumer Protection in Financial Services: Hearing before the Committee on Financial Services, U.S. House of Representatives,* 110th Cong. (2007) (statement of Sheila Bair). http://archives.financialservices.house.gov/hearing110/ht061307.shtml.

35. *Legislative Proposals On Reforming Mortgage Practices: Hearing before the Committee on Financial Services,* U.S. House of Representatives, 110th Cong. (2007) (statement of Sheila Bair). http://archives.financialservices.house.gov/hearing110/htbair102407.pdf.

Two years later, in June 2009, Professor Warren told the same House Committee: "If we don't feed high-risk, high-profit loans into the system, those risks will not get sliced and diced into questionable asset-backed securities and sold throughout the financial system. If we had had a Consumer Financial Protection Agency five years ago, Liar's Loans and no-doc loans would never have made it into the financial marketplace—and never would have brought down our banking system. The economic system took on so much risk—one household at a time—that it destabilized our entire economy." *Regulatory Restructuring: Enhancing Consumer Financial Products Regulation: Hearing before the Committee on Financial Services,* U.S. House of Representatives, 111th Cong. (2009) (statement of Elizabeth Warren). http://archives.financialservices.house.gov/Hearings/hearingDetails.aspx?NewsID=1162.

36. Ezra Klein, "Elizabeth Warren on Elizabeth Warren," *Washington Post,* September 17, 2010, http://voices.washingtonpost.com/ezra-klein/2010/09/elizabeth_warren_on_elizabeth.html.

37. Michael Tomasky, "The Elizabeth Warren Story," *Guardian.co.uk,* July 20, 2010, http://www.guardian.co.uk/commentisfree/michaeltomasky/2010/jul/20/obama-administration-finreg-consumers-warren.

38. Katie Benner, "Elizabeth Warren's War." *Fortune,* March 17, 2010, http://money.cnn.com/2010/03/17/news/economy/elizabeth_warren.fortune/.

Speaking about the new business model in which banks took incalculable risks and reaped extraordinary profits, Benner quotes Warren on the *Charlie Rose* show as saying, "It will not save us if a handful of Wall Street banks prosper and the rest of America fails."

39. John Edwards, "Remarks," *Talking Points Memo* (blog), April 14, 2005, http://talkingpointsmemo.com/bankruptcy/archives/2005/04/guest-blogger-j.php.

40. John Edwards, "Building One America," (presentation, Cooper Union Dialog Series, New York, NY, June 21, 2007). http://dominantreality.blogspot.com/2007/06/john-edwards-cooper-union-excerpts.html.

41. Elizabeth Warren, "Edwards Steps Up on Middle Class," *Talking Points Memo* (blog), June 21, 2007.

42. Hilary Clinton, "Comprehensive Plan to Address Credit Card Abuses, Promote Fair Lending, and Expand Access to Fair Credit," January 30, 2008, accessed May 12, 2011, http://www.democraticunderground.com/discuss/duboard.php?az=view_all&address=132x4292818#4292936).

43. Barack Obama, "Remarks," (presentation at the General Motors Plant, Janesville, Wisconsin, February 13, 2008). http://www.cfr.org/us-election-2008/obamas-speech-janesville-wisconsin/p15492.

44. Bob Sullivan, "Where Candidates Stand on Consumer Issues," *Red Tape Chronicles* (blog), March 25, 2008. http://redtape.msnbc.msn.com/_news/2008/03/25/6345888-where-candidates-stand-on-consumer-issues.

45. Elizabeth Warren, "Obama Speaks Out on Bankruptcy," *Talking Points Memo Blog,* July 8, 2008.

46. U.S. Department of the Treasury, *Blueprint for a Modernized Financial Structure,* Washington D.C.: Government Printing Office, March 2008. http://www.treasury.gov/press-center/press-releases/Documents/Blueprint.pdf.

47. Damon Silvers, interview by authors, March 14, 2011.

48. U.S. Congressional Oversight Panel, *Special Report on Regulatory Reform,* Washington D.C.: Government Printing Office, January 29, 2009. http://cybercemetery.unt.edu/archive/cop/20110401232141/http://cop.senate.gov/reports/library/report-012909-cop.cfm.

49. *Credit Card Practices: Current Consumer and Regulatory Issues: Hearing before the Committee on Financial Services,* U.S. House of Representatives, 110th Cong. (2007) (statement of Arthur Wilmarth Jr.). http://archives.financialservices.house.gov/hearing110/htwilmarth042607.pdf.

50. U.S. Congressional Oversight Panel, *Special Report on Regulatory Reform.*

51. Ibid.

52. Ibid.

53. The special importance of an independent consumer financial protection agency to minorities and labor organizations was emphasized in remarks presented by Tamara Draut of DEMOS to members of the Tobin Project at Harvard in May 2009. See, Tamara Draut, "A Financial Product Safety Commission: The Need and the Challenge" (presentation, Meeting of the Tobin Project, Harvard University, Cambridge, Massachusetts, May 2009). http://people.hmdc.harvard.edu/~dcarpent/finreg/FPSC-Tobin.pdf. She pointed out that "In a 2008 survey of low- and middle-income Americans, Demos, a nonpartisan public policy center, found that Hispanic and African American households carried credit card debt twice the total value of their financial assets. White households, by comparison, tend to have more financial assets than credit card debt. The group United for a Fair Economy estimates that the total loss of wealth among households of color is between $164 billion and $213 billion as a result of subprime loans

taken out during the past eight years—many of whom qualified for prime-rate products."

54. "There is ample evidence that African Americans and Hispanics have been targets for certain deceptive products, much to their injury and to the injury of a country that prizes equality of opportunity for all its citizens." U.S. Congressional Oversight Panel, *Special Report on Regulatory Reform.*

55. Elizabeth Warren, "The Economics of Race: When Making It to the Middle Is Not Enough." *Washington & Lee Law Review* 61 (2004): 1777–99.

56. Ibid., p. 1794.

57. Janis Bowdler, interview by authors, May 9, 2011.

58. National Consumer Law Center, "56 Diverse National, State Organizations Support Financial Product Safety Commission," unpublished letter, March 10, 2009, accessed May 12, 2010. http://www.nclc.org/images/pdf/regulatory_reform/ltr-senate-acts566.pdf/.

59. "Transcript: President Barack Obama on the 'Tonight Show With Jay Leno'," *New York Times*, March 19, 2009.

60. *Statement: Hearing before the Committee on Financial Services,* U.S. House of Representatives, 111th Cong. (2009) (statement of Timothy Geithner, Secretary of the Treasury). http://democrats.financialservices.house.gov/media/file/hearings/111/geithner032609.pdf.

Chapter 3

1. Lisabeth Cohen, "Colston E. Warne Lecture: Is It Time for another Round of Consumer Protection? The Lessons of Twentieth Century U.S. History," *The Journal of Consumer Affairs* 44, no. 1 (2010): 234; Lawrence B. Glickman, *Buying Power* (Chicago: University of Chicago Press, 2009); Nils V. Montan, "The Agency for Consumer Advocacy," *American University Law Review* 26, no. 4 (1976): 1062; George Schwartz, "The Successful Fight against a Federal Consumer Protection Agency," *MSU Business Topics* 27, Summer (1979): 45.

2. According to Federal Reserve statistics, the net worth of U.S. households fell by $16.4 trillion (from $65.8 trillion to $49.4 trillion), or 25 percent, from its peak in the spring of 2007 to its trough in the first quarter of 2009. Chris Isidore, "America's Lost Trillions," *CNNMoney,* June 9, 2011. http://money.cnn.com/2011/06/09/news/economy/household_wealth/index.htm.

3. Simon Johnson calls it the "financial oligarchy" in "The Quiet Coup," *The Atlantic,* May 2009.

4. Eric Janszen, "The Next Bubble," *Harper's,* February 2008.

5 U.S. Department of Labor, Bureau of Labor Statistics, *Employment Projections,* Table 2.1: Employment by Major Industry Sector, 1998, 2008, Projected 2018, accessed September 22, 2012, http://www.bls.gov/emp/ep_table_201.htm. Michael Spence and Sandile Hlatshwayo estimate that the finance and insurance industries produced over a million new jobs between 1990 and 2008 in "The Evolving Structure of the American Economy and the Employment Challenge," *Working*

Paper, Council on Foreign Relations, March 2011, http://thebrowser.com/articles/evolving-structure-us-economy-and-employment-challenge.

6. U.S. Department of Commerce, Bureau of Economic Analysis, *National Income and Products Accounts,* Table 6.16D, accessed September 22, 2012, http://www.bea.gov/iTable/iTable.cfm?ReqID=9&step=1

7. Kathleen Madigan, "Like the Phoenix, U.S. Finance Profits Soar," *Wall Street Journal,* March 25, 2011, http://blogs.wsj.com/economics/2011/03/25/like-the-phoenix-u-s-finance-profits-soar/.

8. Deniz Egan and Prachi Mishra, "Making Friends," *Finance and Development* 8, no. 2 (2011): 27.

9. Center for Responsive Politics, "Annual Lobbying Expenditures by Finance, Insurance, and Real Estate Industries 2008," (undated), accessed June 18, 2012, http://www.opensecrets.org/lobby/indus.php?id=F&year=2008.

10. Center for Responsive Politics, "Contribution Trends, 1990–2010, Finance, Insurance, and Real Estate Industries," (undated), accessed August 28, 2012, http://www.opensecrets.org/industries/indus.php?ind=F.

11. Aaron Kiersh, "Finance/Insurance/Real Estate: Background," Center for Responsive Politics (July 2009), accessed August 28, 2012, http://www.opensecrets.org/industries/background.php?cycle=2010&ind=F.

12. Michael Beckel, "House Financial Services Committee: Hotbed of Money from Financial Sector Interests," (April 15, 2011), accessed August 28, 2012, http://www.opensecrets.org/news/2011/04/house-financial-services-committee.html; Ryan Grim and Arthur Delaney, "The Cash Committee: How Wall Street Wins on the Hill," *Huffington Post,* December 29, 2009, http://www.huffingtonpost.com/2009/12/29/the-cash-committee-how-wa_n_402373.html.

13. Edmund Mierzwinski, "Consumer Protection 2.0—Protecting Consumers in the 20th Century," *Journal of Consumer Affairs* 44, no. 3 (2010): 578.

14. Ryan Grim and Arthur Delaney, "The Cash Committee: How Wall Street Wins on the Hill," Huffington Post, March 18, 2010, http://www.huffingtonpost.com/2009/12/29/the-cash-committee-how-wa_n_402373.html

15. Ibid.

16. Public Citizen, "Financial Industry Invests Heavily in Key Lawmakers," December 28, 2009, http://www.citizen.org/documents/Financial_Industry_Invests_Heavily_in_Key_Lawmakers.pdf.

17. Anthony Ramirez, "Consumer Crusader Feels a Chill in Washington," *New York Times,* December 31, 1995, http://www.nytimes.com/1995/12/31/business/consumer-crusader-feels-a-chill-in-washington.html.

18. Anne Thompson, "Credit Card Companies Able to Raise Rates at Will," *NBC Nightly News,* January 4, 2005, http://www.msnbc.msn.com/id/6786867/ns/nightly_news/t/credit-card-companies-able-raise-rates-will/. Johnson was the only Senate Democrat to vote against the Credit CARD Act in May, 2009. Ann Flaherty, "Senate OK's Bill to Rein in Credit-Card Practices," *Deseret News,* May 20, 2009, http://www.deseretnews.com/article/705305363/Senate-OKs-bill-to-rein-in-credit-card-practices.html.

19. Brian Wingfield, "Wall Street's Favorite Congressman," *Forbes,* June 1, 2010; Cyrus Sanati, "Wall St. Puts Its Campaign Money on Schumer," *New York Times,* September 28, 2009, http://dealbook.nytimes.com/2009/09/28/wall-st-puts-its-campaign-money-on-schumer/; The Center for Responsive Politics presents the exact campaign donation amounts in "Finance/Insurance/Real Estate: Money to Congress-2010," (undated) accessed August 30, 2012, http://www.opensecrets.org/industries/summary.php?ind=F&recipdetail=S&sortorder=A&cycle=2010.

20. The most notable examples are Robert Rubin and Henry Paulson, both heads of Goldman Sachs who became Secretary of the Treasury. A CBS News investigation cites many other cases. CBS News Investigates, "Goldman Sachs' Revolving Door," April 7, 2010. http://www.cbsnews.com/8301-31727_162-20001981-10391695.html. The international dimensions of the relationship are examined by Andrew Baker, "Restraining Regulatory Capture? Anglo-America, Crisis Politics and Trajectories of Change in Global Financial Governance," *International Affairs* 86, no. 3 (2010): 647, and Stephen Foley, "How Goldman Sachs Took Over the World," *The Independent* (*UK*), July 22, 2008, http://www.independent.co.uk/news/business/analysis-and-features/how-goldman-sachs-took-over-the-world-873869.html.

21. Ryan Grim and Arthur Delaney, "The Cash Committee: How Wall Street Wins on the Hill."

22. Simon Johnson and James Kwak, *13 Bankers: The Wall Street Takeover and the Next Financial Meltdown* (New York: Pantheon, 2010); Marcus Baram, "Government Sachs," *Huffington Post,* June 11, 2009, http://www.huffingtonpost.com/2009/06/02/government-sachs-goldmans_n_210561.html.

23. Center for Responsive Politics and Public Citizen, "Banking on Connections," June 3, 2010, http://www.opensecrets.org/news/FinancialRevolvingDoors.pdf.

24. Ryan Grim and Arthur Delaney, "The Cash Committee: How Wall Street Wins on the Hill."

25. Tim Fernholz, "Who's Leading the Fight against Consumer Financial Regulation?" *American Prospect,* September 9, 2009.

26. Rachelle Younglai, "Obama's Consumer Watchdog in Jeopardy," *Reuters,* September 10, 2009, http://www.reuters.com/article/2009/09/10/us-financial-regulation-consumeragency-a-idUSTRE5894MT20090910.

27. Lizabeth Cohen, *A Consumers' Republic* (New York: Alfred A. Knopf, 2003).

28. Robert O. Herrmann, "Consumerism: Its Goals, Organizations and Future," *Journal of Marketing* 34, no. 4 (1970): 55; Robert O. Herrmann and Robert N. Mayer, "U.S. Consumer Movement: History and Dynamics," in *Encyclopedia of the Consumer Movement,* ed. Stephen Brobeck (Santa Barbara, CA: ABC-CLIO, 1997): 584; David P. Thelen, "Patterns of Consumer Consciousness in the Progressive Movement," in *The Quest for Social Justice: The Morris Fromkin Memorial Lectures,* ed. Ralph M. Aderman (Madison, WI: University of Wisconsin Press, 1983):19.

29. Herbert J. Rotfeld, "A Pessimist's Simplistic Historical Perspective on the Fourth Wave of Consumer Protection," *Journal of Consumer Affairs* 44, no. 2 (2010): 423.

30. As of the spring of 2009, Jim Guest of Consumers Union, Steve Brobeck of the Consumer Federation of America, and Joan Claybrook of Public Citizen were 69, 65, and 71, respectively.

31. James Bovard, "The Growing Farce of Fair Housing," *Freedom Daily*, July 1998, http://www.fff.org/freedom/0798d.asp; Lawrence J. White, "The Community Reinvestment Act: Good Goals, Flawed Concept," Federal Reserve Bank of San Francisco, (February 2009): 185. http://www.frbsf.org/publications/community/cra/cra_good_goals_flawed_concept.pdf; Michael S. Barr, a supporter of the CRA, reviews the arguments of its critics in "Credit Where it Counts: The Community Reinvestment Act and its Critics," *New York University Law Review* 80, no. 2 (2005): 513.

32. Stephanie Strom, "Funds Misappropriated at 2 Nonprofit Groups," *New York Times*, July 9, 2008, http://www.nytimes.com/2008/07/09/us/09embezzle.html?pagewanted=all; Susan Kinzie, "ACORN's Capitol Hill Office Shutting Down," *Washington Post*, March 25, 2010, http://www.washingtonpost.com/wp-dyn/content/article/2010/03/24/AR2010032402947.html; John Atlas, *Seeds of Change: The Story of ACORN, America's Most Controversial Antipoverty Community Organizing Group* (Nashville, TN: Vanderbilt University Press, 2010).

33. Jelle Visser, "Union Membership Statistics in Twenty-four Countries," *Monthly Labor Review* 129, no. 1 (2006): 38.

34. Bureau of Labor Statistics, "Union Members—2010," U.S. Department of Labor News Release, January 21, 2011, (USDL-12-0094) http://www.bls.gov/news.release/pdf/union2.pdf.

35. *How Unions Can Help Restore the Middle Class: Hearing Before the Committee on Health, Education, Labor and Pensions*, U.S. Senate 111th Cong. (2009) (statement of Paula B. Voos). http://www.epi.org/page/-/pdf/20090310_voos_efca_testimony.pdf; David Madland, Karla Walter, and Nick Bunker, "Unions Make the Middle Class," Center for American Progress Action Fund, American Worker Project, (April 2011) accessed September 12, 2012, http://www.americanprogressaction.org/issues/2011/04/pdf/unionsmakethemiddleclass.pdf.

36. Karlyn H. Bowman and Andrew Rugg, "Taking Stock of Business," American Enterprise Institute for Public Policy Research, April 22, 2010, http://www.aei.org/papers/politics-and-public-opinion/polls/taking-stock-of-business-paper/.

37 Several interviewees commented on the difficulty of drawing attention to financial reform during the health care debate. Columnist Michael Hirsh makes the same point in "The Politics of Hubris," *The Daily Beast* (blog), January 19, 2010, http://www.newsweek.com/2010/01/19/the-politics-of-hubris.html.

Climate change activists felt similarly challenged by the health care debate. Richard Cowan, "U.S. Climate Change Bill to Compete with Healthcare," *Reuters U.S. Edition*, September 7, 2009, http://www.reuters.com/article/2009/09/07/us-climate-usa-congress-idUSTRE5850NI20090907.

38. The legislative history of H.R. 4173, the Dodd-Frank Wall Street Reform and Consumer Protection Act, 111th Congress: 2009–2010, is available on Govtrack.us. http://www.govtrack.us/congress/bill.xpd?bill=h111-4173. The legislative history of H.R. 3590, the Patient Protection and Affordable Care Act, 111th

Congress: 2009–2010, is available on Govtrack.us. http://www.govtrack.us/congress/bill.xpd?bill=h111-3590.

39. Bill Ragen, interview by authors, March 17, 2011.

40. Janis Bowdler, interview by authors, May 9, 2011. Indeed, it was even worse than that for staffers at La Raza. In addition to Dodd-Frank and healthcare, they were also working on the immigration reform bill.

41. Kathleen C. Engel and Patricia A. McCoy, *The Subprime Virus* (New York: Oxford University Press, 2011); Nomi Prins, *It Takes a Pillage* (Hoboken, NJ: John Wiley & Sons, 2009); *Community and Consumer Advocates' Perspectives on the Obama Administration's Financial Regulatory Reform Proposals: Hearings Before Committee on Financial Services,* U.S. House of Representatives, 111th Cong. (2009) (statement of Travis Plunkett).

42. S. E. Cupp, "What About Irresponsible Consumers?" *New York Daily News,* October 17, 2008, http://www.nydailynews.com/opinions/2008/10/17/2008-10-17_what_about_irresponsible_consumers.html.

43. Ibid.

44. Thomas Sowell, *The Housing Boom and Bust* (New York: Basic Books, 2009), 67.

45. Richard Sylla, "Anatomy of a Financial Crisis: The Consumer's Role in the Financial Crisis," Panel Discussion, Nightly Business Report, PBS Television, October 30, 2008. http://www.pbs.org/nbr/site/onair/transcripts/081030d/

46. Elizabeth Warren and Amelia Warren Tyagi, *The Two-Income Trap* (New York: Basic Books, 2003); Teresa A. Sullivan, Elizabeth Warren, and Jay Westbrook, *The Fragile Middle Class* (New Haven, CT: Yale University Press, 2001); David U. Himmelstein, Elizabeth Warren, Deborah Thorne, and Steffie J. Woolhandler, "Illness and Injury as Contributors to Bankruptcy," *Health Affairs* 24, February 2 (2005): Web Supplement, w63–w73.

47. Elizabeth Warren rebutted this claim in "The Phantom $400," *Journal of Bankruptcy Law & Practice* 13, no. 2 (2004):77.

48. Edmund Mierzwinski, interview by authors, December 31, 2010.

49. Todd J. Zywicki and Stefanie Haeffele-Balch, "Loans are not Toasters: The Problem with a Consumer Financial Protection Agency," *Mercatus on Policy,* no. 60, Mercatus Center, George Mason University, October 2009 http://mercatus.org/sites/default/files/publication/MOP_-_60_Loans_are_not_Toasters_web.pdf.

50. Lowell Bergmann, "Secret Life of the Credit Card," PBS Television, Frontline, first aired November 24, 2004, http://www.pbs.org/wgbh/pages/frontline/shows/credit/view/?autoplay. During the documentary, Elizabeth Warren said, "There's no regulator, and there's no customer who can bring this industry to heel."

51. Edmund Mierzwinski, interview by authors, December 31, 2010.

52. *Credit Card Practices that Undermine Consumer Safety: Hearing Before the Sub-Committee on Financial Institutions and Consumer Credit of the Committee on Financial Services,* U.S. House of Representatives, 110th Cong. (2008) (statement of Elizabeth Warren). http://archives.financialservices.house.gov/hearing110/warren031308.pdf.

53. *The Credit Cardholders' Bill of Rights (H.R. 5244): Hearing of the Sub-Committee on Financial Institutions and Consumer Credit of the Committee on Financial Services,* U.S. House of Representatives, 110th Cong. (2008). http://www.gpo.gov/fdsys/pkg/CHRG-110hhrg42721/html/CHRG-110hhrg42721.htm

54. Peter Garuccio of the American Bankers Association communicated this point to journalists. Jessica Dickler, "Credit Card Crackdown Coming Soon," *CNNMoney,* December 16, 2008, http://money.cnn.com/2008/12/16/pf/credit_card_rules/index.htm, and Connie Prater, "Will New Credit Card Law Hurt More People than it Helps?" *Creditcards.com,* December 2008, http://www.creditcards.com/credit-card-news/credit-card-law-consequences-1282.php. Several studies have contested the view that restrictions on credit card companies are detrimental to consumers in general and low-income consumers in particular. See Angela Littwin, "Testing the Substitution Hypothesis: Would Credit Card Regulations Force Low-Income Borrowers into Less Desirable Lending Alternatives?" *University of Illinois Law Review,* no. 1 (2009): 403; Pew Health Group, "A New Equilibrium: After Passage of Landmark Credit Card Reform, Interest Rates and Fees Have Stabilized," Report of the Credit Cards Project, May 2001, http://www.pewtrusts.org/uploadedFiles/wwwpewtrustsorg/Reports/Credit_Cards/Report_Equilibrium_web.pdf.

55. John Poirier and Nancy Waitz, "White House Says [It] Opposes Credit Card Bill," *Reuters,* September 22, 2008, http://www.reuters.com/article/2008/09/22/us-creditcards-whitehouse-idUSN2234253220080922.

56. Board of Governors of the Federal Reserve System, Press Release, December 18, 2008, http://www.federalreserve.gov/newsevents/press/bcreg/20081218a.htm; Office of the Comptroller of the Currency, Press Release, December 18, 2008, http://www.ots.treas.gov/?p=PressReleases&ContentRecord_id=4a2b42c5-1e0b-8562-eb93-76deb8152159.

57. Travis Plunkett, "The Regulatory Structure and Consumer Credit Protections," Harvard University Joint Center for Housing Studies, August 2010, http://www.jchs.harvard.edu/sites/jchs.harvard.edu/files/mf10-13.pdf.

58. *Improving Federal Consumer Protection in Financial Services: Hearing Before the Committee on Financial Services,* U.S. House of Representatives, 110th Cong. (2007). http://frwebgate.access.gpo.gov/cgibin/getdoc.cgi?dbname=110_house_hearings&docid=f:37556.pdf.

59. See a list of signees on letters to the House Financial Services Committee on March 30, 2009, and April 21, 2009. http://maloney.house.gov/documents/financial/creditcards/maloneysupport2009.pdf and http://www.creditcardreform.org/pdf/HR627-42109.pdf.

60. The legislative history of H.R. 627, the Credit Card Accountability Responsibility and Disclosure Act, 111th Congress: 2009–2010 is available on Govtrack.com. http://www.govtrack.us/congress/bill.xpd?bill=h111-627. Rather than being watered down to pass the Senate, the bill was slightly strengthened there. See: "Editorial: Safer Credit Cards," *The New York Times,* May 19, 2009.

61. A possible exception to this rule was the FACT Act, but it took on the relatively weak credit reporting agencies, not the big banks or investment companies.

62. Americans for Fairness in Lending, "About Us," http://americansforfair nessinlending.wordpress.com/about-2/.

63. Edmund Mierzwinski, interview by authors, December 31, 2010.

64. Both types of groups signed a letter on January 12, 2009, addressed to members of the House of Representatives and urging them to cosponsor the Credit CARD Act. The letter is available online at the Consumers Union website. http://www.consumersunion.org/pdf/Maloney-group-letter09.pdf. They also were co-signers of a February 25, 2008 letter to members of the U.S. Senate in favor of addressing mortgage modifications through the bankruptcy courts. http://www.consumerfed.org/elements/www.consumerfed.org/file/finance/S_2636_cloture_vote_letter_FINAL. pdf.

65. National Consumers League, "Consumer Groups Call on Congress to Support Employee Free Choice Act and Help Rebuild the Middle Class," press release, December 19, 2008. http://www.nclnet.org/newsroom/press-releases/325-consumer-groups-call-on-congress-to-support-employee-free-choice-act-and-help-rebuild-the-middle-class. The full list of organizations supporting the Act is available on AFL-CIO's website, http://www.aflcio.org/joinaunion/voiceatwork/efca/allies.cfm.

66. Gary Kalman, interview by authors, February 10, 2011.

67. Maureen Thompson, interview by authors, January 14, 2011.

68. David Arkush, interview by authors, February 16, 2011.

69. Susan Weinstock, interview by authors, March 15, 2011.

70. Marie Hojnacki, "Organized Interests' Advocacy Behavior in Alliances," *Political Research Quarterly* 51, no. 2 (1998): 437.

71. Travis Plunkett, interview by authors, December 21, 2010.

72. Lisa Rice, interview by authors, February 18, 2011.

73. Congressional Oversight Panel, Special Report on Regulatory Reform, January 2009, http://cybercemetery.unt.edu/archive/cop/20110402010517/http://cop.senate.gov/documents/cop-012909-report-regulatoryreform.pdf

74. Steve Abrecht, interview by authors, May 23, 2011.

75. Part of the Call to Action document is contained in a message dated April 8, 2009, from Ed Mierzwinksi, U.S. PIRG, and available from U.S. PIRG.

Chapter 4

1. Americans for Financial Reform, "Americans for Financial Reform Launch Campaign to Clean Up Wall Street, Protect Your Pocketbook," press release, June 16, 2009, http://ourfinancialsecurity.org/2009/06/americans-for-financial-re form-launch-campaign-to-clean-up-wall-street-protect-your-pocketbook/. The re-maining members of initial AFR's Steering Committee were: Stephen Abrecht (Service Employees International Union), David Arkush (Public Citizen), Janis Bowdler (National Council of La Raza), Alan Charney (USAction), Nita Chaud-hary (MoveOn.org Political Action), Richard Ferlauto (American Federation

of State, County and Municipal Employees), Gary Kalman (U.S. PIRG), Robert Kuttner (Demos), Daniel Pedrotty (AFL-CIO), Travis Plunkett (Consumer Federation of America), Lisa Rice (National Fair Housing Alliance), Jennifer Vasiloff (Opportunity Finance Network), Ryan Wilson (AARP), and Nancy Zirkin (Leadership Conference on Civil Rights).

2. Booth has her critics as well. Stanley Kurtz, *Radical in Chief* (New York: Threshold Editions, 2010).

3. Harry C. Boyte, Heather Booth, and Steve Max, *Citizen Action and the New American Populism* (Philadelphia: Temple University Press, 1986), 54.

4. Gina Caneva, ed. "Heather Booth: Living the Movement Life, Memoirs and Biographies," interview (undated) conducted by Becky Kluchin, Chicago Women's Liberation Union Herstory Website, http://www.uic.edu/orgs/cwluher story/CWLUMemoir/Booth.html.

5. "Heather Booth" Statement, undated, Women's Archive Website, http://jwa.org/feminism/_html/JWA004.htm.

6. Gina Caneva, ed. "Heather Booth."

7. Ibid.

8. Amy Kesselman, Heather Booth, Vivian Rothstein, and Naomi Weisstein, "Our Gang of Four: Friendships and Women's Liberation," in *The Feminist Memoir Project: Voices from Women's Liberation,* ed. by Rachel Blau Duplessis and Ann Snitow (New York: Three Rivers Press, 1998), 25–53.

9. Heather Booth, "Heather Tobis Booth," statement, June 12, 2002, Veterans of the Civil Rights Movement Website, http://www.crmvet.org/vet/booth.htm.

10. Amanda I. Seligman, *Block by Block: Neighborhoods and Public Policy on Chicago West Side* (Chicago: University of Chicago Press, 2005), 134.

11. Amy Kesselman, Heather Booth, Vivian Rothstein, and Naomi Weisstein, "Our Gang of Four."

12. Howard Ball, *Justice in Mississippi: The Murder Trial of Edgar Ray Killen* (Lawrence, KS: University Press of Kansas, 2006); Bill Schelppler, *The Mississippi Burning Trial: A Primary Source Account* (New York: Rosen Publishing Group, 2003).

13. David and Linda Beito, *Black Maverick: T.R.M. Howard's Fight for Civil Rights and Economic Power* (Urbana, IL: University of Illinois Press, 2009).

14. Gina Caneva, ed. "Heather Booth."

15. Natalie Doss, "The Progressive: For Over Forty Years, Heather Booth has Worked to Build a Small-d Democracy," *Chicago Weekly,* January 7, 2010, http://chicagoweekly.net/2010/01/07/the-progressive-for-over-forty-years-heather-booth-has-worked-to-build-a-small-d-democracy.

16. Todd Gitlin, *The Whole World is Watching* (Berkeley, CA: University of California Press, 2003); James Miller, *Democracy in the Streets* (New York: Simon and Schuster, 1987).

17. Stephen D. Lerner, "Silhouette: Paul Booth," *Harvard Crimson,* November 2, 1965, http://www.thecrimson.com/article/1965/11/2/paul-booth-ppaul-booth-is-a/.

18. James Miller, *Democracy in the Streets.*

19. Gina Caneva, ed. "Heather Booth."

20. Susan Brownmiller, *In Our Time: Memoir of a Revolution* (New York: Dial Press, 1999).

21. Amy Kesselman, Heather Booth, Vivian Rothstein, and Naomi Weisstein, "Our Gang of Four."

22. Amy Kesselman, Heather Booth, Vivian Rothstein, and Naomi Weisstein, "Our Gang of Four," and Susan Brownmiller, *In Our Time*. The New Left refers to the largely middle-class protesters (especially college students) of the 1960s and 1970s who sought traditional left-wing goals of economic and social justice but with less emphasis on Marxian theory, class consciousness, and mobilization of the working class via unions as earlier generations of activists.

23. Amy Kesselman, Heather Booth, Vivian Rothstein, and Naomi Weisstein, "Our Gang of Four."

24. Booth, personal communication with the authors, December 4, 2011.

25. Amy Kesselman, Heather Booth, Vivian Rothstein, and Naomi Weisstein, "Our Gang of Four."

26. Herstory Editorial Committee, "The Chicago Women's Liberation Union: An Introduction," unpublished editorial, 2000, http://www.uic.edu/orgs/cwluherstory/CWLUAbout/cwluintro.html.

27. Donald C. Reitzes and Dietrich C. Reitzes, *The Alinsky Legacy: Alive and Kicking* (Greenwich, CT: JAI Press Inc., 1987).

28. Donald C. Reitzes and Dietrich C. Reitzes, *The Alinsky Legacy,* 84–85. A video about the campaign can be found at http://www.uic.edu/depts/pols/ChicagoPolitics/cpef.htm.

29. University of Illinois at Chicago, Manuscripts and Rare Books, "Citizen Action Program Records, 1970–1975," unpublished catalog and introduction to Folders 1–25; http://www.uic.edu/depts/lib/specialcoll/services/rjd/findingaids/CAP.pdf; http://www.uic.edu/depts/lib/specialcoll/services/rjd/findingaids/CAPf.html.

30. Jean-Paul D. Addie, "A Century of Chicago's Crosstown Corridor," (presentation, Transport Chicago Conference, Chicago, Illinois, June 7, 2009). http://www.transportchicago.org/uploads/5/7/2/0/5720074/6-a_century_of_chicagos_crosstown_corridor.pdf.

31. Donald C. Reitzes and Dietrich C. Reitzes, *The Alinsky Legacy,* 151.

32. Ibid., 153.

33. Kennedy Wheatley and Bob Nicklas, "Midwest Academy: Ten Years," cited in Donald C. Reitzes and Dietrich C. Reitzes, *The Alinsky Legacy: Alive and Kicking,* 154.

34. Donald C. Reitzes and Dietrich C. Reitzes, *The Alinsky Legacy,* 152.

35. Ibid., 156; John Herbers, "Grass-roots Groups Go National," *New York Times Magazine,* September 14, 1983, 22.

36. Donald C. Reitzes and Dietrich C. Reitzes, *The Alinsky Legacy,* 164.

37. Andrew Battista, *The Revival of Labor Liberalism* (Urbana, IL: University of Illinois Press, 2008), 103–21; Harry C. Boyte, Heather Booth, and Steve Max, *Citizen Action and the New American Populism.*

38. Karen R. Merrill, *The Oil Crisis of 1973–1974* (New York: Bedford/St. Martin's, 2007).

39. Patrick Halley, *Wimpy* (Charleston, SC: BookSurge Publishing, 2008).

40. Andrew Battista, *The Revival of Labor Liberalism,* 104.

41. Ibid., 107.

42. Ibid., 105.

43. Americans for Financial Reform, "Our Coalition," document (undated), http://ourfinancialsecurity.org/about/our-coalition/.

44. Donald C. Reitzes and Dietrich C. Reitzes, *The Alinsky Legacy: Alive and Kicking,* 164.

45. Harry C. Boyte, Heather Booth, and Steve Max, *Citizen Action and the New Populism,* 105.

46. Kristen Schorsch, "Durbin Calls for Bailed-Out Banks to Help in Foreclosures," *Chicago Tribune,* October 26, 2009, 1. Esther Kaplan, "Anger, At Last," *The Notion: The Nation's Group (blog),* October 26, 2009, http://www.thenation.com/blog/anger-last.

47. Mary Bottari, "LIVE! From the Big Showdown in Chicago," *PRWatch,* October 26, 2009. http://www.prwatch.org/node/8654; "Slide Show: Showdown in Chicago," *The Nation,* October 27, 2009. http://www.thenation.com/slideshow/slide-show-showdown-chicago.

48. Stanley Kurtz, *Radical in Chief.*

49. Donald C. Reitzes and Dietrich C. Reitzes, *The Alinsky Legacy: Alive and Kicking,* 154–55.

50. Heather Booth, interview by authors, January 6, 2011.

51. "Heather Booth: On Canvassing & Canvassers," *ConvassingWorks.org,* March 19, 2007, http://www.canvassingworks.org/canvassingworks/2007/03/for_40_years_he.html

52. Heather Booth Interview, January 6, 2011.

53. Heather Booth, "Intro and Non-Profits/Advocacy," (presentation, New Organizing Institute, Washington, D.C., February 26, 2009). http://www.youtube.com/watch?v=Q0m1hhivauY.

54. President Obama's chief of staff Rahm Emanuel had worked early in his career for the Illinois Public Action Council and would almost certainly have been aware of Heather Booth's work. See: Mark Jannot, "A Rahm for the Money," *Chicago Magazine,* August 1992, http://www.chicagomag.com/Chicago-Magazine/August-1992/Rahm-Emanuel-during-the-Bill-Clinton-Years/.

55. Jennifer Liberto, "Consumers Gain Clout in Washington," *CNNMoney.com,* May 29, 2009, http://money.cnn.com/2009/05/29/news/economy/consumer_advocates_obama/?postversion=2009052916.

56. Heather Booth, interview by authors, January 11, 2011; Ben Smith, "Liberal Coalition Takes Shape," *Politico,* March 29, 2009, http://www.politico.com/blogs/bensmith/0309/Liberal_coalition_takes_shape.html.

57. Heather Booth, interview by authors, January 11, 2011.

58. Gary Kalman, interview by authors, February 10, 2011.

59. Heather Booth, interview by authors, January 11, 2011.

60. Edmund Mierzwinski, interview by authors, December 31, 2010.

61. Heather Booth, personal communication with the authors, December 4, 2011.

62. ARCA Foundation, "2009 Grantees," http://www.arcafoundation. org/2009grantees.html; Atlantic Philanthropies, "Grantee Profile: Public Interest Projects Action Fund," http://www.atlanticphilanthropies.org/grantee/public-in terest-projects-action-fund-inc; Janet Shenk (Panta Rhea Foundation), personal communication with authors, July 5, 2011.

63. Lisa Donner, interview by authors, December 3, 2010.

64. Claire Suddath, "A Brief History of ACORN," *Time Magazine,* October 14, 2008, http://www.time.com/time/politics/article/0,8599,1849867,00.html; Ian Urbina, "Acorn on Brink of Bankruptcy, Officials Say," *New York Times,* March 19, 2010, http://www.nytimes.com/2010/03/20/us/politics/20acorn.html?_ r=1&pagewanted=all; John Atlas, *Seeds of Change*; Robert Fisher, ed., *The People Shall Rule* (Nashville, TN: Vanderbilt University Press, 2009). Peter Dreier and Christopher Martin argue that ACORN's good name was deliberately destroyed by business and conservative "opinion entrepreneurs." See: "How ACORN was Framed: Political Controversy and Media Agenda Setting," *Perspectives on Politics* 8, no. 3 (2010): 761.

65. Lee Staples and Richard A. Cloward, *Roots to Power: A Manual for Grassroots Organizing* (Westport, CT: Greenwood Publishing, 2004), 170–83; Kari Lydersen, "Big Campaigns Sprout from Little ACORN," *AlterNet* (blog), July 2, 2002,http://www.alternet.org/story/13508/big_campaigns_sprout_from_little_ac orn/?page=entire; Linda Ostreicher, "A Tax Shelter for the Working Poor," *Gotham Gazette,* February 2004, http://www.gothamgazette.com/article/socialser vices/20040223/15/888.

66. Lisa Donner, interview by authors, December 3, 2010.

67. Heather Booth, interview by authors, January 11, 2011.

68. Ibid.

Chapter 5

1. Phillip Swagel, "The Cost of the Financial Crisis: The Impact of the September 2008 Economic Collapse," Pew Financial Reform Project (April 28, 2010), http://www.pewfr.org/project_reports_detail?id=0033.

2. Natalie Doss, "The Progressive: For Over Forty Years, Heather Booth Has Worked to Build a Small-d Democracy," *Chicago Weekly Online,* January 7, 2010, http://chicagoweekly.net/2010/01/07/the-progressive-for-over-forty-years- heather-booth-has-worked-to-build-a-small-d-democracy/.

3. Gary Kalman, interview by authors, February 10, 2011.

4. Travis Plunkett, interview by authors, December 21, 2010.

5. Ibid.

6. Lisa Donner, interview by authors, December 3, 2010.

7 Stephen Abrecht, interview by authors, May 23, 2011.

8 The Steering Committee included: AARP, ACORN, AFL-CIO, AFSCME, Campaign for America's Future, Consumer Federation of America, Demos, Leadership Conference for Civil and Human Rights, MoveOn, National Coalition of

La Raza, National Community Reinvestment Coalition, National Fair Housing Alliance, National People's Action, Public Citizen, Rob Johnson (for the Roosevelt Institute), SEIU, USAction, U.S. PIRG, and AFR's Director.

9. Lisa Rice, interview by authors, February 18, 2011.

10. Center for Responsible Lending, "Top Priorities for Real Financial Reform Reconciling H.R. 4173 and S. 3217," policy brief (June 2010) http://www.responsiblelending.org/mortgage-lending/policy-legislation/regulators/Overview-Priorities-for-Financial-Reform-FINAL.pdf.

11. Travis Plunkett, interview by authors, December 21, 2010.

12. Lake Research Partners, "Response to Frank Luntz Memo on Financial Reform," memorandum (February 22, 2010), http://ourfinancialsecurity.org/blogs/wp-content/ourfinancialsecurity.org/uploads/2010/01/luntz_response.f.022210.pdf.

13. Cora Ganzglass, interview by authors, February 16, 2011.

14. Stan Greenberg, "Why Voters Tune Out Democrats," *New York Times*, p. SR-1, July 31, 2011.

15. Pat Garofalo, "Chamber of Commerce Launches $100 Million Campaign To Defend and Advance Economic Freedom," *Think Progress Economy Blog*, June 10, 2009, http://thinkprogress.org/economy/2009/06/10/172814/coc-economic-freedom-campaign/.

16. Americans for Financial Reform, "Staff," http://ourfinancialsecurity.org/about/our-structure/.

17. Dean Baker et al., "Restoring Oversight and Accountability to Financial Markets," position paper from Americans for Financial Reform (July 10, 2009), http://ourfinancialsecurity.org/2009/07/position-papers/.

18. "Austin Powers: The Spy Who Shagged Me," IMDb, Austin Powers (Character) Quotes, (undated), http://www.imdb.com/character/ch0002425/quotes.

19. David Meyer and Suzanne Staggenborg, "Thinking about Strategy," (presentation, American Sociological Association, Collective Behavior/Social Movement Section's Workshop, "Movement Cultures, Strategies, and Outcomes," Hofstra University, Hempstead, New York, August 9–10, 2007). http://www.hofstra.edu/pdf/cbsm_plenary_3.pdf

The authors emphasize the interplay between the choice of strategic objectives, the goals of the coalition's members and the coalition's need to retain organizational support. In this case, it was important to assure AFR's partner organizations that their key objectives would not be traded away in favor of different objectives.

20. Jane Hamscher, "Americans for Financial Reform: Waste. Of. Time.," *Firedoglake* (blog), June 29, 2009, http://fdlaction.firedoglake.com/2009/06/29/americans-for-financial-reform-waste-of-time/.

21. Ken Kollman, *Outside Lobbying* (Princeton, NJ: Princeton University Press, 1998), 27.

22. Michael Calhoun, personal communication with the authors, January 4, 2012.

23. *Civil and Human Rights Perspective on the Obama Administration's Financial Regulatory Reform Proposals: Hearing Before Financial Services Committee,*

United States House of Representatives, 111th Cong. (2009) (statement of Nancy Zirkin). http://www.civilrights.org/advocacy/testimony/zirkin-financial.html.

24. Janis Bowdler, interview by authors, May 9, 2011.

25. Connie Koenenn, "The Buyer's Best Friend: You Name it—TVs, Cars, Even Toilets—and Consumer Reports Will Test it. After All, What is a Shopper's Bible for?" *Los Angeles Times,* December 16, 1994, http://articles.latimes.com/1994-12-16/news/ls-9774_1_consumer-reports/2.

26. EileenToback, interview by authors, February 5, 2011.

27. Ibid.

28. Gary Kalman, interview by authors, February 10, 2011.

29. Eileen Toback, interview by authors, February 5, 2011; Heather Booth, interview by authors, January 6, 2011.

30. Adam Goode, "Mainers Make Final Push for Financial Reform," press release (July 10, 2010), http://ourfinancialsecurity.org/2010/07/mainers-make-final-push-for-financial-reform/.

31. Bill Ragan, interview by authors, March 17, 2011.

32. Eileen Toback, interview by authors, February 5, 2011.

33. Ibid.

34. Ibid.

35. "We've learned to play an inside and outside game as we did on stopping Social Security privatization, which was the first effective stopping of the Bush juggernaut and the first indication of this new democratic promise. Their union (AFSCME and AFL-CIO and others) and community and state-based groups (USAction) and MoveOn and think tanks (Campaign for America's Future) and others came together working with the Democratic leadership with a common message, common purpose and common strategy. "Radical Alinsky-Style Teaching School: The Midwest Academy," *Romantic Poet's Weblog,* March 27, 2010, http://romanticpoet.word press.com/2010/03/27/radical-alinsky-style-teaching-school-midwest-academy.

36. Heather Booth, interview by authors, January 6, 2011.

37. Travis Plunkett, personal communication with the authors, November 28, 2011.

38. Jane Hamscher, "Rahm Goes Apeshit on Liberals in the Veal Pit," *Firedoglake* (blog), August 7, 2009, http://fdlaction.firedoglake.com/2009/08/07/rahm-goes-apeshit-on-liberals-in-the-veal-pen/.

39. Other initial staff included Kimberly Miller, a lawyer who gave up a lucrative job in the insurance industry to work on a cause she believed in, and Grace Garner, who was working for the Unitarian Universalists and saw the opportunity to play a role in an exciting new venture.

40. Heather Booth, interview by authors, January 6, 2011; Gary Kalman, interview by authors, February 10, 2011.

41. Donald Reitzes and Dietrich Reitzes, *The Alinsky Legacy.*

42. Janis Bowdler, interview by authors, May 9, 2011.

43. Susan Webb, "Coalition Will Battle Banks Over New Consumer Protection Agency," *Peoples World,* July 8, 2009, http://peoplesworld.org/co alition-will-battle-banks-over-new-consumer-protection-agency.

44. Tim Fernholz, "Why Don't People Trust Financial Reform?" *The American Prospect,* July 15, 2010.

45. David Corn, "Thank You, Wall Street. May We Have Another?" *Mother Jones,* January-February 2010.

46. Evan Allen, "Barney Frank Laments Political Attacks," *Boston Globe Online,* January 4, 2012, http://articles.boston.com/2012-01-04/metro/30585321_1_barney-frank-independent-political-action-committees-newton.

47. Janis Bowdler, interview by authors, May 9, 2011.

48. Heather Booth, interview by authors, January 11, 2001.

49. Ibid.

50. Press coverage of AFR's launch described it as having 200 members and a budget of $5 million. Silla Brush, "Lobbyists Dig in as Obama Pushes Financial Overhaul," *The Hill,* June 16, 2009, http://thehill.com/business-a-lobbying/47070-lobbyists-dig-in-as-obama-pushes-financial-overhaul; Kate Ackley, "K Street Files: Wall Street Watchdog?" *Roll Call,* June 16, 2009, http://www.rollcall.com/issues/54_146/-35886-1.html. Chris Hayes came closer to the truth when he wrote that AFR had a *projected* budget of $5 million. Chris Hayes, "Bucking the Banks," *The Nation,* July 13, 2009. AFR ended up spending only about $1.5 million. Heather Booth, interview by authors, January 6, 2011.

51. Heather Booth, interview by authors, January 6, 2011.

52. Michael Calhoun, interview by authors, February 4, 2011.

53. Bill Ragen, interview by authors, March 17, 2011.

54. Heather Booth, interview by authors, January 11, 2011.

55. David Arkush, interview by authors, February 16, 2011.

56. Janis Bowdler, interview by authors, May 9, 2011.

57. This type of in-kind contribution, while likely substantial, is not counted in any reckoning of AFR's formal budget of around $1.5 million.

58. Janis Bowdler, interview by authors, May 9, 2011.

59. Organizational research suggests that exposing people's work product to others in the relevant peer group represents a form of reputational incentive and discourages shirking or freeriding. Marie Hojnacki, "Organized Interests' Advocacy Behavior in Alliances," *Political Research Quarterly* 51, no. 2 (1998): 437–59.

60. David Arkush, interview by authors, February 16, 2011.

61. Jan Gaudio, interview by authors, April 14, 2011.

62. Frank was also highly sensitive about comments he regarded as questions about his motives and commitments, even those raised by constituents who were important long-time supporters. An example was a colloquy with the president of a Boston-based SEIU public employee's local about pending credit card legislation. Stephanie Mencimer, "Banking on Barney Frank," *Mother Jones,* April 16, 2008.

63. One controversial exception was the exclusion of the Community Reinvestment Act from CFPB authority. Martin N. Baily, "Consumer Financial Protection: Advantages, Dangers and Should it be a New Agency?" briefing paper (September 29, 2009), http://fic.wharton.upenn.edu/fic/policy%20page/Baily-CFPA-Final.pdf.

64. Heather Booth, interview by authors, January 6, 2011.

65. Eileen Toback, interview by authors, February 5, 2011.

66. Pam Banks, interview by authors, February 1, 2011.

67. The concurrent health care debate periodically spilled over into the Dodd-Frank deliberations, as for example when difficulties with the health bill in the Senate Committee gave national banks and other supporters of federal preemption more time to muster support for their faltering position in the House Committee.

68. Charlie Rose, "Interview of Elizabeth Warren," (March 3, 2010), http://www.charlierose.com/download/transcript/10895.

Chapter 6

1. Jonathan D. Salant and Lizzie O'Leary, "Citigroup Taxpayer Ownership Doesn't Prevent Lobbying," *Bloomberg News*, October 23, 2009, http://www.bloomberg.com/apps/news?pid=newsarchive&sid=axiOjGkS2zYY.

2. Consumer Federation of America, "Bank Lobbyists Try to Gut Consumer Financial Protection Agency, press release, October 9, 2009, http://www.consumerfed.org/elements/www.consumerfed.org/file/CFA%20PR%20Pre-House%20Mark%20up%20CFPA%20October%209_09.pdf; Heather C. McGhee and Tamara Draut, "Why We Need an Independent Consumer Financial Protection Agency Now," DEMOS Briefing Paper, March 1, 2010, http://www.demos.org/publication/why-we-need-independent-consumer-protection-agency.

3. The position paper might have legitimately included an additional phrase "or subsequent action by Congress to renege." Americans for Financial Reform, "Restoring Oversight and Accountability to Financial Markets," July 10, 2009, http://ourfinancialsecurity.org/2009/07/position-papers/.

4. Americans for Financial Reform et al., Letter to Christopher Dodd, Chairman, Senate Committee on Banking, Housing and Urban Affairs, February 19, 2010, http://ourfinancialsecurity.org/2010/02/afr-strongly-supports-an-independent-cfpa/.

5. *Regulatory Restructuring: Enhancing Consumer Financial Products Regulation: Hearing Before the Committee on Financial Services,* U.S. House of Representatives, 111th Cong., June 24, 2009 (Washington, D.C.: Government Printing Office, 2009); *The Proposed Consumer Financial Protection Agency: Implications for Consumers and FTC: Hearings of the Subcommittee on Commerce, Trade and Consumer Protection of the Committee on Energy and Commerce.* U.S. House of Representatives, 111th Cong., July 8, 2009 (Washington, D.C.: Government Printing Office, 2012); *Creating a Consumer Financial Protection Agency: A Cornerstone of America's New Foundation: Hearing Before the Committee on Banking, Housing, and Urban Affairs,* U.S. Senate, 111th Cong., July 14, 2009 (Washington, D.C.: U.S. Government Printing Office); *Regulatory Restructuring: Safeguarding Consumer Protection and the Role of the Federal Reserve: Hearing Before the Subcommittee on Domestic Monetary Policy and Technology of the Committee on Financial Services,* U.S. House of Representatives, 111th Cong., July 16, 2009 (Washington, D.C.: Government Printing Office, 2009); *Community and Consumer Advocates'*

Perspectives on the Obama Administration's Financial Regulatory Reform Proposals: Hearings Before the Committee on Financial Services, U.S. House of Representatives, 111th Cong. 62, July 16, 2009 (Washington, D.C.: Government Printing Office, 2009); *Regulatory Perspectives on the Obama Administration's Financial Regulatory Reform Proposals, Part II: Hearing Before the Committee on Financial Services,* U.S. House of Representatives, 111th Cong., July 24, 2009 (Washington, D.C.: Government Printing Office, 2010); *Strengthening and Streamlining Prudential Bank Supervision: Hearing Before the Committee on Banking, Housing, and Urban Affairs,* U.S. Senate, 111th Cong. 407, August 4, 2009 (Washington, D.C.: Government Printing Office, 2010); *Perspectives on the Consumer Financial Protection Agency: Hearing Before the Committee on Financial Services,* U.S. House of Representatives, 111th Cong., September 30, 2009 (Washington: Government Printing Office, 2010).

6. *Regulatory Perspectives on the Obama Administration's Financial Regulatory Reform Proposals, Part II: Hearing Before the Committee on Financial Services,* U.S. House of Representatives, 111th Cong. 68, July 24, 2009 (Washington, D.C.: Government Printing Office, 2010) (statements of Hon. Ben S. Bernanke, Hon. John C. Dugan); William E. Kovacic, "The Consumer Financial Protection Agency and the Hazards of Regulatory Restructuring, Lombard Street," September 14, 2009, http://www.ftc.gov/speeches/kovacic/090914hazzrdsrestructuring.pdf.

7. In speaking at the January 2010 meetings of the American Economics Association, Bernanke touted the Fed's strengthened commitment to consumer protection but stopped short of endorsing the CFPB. See Ben S. Bernanke, "Monetary Policy and the Housing Bubble," speech at the annual meeting of the American Economics Association, Atlanta, Georgia, January 3, 2010, http://www.federalreserve.gov/newsevents/speech/bernanke20100103a.htm.

8. These justifications had been stated many times by the advocates, including as members of the Federal Reserve's Consumer Advisory Council. See Carol A. Needham, "Listening to Cassandra: The Difficulty of Recognizing Risks and Taking Action," *Fordham Law Review* 78, no. 5 (2010): 2329–55.

9. U.S. Department of Treasury, *Financial Regulatory Reform, A New Foundation: Rebuilding Financial Supervision and Regulation,* June 17, 2009, http://www.treasury.gov/initiatives/Documents/FinalReport_web.pdf.

10. Ibid., 56.

11. U.S. Department of Treasury, "Title X—Consumer Financial Protection Agency Act of 2009," draft legislation, June 30, 2009.

12. U.S. Department of Treasury, *Financial Regulatory Reform,* 57.

13. Ibid., 55–75.

14. *Regulatory Restructuring: Enhancing Consumer Financial Products Regulation: Hearing Before the Committee on Financial Services,* statement of Elizabeth Warren, 12.

15. "Washington Watch with Roland Martin," transcript of podcast with Elizabeth Warren, March 14, 2010, http://www.rolandsmartin.com/blog/index.php/2010/03/14/washington-watch-wroland-martin-03-14-10-transcript/.

16. *Regulatory Restructuring: Enhancing Consumer Financial Products Regulation,* statement of Elizabeth Warren, 11. In the same vein, Gail Hillebrand of Consumers Union, the largest consumer organization in the United States, said: "The complex financial instruments that sparked the financial crisis were based on home loans that were poorly underwritten, unsuitable to the borrower, were arranged by persons not bound to act in the best interest of the borrower and who lacked a sufficient stake in the success of the borrower, or contained terms so complex that many individual homeowners had little opportunity to fully understand the nature or magnitude of the risks of these loans." *The Proposed Consumer Financial Protection Agency: Implications for Consumers and FTC,* statement of Gail Hillebrand, http://democrats.energycommerce.house.gov/Press_111/20090708/tes timony_hillebrand.pdf, 80.

17. *Perspectives on the Consumer Financial Protection Agency,* statement of Hilary Shelton, 10.

18. *Community and Consumer Advocates' Perspectives on the Obama Administration's Financial Regulatory Reform Proposals,* statement of Janet Murguia, 13.

19. Ibid.

20. Ibid., statement of Nancy Zirkin, 170.

21. *Creating a Consumer Financial Protection Agency: A Cornerstone of America's New Foundation,* statement of Michael S. Barr, 6.

22. *Regulatory Restructuring: Enhancing Consumer Financial Products Regulation,* statement of Edmund Mierzwinski, 18.

23. Ibid., statement of Kathleen E. Keest, 95.

24. Ibid., statement of Hon. Ellen Seidman, 16.

25. Americans for Financial Reform, "Restoring Oversight and Accountability to Financial Markets," July 10, 2009, http://ourfinancialsecurity.org/2009/07/position-papers/.

26. Consumer Financial Protection Agency Act of 2009, H.R. 3126, 111th Cong. (2009); see also Michael Barr, Sendhil Mullainathan, Edlar Shafir, "Behaviorally Informed Financial Services Regulation," Asset Building Program of the New America Foundation, Washington, D.C., October 2008, and Ann Graham, "The Consumer Financial Protection Agency: Love It Or Hate It, U.S. Financial Regulation Needs It," *Villanova Law Review* 55, no. 3 (2010): 603–26.

27. "Prof. Elizabeth Warren on Why We Need the CFPA, Part 2," *Consumer-Reports.org,* August 17, 2009, http://news.consumerreports.org/money/2009/08/consumer-reports-consumer-financial-protection-agency-elizabeth-warren-interview-cfpa-plain-vanilla-mortgage-banks-lenders-fi.html.

28. *Banking Industry Perspectives on the Obama Administration's Financial Regulatory Reform Proposals: Hearings Before the Committee on Financial Services,* U.S. House of Representatives, 111th Cong. 58, July 15, 2009 (Washington: Government Printing Office, 2010) (statements of Hon. Steve Bartlett, Chris Stinebert, and Steven I. Zeisel).

29. *Compensation in the Financial Industry: Hearing before the House Comm. on Financial Services,* 111th Cong. 98, January 22, 2010 (Washington: U.S. Government Printing Office, 2010) (statement of Joseph E. Stiglitz).

30. Elizabeth Warren, "Professor Elizabeth Warren Speaks about the Consumer Financial Protection Agency," Youtube video, 7:34, July 16, 2009, http://www.youtube.com/watch?v=lYd08e5Cjvs.

31. Elizabeth Warren, "Consumers Need a Credit Watchdog," *BusinessWeek*, July 27, 2009, 76.

32. Elizabeth Warren, "Three Myths about the Consumer Financial Protection Agency," The Baseline Scenario, July 21, 2009, http://baselinescenario.com/2009/07/21/three-myths-about-the-consumer-financial-product-agency/.

33. Americans for Financial Reform, Statement on the President's Plan to Create a Consumer Financial Protection Agency, press release, Washington, D.C., June 29, 2009, http://ourfinancialsecurity.org/2009/07/statement-from-americans-for-financial-reform-on-the-president%E2%80%99s-plan-to-create-a-consumer-financial-protection-agency/.

34. Professors of Consumer Law and Banking Law, "A Communication from Academic Faculty Who Teach Courses Related to Consumer Law and Banking Law at American Law Schools," letter to the honorable Christopher J. Dodd, Barney Frank, Richard C. Shelby, and Spencer Bachus in support of legislation creating a Consumer Financial Protection Agency, September 29, 2009, http://law.hofstra.edu/pdf/Media/consumer-law%209-28-09.pdf.

35. Bob Herbert, "Chutzpah on Steroids," *New York Times*, July 14, 2009, A25.

36. "Reforming the Financial System," Editorial, *New York Times*, September 9, 2009, 20.

37. "Our View on Consumer Protection: How the Banking Lobby Tries to Undermine Loan Reform," Editorial, *USA Today*, October 7, 2009, 8; Errol Louis, "How to Spear Credit Sharks: Create a Potent New Federal Agency to Protect Consumers," *New York Daily News*, October 11, 2009, 39.

38. Consumer Federation of America, "Survey: Americans Want Consumer Agency for Financial Products and Services," press release, September 9, 2009, http://www.consumerfed.org/elements/www.consumerfed.org/file/CFPA_Poll_Release_3_Sep_09_2009_final.pdf.

39. Celinda Lake, David Mermin, Rick Johnson, and Zach Young, "Recent Polling Data on Financial Reform Legislation," Memorandum to Interested Parties, Lake Research Partners, October 13, 2009, http://ourfinancialsecurity.org/blogs/wp-content/ourfinancialsecurity.org/uploads/2009/10/pacmemo_AFR_f_10130912.pdf.

40. Frank Luntz, "The Language of Financial Reform," theworddoctors, Alexandria, Virginia, January 2010, http://ourfinancialsecurity.org/blogs/wp-content/ourfinancialsecurity.org/uploads/2009/10/pacmemo_AFR_f_10130912.pdf.

41. Trade Association Letter to congressmen Barney Frank and Spencer Bachus regarding H.R. 3126, July 20, 2009, http://businessroundtable.org/news-center/business-roundtable-letter-to-chairman-frank-and-ranking-member-bachus-rega/.

42. *Banking Industry Perspectives on the Obama Administration's Financial Regulatory Reform Proposals*, statement of John A. Courson, 14. This note of caution came from a leader of an industry that rushed headlong into offering billions

of dollars of mortgages to people who had no reasonable chance of making their payments. So, one could say that Mr. Courson had learned from experience. http://www.house.gov/apps/list/hearing/financialsvcs_dem/courson_testimony.pdf

43. *Banking Industry Perspectives on the Obama Administration's Financial Regulatory Reform Proposals,* statement of Edward L. Yingling, 37.

44. Brody Mullins, "Chamber Ad Campaign Targets Consumer Agency," *Wall Street Journal,* September 8, 2009, A4.

45. The U.S. Chamber of Commerce declined our request to reprint their ads in this book. As of September 2012, the butcher ad could be found at the following website: http://www.cfpbspotlight.com/wp-content/uploads/2009/09/Butcher.pdf. The baker and orthodontist ads can be viewed, respectively, at http://news.consumerreports.org/money/2009/09/cfpa-consumer-financial-protection-agency-white-house-water-down-barney-frank-proposed-no-plain-vanilla-requirement-exempt-sm.html and http://www.revolution-agency.com/2010/cfpa-print1.php.

46. U.S. Department of Treasury, *Financial Regulatory Reform,* 15.

47. Independent Community Bankers of America, Letters to the Honorable Barney Frank and Spencer Bachus on "Hearings on Regulatory Restructuring: Enhancing Consumer Financial Products Regulation," Washington, D.C., June 24, 2009, http://www.icba.org/files/ICBASites/PDFs/ltr062409.pdf; Peter J. Wallison, "Unfree to Choose," American Enterprise Institute, July 9, 2009, http://www.aei.org/outlook/100056; *Banking Industry Perspectives on the Obama Administration's Financial Regulatory Reform Proposals: Hearings Before the Committee on Financial Services,* statements of Edward L. Yingling and Todd Zywicki.

48. Committee on Financial Services: Democrats, "Frank Introduces Obama Administration's Plan to Increase Consumer Protection," press release, July 8, 2009, http://democrats.financialservices.house.gov/press/PRArticle.aspx?NewsID=510.

49. Edmund Mierzwinski, interview by authors, December 31, 2010.

50. *Community and Consumer Advocates' Perspectives on the Obama Administration's Financial Regulatory Reform Proposals: Hearings Before the Committee on Financial Services,* U.S. House of Representatives, 111th Cong. 62, July 16, 2009 (Washington: Government Printing Office, 2009) (statement of John Taylor). http://ourfinancialsecurity.org/blogs/wp-content/ourfinancialsecurity.org/uploads/2009/07/Click-Here1.pdf

51. National Community Reinvestment Coalition, "Efforts to Weaken Consumer Protection Agency Underway," press release, Washington, D.C., July 9, 2009, http://www.ncrc.org/media-center/press-releases/item/400-efforts-to-weaken-consumer-protection-agency-underway.

52. John Taylor, interview with authors, March 16, 2011.

53. Heather Booth, interview by authors, January 6, 2011.

54. Nancy Zirkin, interview by authors, Washington, D.C., April 15, 2011.

55. Mierzwinski, interview.

56. The data was compiled by comparing members of the House Financial Services Committee with member lists of the two caucuses. For the Committee's members, see "Member Money: House Financial Services Committee," *OpenSecrets,*

http://www.opensecrets.org/cmteprofiles/profiles.php?cmteid=&cmte=HFIN%20 %20&congno=111. Members of the two causes are listed here: "U.S. Congress: One Week after Election Day—A Snapshot of the New Congressional Landscape," Residents Against Wood Smoke Emission Particulates (RAWSEP), November 9, 2010, http://rawsep.wordpress.com/2010/11/09/2010-nov-9-u-s-congress-one-week-after-election-day-a-snapshot-of-the-new-congressional-landscape/. The following members of the House Financial Services Committee were during the 111th Congress members of either or both caucus groups: Joe Baca, Melissa Bean, Andre Carson, Travis Childers, Joe Donnelly, Bill Foster, Jim Himes, Ron Klein, Suzanne Kosmas, Dan Maffei, Gregory Meeks, Walt Minnick, Dennis Moore, Gary Peters, Edwin Perlmutter, David Scott, and Charlie Wilson.

57. Maureen Thompson, interview by authors, February 4, 2011.

58. Later, in December, the New Democrat and Blue Dog Caucuses opposed the narrow rule offered by the House Rules Committee which would have prevented consideration of floor amendments on preemption, carve-outs, and other moderate Democratic favorites. The two Caucuses threatened to vote as a bloc to defeat the rule and thereby ruin the chances for the entire bill. This warning was treated seriously and delayed a vote while further negotiations could take place. See David Dayen, "Hijack: Bank-Friendly Dems Revolt on Financial Regulatory Reform," *Firedoglake,* December 9, 2009, http://news.firedoglake.com/2009/12/09/ hijack-bank-friendly-dems-revolt-on-financial-regulatory-reform/.

59. The White House, "Weekly Address: President Obama Promotes Tougher Rules on Wall Street to Protect Consumers," press release, September 19, 2009. http://www.whitehouse.gov/the_press_office/Weekly-Address-President-Obama-Promotes-Tougher-Rules-on-Wall-Street-to-Protect-Consumers/.

60. Victoria McGrane, "Moderate Democrats May Buck Barack Obama's Plan," *Politico,* September 21, 2009, http://www.politico.com/news/stories/0909/27367. html.

61. The memo is reprinted in: Ryan Grimm, "Greenspan Backs Key Obama Wall Street Reform Effort," *Huffington Post,* November 28, 2009, http://www. huffingtonpost.com/2009/09/28/greenspan-backs-key-obama_n_302018.html.

62. "Obama Administration to Scale Back Consumer Financial Protection Agency Powers," Ballard Spahr, September 24, 2009, http://www.ballardspahr.com/ alertspublications/legalalerts/2009-09-24_obamaadministration.aspx.

63. Keith Whann, letter to Hon. Barney Frank, National Independent Automobile Dealers Association, Arlington, TX, undated, http://taxdollars.ocregister. com/files/2009/10/niada-letter-to-frank.pdf

64. Jennifer Liberto, "Banks Win Round 1 in Consumer Fight," *CNNMoney,* September 23, 2009, http://money.cnn.com/2009/09/23/news/economy/consumer_ financial_protection_agency/index.htm.

65. Richard A. Posner, "Treating Financial Consumers as Consenting Adults," *Wall Street Journal,* July 22, 2009, http://online.wsj.com/article/SB1000142405297 0203946904574302213213148166.html.

66. "'Plain Vanilla' Provision's Out, But CFPA Proposal is Still Worthwhile," *ConsumerReports,* September 24, 2009, http://news.consumerreports.org/

money/2009/09/cfpa-consumer-financial-protection-agency-white-house-water-down-barney-frank-proposed-no-plain-vanilla-requirement-exempt-sm.html.

67. U.S. Department of Treasury, *Financial Regulatory Reform*; H.R. 3126: Consumer Financial Protection Agency, 111th Cong., introduced July 8, 2009, http://www.govtrack.us/congress/bills/111/hr3126/text.

68. Ryan Grimm, "Greenspan Backs Key Obama Wall Street Reform Effort," *Huffington Post,* November 28, 2009, http://www.huffingtonpost.com/2009/09/28/greenspan-backs-key-obama_n_302018.html.

69. Anne Flaherty, "Planned Consumer Protection Agency Scaled Back," *MainStreet,* September 24, 2009, http://www.mainstreet.com/article/lifestyle/planned-consumer-protection-agency-scaled-back.

70. National Community Reinvestment Coalition, "Changes to CFPA Weaken an Already Compromised Bill," press release, September 24, 2009, http://www.ncrc.org/media-a-resources-mainmenu-118/press-releases-mainmenu-75/518-changes-to-cfpa-weaken-an-already-compromised-bill.

71. Anne Flaherty, "Planned Consumer Protection Agency Scaled Back," *MainStreet,* September 24, 2009, http://www.mainstreet.com/article/lifestyle/planned-consumer-protection-agency-scaled-back

72. Stephen Labaton, "White House Pares Its Financial Reform Plan," *New York Times,* September 23, 2009, http://www.nytimes.com/2009/09/24/business/24regulate.html.

73. Tim Fernholz, "What Do Barney Frank's Changes Mean for Consumer Financial Protection," *The American Prospect,* September 24, 2009, http://prospect.org/csnc/blogs/tapped_archive?month=09&year=2009&base_name=what_do_barney_franks_changes.

74. Sam Stein, "White House Hints at Veto Threat of 'Weak' Consumer Protection Bill," *Huffington Post,* November 29, 2009, http://www.huffingtonpost.com/2009/09/29/white-house-hints-at-veto_n_303219.html.

75. In a February 29, 2012 interview by the authors, Assistant Treasury Secretary Barr described Eric Stein as "off-the-charts fabulous" and responsible for day-to-day contact with AFR's advocates, including Heather Booth.

76. Democrats Travis Childers of Mississippi and Minnick voted against the bill, and Republican Michael Castle of Delaware voted for it. See Michael Beckel, "Congressional Opponents of Consumer Financial Protection Bill Got Big Money from Wall Street Interests," *OpenSecrets* (blog), October 26, 2009, http://www.opensecrets.org/news/2009/10/congressional-opponents-of-con.html; Jason M. Rosenstock and Bryan M. Stockton, "Financial Services Regulatory Reform Update," ML Strategies, October 26, 2009, http://www.mintz.com/media/pnc/4/media.2024.pdf.

77. "The Reformed CFPA—New Paint, Same Old Clunker," *GOP.gov,* October 1, 2009, http://www.gop.gov/policy-news/09/10/01/the-reformed-cfpa-new-paint

78. Binyamin Appelbaum, "Big Financial Firms Losing Power on Capitol Hill," *Washington Post,* October 19, 2009, http://www.washingtonpost.com/wp-dyn/content/article/2009/10/18/AR2009101802156_pf.html

79. Mierzwinski, interview.

80. Heather Booth, interview by authors, January 6, 2011.

81. Off-the-record interview by authors.

82. As early as June 24, 2009, Representative Frank said, "Ultimately, the financial regulation is going to be one bill, in part because of the United States Senate." *Regulatory Restructuring: Enhancing Consumer Financial Products Regulation: Hearing before the Committee on Financial Services,* U.S. House of Representatives, 111th Cong., June 24, 2009 (Washington, D.C.: Government Printing Office, 2009), 2.

83. Discussion Draft of Senate bill on financial reform, 111th Congress, undated, http://banking.senate.gov/public/_files/AYO09D44_xml.pdf.

84. H.R. 4173, 111th Cong. (December 2, 2009), http://www.gpo.gov/fdsys/pkg/BILLS-111hr4173ih/pdf/BILLS-111hr4173ih.pdf.

85. Digest for H.R. 4173 Amendments, 111th Congress, GOP.gov, http://www.gop.gov/bill/111/1/hr4173amendments.

86. Victoria McGrane, "Moderates Win Wall St. Bill Changes," *Politico,* December 9, 2009, http://www.politico.com/news/stories/1209/30429.html.

87. Silla Brush, "Minnick Amendment to Scrap Proposed Consumer Protection Agency Fails," *The Hill,* December 11, 2009, http://thehill.com/homenews/house/71871-minnick-amendment-to-scrap-consumer-agency-proposal-fails.

88. "On Agreeing to the Amendment: Amendment 22 to H.R. 4173," *Govtrack. us,* http://www.govtrack.us/congress/vote.xpd?vote=h2009-965.

89. "H.R. 4173: Dodd-Frank Wall Street Reform and Consumer Protection Act (On Passage of the Bill), 111th Congress, December 11, 2009, http://www.govtrack. us/congress/votes/111-2009/h968.

90. Michael Barr, interview by authors, February 29, 2012.

Chapter 7

1. Ryan Grimm, "GOP, Warning of a 'New EPA', Oppose Independent CFPA," *Huffington Post,* March 18, 2010, http://www.huffingtonpost.com/2010/01/04/gop-warning-of-a-new-epa_n_410750.html.

2. Alison Vekshin and Robert Schmidt, "Dodd Said to Weigh Dropping Consumer Agency from Overhaul Plan," *Bloomberg,* January 15, 2010, http://www.bloomberg.com/apps/news?pid=newsarchive&sid=aUTeWAK__CBI&pos=9; Damian Paletta, "Consumer Protection Agency in Doubt," *Wall Street Journal,* January 15, 2010, http://online.wsj.com/article/SB10001424052748704363504575003360632239020.html?mod=WSJ_newsreel_us.

3. Americans for Financial Reform, "AFR Urges Chairman Dodd Not to Dump Cornerstone of Reform: Consumer Financial Protection Agency," January 15, 2010, http://ourfinancialsecurity.org/2010/01/afr-urges-chairman-dodd-not-to-dump-cornerstone-of-reform-consumer-financial-protection-agency/.

4. Jackie Calmes and Sewell Chan, "Obama Pressing for Protections against Lenders," *New York Times,* January 12, 2010, http://www.nytimes.com/2010/01/20/us/politics/20regulate.html?dbk.

5. Chan, Sewell, "Talks with G.O.P. on Financial Bill at 'Impasse,' Dodd Says," *New York Times*, February 5, 2010. http://www.nytimes.com/2010/02/06/business/06regulate.html.

6. Ibid.

7. Silla Brush, "Dodd to Move Forward as Financial Talks with Shelby at 'Impasse,'" *The Hill*, February 5, 2010, http://thehill.com/homenews/senate/79943-dodd-to-move-rforward-alone-talks-with-shelby-at-impasse.

8. Felix Salmon, "Has Corker Killed the CFPA?" *Reuters*, February 24, 2010, http://blogs.reuters.com/felix-salmon/2010/02/24/has-corker-killed-the-cfpa/.

9. The idea of placing a Bureau of Financial Protection inside Treasury was floated in late February. Using the Fed as the Bureau's home apparently emerged a bit later. Sewell Chan, "Dodd Proposes Financial Protection Agency," *New York Times*, February 27, 2010, http://www.nytimes.com/2010/02/27/business/economy/27regulate.html; Alison Vekshin and Robert Schmidt, "Dodd Scraps Obama's Consumer Agency, Proposed Treasury Bureau," *Bloomberg*, February 28, 2010, http://www.bloomberg.com/apps/news?pid=newsarchive&sid=aUmOFjhv8kOE; Binymain Appelbaum and David Cho, "Dodd Wants Democratic Support for Consumer-Protection Regulator at Fed," *Washington Post*, March 3, 2010, http://www.washingtonpost.com/wp-dyn/content/article/2010/03/01/AR2010030102049.html. An undated and unsigned memo proposing the Treasury home can be found at: http://www.capitalgainsandgames.com/files/Dodd%20consumer%20protection%20proposal%20feb%2026_0.pdf.

10. Pat Garofalo, "Why Is Dodd Reopening Reg Reform Negotiations with Corker," *ThinkProgress.org*, February 12, 2010, http://thinkprogress.org/economy/2010/02/12/173129/dodd-corker-nonstart/.

11. David Cho and Brady Dennis, "Obama May Compromise on Consumer Agency to Pass Financial Regulation," *Washington Post*, February 25, 2010, http://www.washingtonpost.com/wp-dyn/content/article/2010/02/24/AR2010022405573.html?hpid=topnews.

12. Michael Barr, interview by authors, February 29, 2012.

13. Sewell Chan, "Dodd Proposes Giving Fed the Task of Consumer Protection," *New York Times*, March 2, 2010, http://www.nytimes.com/2010/03/02/business/02regulate.html?dbk.

14. Eamon Javers and Victoria McGrane, "Barney Frank: Chris Dodd Deal Like 'A Bad Joke,'" *Politico*, March 2, 2010, http://www.politico.com/news/stories/0310/33777.html; Craig Torres and Yalman Onaran, "Consumer Agency within Fed Seen as Victory for Banks," *Bloomberg*, March 3, 2010, http://www.bloomberg.com/apps/news?pid=newsarchive&sid=a.E.59TT96Y.

15. Harold Meyerson, "Wall Street's Financial Aftershocks," *Washington Post*, March 3, 2010, http://www.washingtonpost.com/wp-dyn/content/article/2010/03/02/AR2010030202944.html?wprss=rss_opinions.

16. Jodi Kantor, "Behind Consumer Agency Idea, A Tireless Advocate," *New York Times*, March 24, 2010, http://www.nytimes.com/2010/03/25/business/25warren.html.

17. Brian Stelter, "Fake Former Presidents Use Comedy for a Cause," *New York Times,* March 5, 2010, http://www.nytimes.com/2010/03/06/arts/television/06funny.html?dbk.

18. "Heidi Montag Says No to Plastic," video, *FunnyOrDie,* posted March 10, 2010, http://www.funnyordie.com/videos/a1da6ff653/heidi-montag-says-no-to-plastic.

19. Americans for Financial Reform, "New Funny or Die Video on the Need for Financial Reform," press release, March 3, 2010, http://ourfinancialsecurity.org/2010/03/new-funny-or-die-video-on-the-need-for-financial-reform/.

20. Edmund Mierzwinski, interview by authors, December 31, 2010.

21. Ryan Grim, "Bob Corker: Dodd Decision To Go Alone on Wall Street Reform 'Stunning,'" *Huffington Post,* March 11, 2010, http://www.huffingtonpost.com/2010/03/11/dodd-financial-regulation_n_494796.html; Sewell Chan, "Democrats Push Ahead on Financial Bill," *New York Times,* March 11, 2010, http://www.nytimes.com/2010/03/12/business/12regulate.html.

22. Committee Print of Unnumbered Senate Bill, 111th Congress, http://banking.senate.gov/public/_files/ChairmansMark31510AYO10306_xmlFinancialReformLegislationBill.pdf; Jim Puzzanghera, "Dodd Expected to Offer More Modest Financial Reform Legislation," *Los Angeles Times,* March 15, 2010, http://articles.latimes.com/2010/mar/15/business/la-fi-dodd-bill15-2010mar15.

23. Raj Date, "Losing the Last War: Evaluating 'Veto' Powers on Consumer Financial Protection," Cambridge Winter Center for Financial Institutions Policy, March 21, 2010, http://cambridgewinter.org/Cambridge_Winter/Archives/Entries/2010/3/21_LOSING_THE_LAST_WAR_files/cfpa%20veto%20032110_1.pdf.

24. Pat Garofalo, "Shelby and Corker Reject Dodd's Watered-Down Consumer Protection Proposal," *ThinkProgress.org,* March 1, 2010, http://thinkprogress.org/economy/2010/03/01/173152/corker-shelby-reject/.

25. Richard Eskow, "Demand an 'Up or Down Vote' on Real Financial Reform," *Huffington Post,* March 11, 2010, http://www.huffingtonpost.com/rj-eskow/demand-an-up-or-down-vote_b_495497.html?ref=max-baucus.

26. Off-the-record interview by authors.

27. This perspective on events was provided to us by a well-placed interviewee who did not want to be identified or quoted.

28. Americans for Financial Reform, "The 'Restoring American Financial Stability Act of 2010,'" March 15, 2010, http://ourfinancialsecurity.org/2010/03/afr-statement-on-chairman-dodd%E2%80%99s-financial-reform-bill/.

29. Ibid.

30. Americans for Financial Reform, "Take Action to Strengthen 'The Restoring American Financial Stability Act,'" March 22, 2010, http://ourfinancialsecurity.org/2010/03/take-action-to-strengthen-the-restoring-american-financial-stability-act/

31. Lisa Donner, interview by authors, Washington, D.C., December 2, 2011.

32. Edmund Mierzwinski, interview by authors, Washington, D.C., December 2, 2011.

33. Damon Silvers, interview by authors, May 4, 2011.

34. Lisa Donner, interview by authors, Washington, D.C., December 3, 2010.

35. Michael Calhoun, interview by authors, February 4, 2011.

36. National Community Reinvestment Coalition, "Dodd Bill Offers Compromised Consumer Financial Protection Agency," press release, March 16, 2010, http://www.ncrc.org/media-center/press-releases/item/419-dodd-bill-offers-compromised-consumer-financial-protection-agency.

37. Off-the-record interview by authors.

38. H.R. 4173, Section 4111. The House version passed on to the Senate can be found at: Rick McKinney, "Dodd-Frank Wall Street Reform and Consumer Financial Protection Act: A Brief Legislative History with Links, Reports and Summaries," *LLRX.com*, December 10, 2010, http://www.llrx.com/features/doddfrank.htm.

39. *Regulatory Restructuring: Enhancing Consumer Financial Products Regulation: Hearing Before the Committee on Financial Services,* U.S. House of Representatives, 111th Cong. 49, June 24, 2009 (Washington, D.C.: Government Printing Office, 2009) 36.

40. Ibid, 52.

41. Committee Print of Unnumbered Senate Bill, 111th Congress, March 15, 2011, available at: Rick McKinney, "Dodd-Frank Wall Street Reform and Consumer Financial Protection Act: A Brief Legislative History with Links, Reports and Summaries," *LLRX.com*, December 10, 2010, http://www.llrx.com/features/doddfrank.htm.

42. *The Restoring American Financial Stability Act,* a report submitted by Sen. Christopher Dodd from the Committee on Banking, Housing, and Urban Affairs, March 22, 2010, 133, http://banking.senate.gov/public/_files/RAFSAPosted CommitteeReport.pdf.

43. Maureen Thompson, interview by the authors, January 14, 2011.

44. Jim Kuhnhenn, "Dodd Financial Reform Bill Passed by Senate Banking Committee," *Huffington Post,* March 22, 2010, http://www.huffingtonpost.com/2010/03/22/dodd-bill-passed-by-senat_0_n_508935.html.

45. "Corker Claims the Financial Regulation Got a Speedy Vote," *PolitiFact.com,* April 25, 2010, http://www.politifact.com/truth-o-meter/statements/2010/apr/25/bob-corker/corker-claims-financial-regulation-had-speedy-vote/.

46. Jim Kuhnhenn, "Dodd Financial Reform Bill Passed by Senate Banking Committee," *Huffington Post,* March 22, 2010, http://www.huffingtonpost.com/2010/03/22/dodd-bill-passed-by-senat_0_n_508935.html.

47. Travis Plunkett, interview by the authors, December 21, 2010.

48. Edmund Mierzwinski, interview by the authors, December 31, 2010.

49. Lisa Donner, interview by the authors, Washington, D.C., December 3, 2010.

50. Michael Barr, interview by the authors, February 29, 2012.

51. Paul Wiseman, "Dodd's 2nd Shot at Financial Reform Still Leaves Loopholes," *USA Today,* March 19, 2010, http://www.usatoday.com/money/companies/regulation/2010-03-15-financial-reform-cover_N.htm

52. Dana Milbank, "Sen. Dodd Announces Retirement with Dignity—and Honesty," *Washington Post,* January 7, 2010, http://www.washingtonpost.com/wp-dyn/content/article/2010/01/06/AR2010010604137.html.

53. U.S. Chamber of Commerce, "U.S. Chamber Intensifies Campaign for Bipartisan Financial Regulatory Reform," press release, March 26, 2010, http://www.uschamber.com/press/releases/2010/march/us-chamber-intensifies-campaign-bipartisan-financial-regulatory-reform.

54. Ibid.

55. Eric Lichtblau and Edward Wyatt, "Pro-Business Lobbying Blitz Takes On Obama's Wall Street Overhaul," *New York Times*, March 27, 2010, http://www.nytimes.com/2010/03/28/business/28lobby.html?_r=1&dbk.

56. "Stop the CFPA: 'No Sleep,'" U.S. Chamber of Commerce campaign advertisement for television, http://www.revolution-agency.com/advocacy/cfpa-tv1.php.

57. Noah Rothman, "Reed Awards Recognize Top Political and Public Affairs Talent in the World," Campaignsandelections.com, February 5, 2011, http://www.campaignsandelections.com/campaign-insider/172082/-reed-awards-recognize-top-political-and-public-affairs-talent-in-the-world.thtml.

58. Gretchen Morgenson, transcript of "Bill Moyers Journal," PBS television, March 26, 2010, http://www.pbs.org/moyers/journal/03262010/transcript2.html.

59. U.S. Chamber of Commerce, "Consumer Financial Protection Agency Toolkit," undated, http://www.uschamber.com/chambers/consumer-financial-protection-agency-toolkit.

60. AARP Blog, "New AARP Ad on Financial Reform Debuts Today!" April 19, 2010, http://blog.aarp.org/2010/04/19/new_aarp_ad_on_financial_refor/.

61. The video can be viewed at: Brian Beutler, "Pro–Financial Reform Groups Begin Pushback on GOP Filibuster," *TPM*, April 27, 2010, http://tpmdc.talkingpointsmemo.com/2010/04/pro-financial-reform-groups-begin-pushback-on-gop-filibuster-video.php.

62. Tyler Finn, "MoveOn Ad Claims McConnell 'Unfit to Lead,'" *CBS News*, April 21, 2010, http://www.cbsnews.com/8301-503544_162-20003077-503544.html.

63. Americans for Financial Reform, "AFR Joins National Mobilization for Financial Reform; Events across Country," October 26, 2009, http://ourfinancialsecurity.org/2009/10/afr-joins-national-mobilization-for-financial-reform-events-across-country/.

64. Crowd estimates are unreliable, but supporters of the event gravitated to the 5,000 figure. See: David Moberg, "5,000 Protest Bank Power, Abuses, as 'Showdown' Culminates," *In These Times*, October 27, 2009, http://inthesetimes.com/working/entry/5103/5000_protest_bank_power_abuses_as_showdown_culminates/ and "'Showdown in Chicago': Thousands of Protesters Gather at Bankers' Convention, Jess Jackson, Labor Leaders Speak," *Huffington Post*, March 18, 2010, http://www.huffingtonpost.com/2009/10/27/showdown-in-chicago-thous_n_335533.html.

Groups participating in the three days of mobilizations include: A New Way Forward, AFL-CIO, Action Now, Albany Park Neighborhood Council, Alliance to Develop Power (ADP), Americans for Fairness in Lending, Americans for Financial Reform, ARISE Chicago, Brighton Park Neighborhood Council, Central

Illinois Organizing Project (CIOP), Center for Community Change (CCC), Change in Terms, Change to Win, Citizen Action, Chicago Coalition of the Homeless, Communities United for Action (CUFA), Community Voices Heard (CVH), Contra Costa Interfaith Supporting Community Organization (CCISCO), Grassroots Collaborative, Green Party of Nevada, Fuerza Laboral/Power of Workers, Illinois Hunger Coalition, Iowa Citizens for Community Improvement, Jobs with Justice, Gender Just Metanoia Centers, Inc., Michigan People's Action (MPA), MoveOn, National People's Action, Northside Action for Justice, Northside POWER, Northwest Bronx Community & Clergy Coalition, People Organized for West Side Renewal (POWER), PUSH Buffalo, Right to the City Alliance, Rights for All People (RAP), Roomdad Productions, Service Employees International Union (SEIU), SEIU Illinois State Council, SOUL, South Austin Coalition Community Council (SACCC), Sunflower Community Action, Syracuse United Neighbors (SUN), Teach Our Children (TOC), The Grassroots Collaborate, UE, UCLA Undergraduate Students Association, Workers United, and Working In Neighborhoods (WIN). *Source:* http://showdowninamerica.org/showdown-in-chicago.

65. "ABA Showdown: Durbin Urges Bankers to Support CFPA," video, http://www.youtube.com/watch?v=aqVu0kLEMhI.

66. Service Employees International Union, "FDIC Chairman Sheila Bair Addresses Thousands of Taxpayers at Showdown in Chicago in Support of President Obama's New Consumer Protection Agency," press release, October 26, 2009, http://www.seiu.org/2009/10/fdic-chairman-sheila-bair-addresses-thousand-of-taxpayers-at-showdown-in-chicago-in-support-of-presi.php.

67. Esther Kaplan, "Anger, At Last," *The Nation,* October 26, 2009, http://www.thenation.com/blog/anger-last.

68. "Showdown in America: About Us," undated, http://showdowninamerica.org/about-us, accessed April 17, 2010.

69. Americans for Financial Reform, "Financial Reform Events," undated, http://ourfinancialsecurity.org/blogs/wp-content/ourfinancialsecurity.org/uploads/2010/07/AFR-2010-Calendar.pdf.

70. Steven Greenhouse, "Unions Hold a Rally to Protest Wall Street," *New York Times,* April 29, 2010, http://www.nytimes.com/2010/04/30/business/30protest.html.

71. Goerge Goehl, interview by the authors, May 5, 2011.

72. Sam Youngman, "McConnell: White House Trying to 'Jam' GOP on Financial Overhaul Legislation," *The Hill,* April 14, 2010, http://thehill.com/homenews/administration/92153-obama-steps-up-campaign-for-financial-overhaul.

73. Ibid.

74. Americans for Financial Reform, "AFR: Give the People an Up or Down Vote," letter to senators Harry Reid and Mitch McConnell, April 23, 2010, http://ourfinancialsecurity.org/2010/04/afr-says-give-the-people-an-up-or-down-vote/.

75. Americans for Financial Reform, "Showdown: Main Street v. Wall Street: Americans Travel to Capitol Hill to Press for Wall Street Reform," press release, April 27, 2010, http://ourfinancialsecurity.org/2010/04/showdown-main-street-v-wall-street-americans-travel-to-capitol-hill-to-press-for-wall-street-reform/.

76. Brady Dennis and Paul Kane, "Reid Aims to Move Forward with Financial Regulation Bill," *Washington Post,* April 23, 2010, http://www.washingtonpost.com/wp-dyn/content/article/2010/04/22/AR2010042203650.html.

77. Adam Sorensen, "Financial Reform Chicken," *Time,* April 22, 2010, http://swampland.time.com/2010/04/22/financial-reform-chicken/.

78. Sean Lengell, "Filibuster Stalls Financial-Reform Bill," *Washington Times,* April 27, 2010, http://www.washingtontimes.com/news/2010/apr/27/filibuster-stalls-financial-reform-bill/.

79. Donny Shaw, "GOP Again Sustains Filibuster of Financial Reform," *Open Congress* (blog), April 27, 2010, http://www.opencongress.org/articles/view/1845-GOP-Again-Sustains-Filibuster-of-Financial-Reform; Devin Dwyer, "'Anti-American'? Reid Blasts 3rd GOP Filibuster of Financial Reform Bill," *ABC News,* April 28, 2010; http://abcnews.go.com/blogs/politics/2010/04/reid-filibuster-is-antiamerican-gop-blocks-finreg-a-3rd-time/.

80. Democratic senator Ben Nelson of Nebraska was one of the holdouts on cloture. According to Edward Yingling of the American Bankers Association, Nelson decided to change his vote when he realized that the Independent Community Bankers of America, having extracted key concessions, did not object. The community bankers dispute this version of events, but Yingling insists that this was the moment when the battle over regulatory reform was largely lost. See: Rob Blackwell, "The Clash of the Trade Groups over Reg Reform Traces to One Vote," *American Banker* 175, issue 195 (December 2010): 1.

81. Eamon Javers, "Levin's Language Hits the Fan." *Politico,* April 27, 2010, http://www.politico.com/news/stories/0410/36416.html.

82. David M. Herszenhorn and Edward Wyatt, "Republicans Allow Debate on Financial Overhaul," New York Times, April 28, 2010, http://www.nytimes.com/2010/04/29/business/29regulate.html. Political columnist Ezra Klein attributed the end of the filibuster to the coming weekend's Kentucky Derby, an event that McConnell, as a senator from Kentucky, surely wanted to attend. Ezra Klein, "Will the Kentucky Derby End the Republican Filibuster of FinReg?" *Washington Post,* April 28, 2010, http://voices.washingtonpost.com/ezra-klein/2010/04/will_the_kentucky_derby_end_th.html.

83. Stephanie Condon, "GOP Poised to Give Up Financial Reform Filibuster," *CBS News,* April 28, 2010, http://www.cbsnews.com/8301-503544_162-20003704-503544.html.

84. Americans for Financial Reform, "AFR Opposes the Sen. Shelby Substitute on the Consumer Financial Protection Agency," press release, May 5, 2010, http://ourfinancialsecurity.org/2010/05/afr-opposes-the-sen-shelby-substitute-on-the-consumer-financial-protection-agency/.

85. U.S. Congress, *Congressional Record* 156, no. 67 (May 6, 2010): S3305.

86. David Lightman, "Senate Rejects GOP Effort to Weaken Consumer Safeguards," mcclatchy.com, May 6, 2010, http://www.mcclatchydc.com/2010/05/06/v-print/93708/senate-rejects-gop-effort-to-weaken.html. The roll call can be found at http://www.opencongress.org/vote/2010/s/133

87. Securities Industry and Financial Markets Association, "Current Issues," *Washington Weekly,* May 4, 2010, http://www.sifma.org/blastemails/washingtonweekly/washingtonweekly-050710.html.

88. David M. Herszenhorn, "Senate Fails to Advance Financial Reform Bill," *New York Times,* May 19, 2010, http://www.nytimes.com/2010/05/20/business/20regulate.html.

http://cantwell.senate.gov/news/record.cfm?id=325094; http://blogs.alternet.org/speakeasy/2010/05/20/sen-cantwells-courageous-vote/;

89. Carl Hulse, "Maine Senators Break with Republican Party on Stimulus," *New York Times,* February 10, 2009, http://www.nytimes.com/2009/02/11/us/politics/11cong.html.

90. Ben Frumin, "Dems Overcome GOP Filibuster with 60–40 Vote to Advance Financial Reform," *TPM,* May 20, 2010, http://tpmdc.talkingpointsmemo.com/2010/05/senate-votes-to-end-debate-on-financial-reform-bill.php; Matt Loffman, "Wall Street Reform Attains Cloture—60–40," abcnewsgo.com, May 20, 2010, http://abcnews.go.com/blogs/politics/2010/05/wall-street-reform-attains-cloture-senate/.

91. Daniel Indiviglio, "Scott Brown Helps Democrats Push Through Financial Reform," *The Atlantic,* May 20, 2010, http://www.theatlantic.com/business/archive/2010/05/scott-brown-helps-democrats-push-through-financial-reform/57041/; Jia Lynn Yang, "Scott Brown's Key Vote Gives Massachusetts Firms Clout in Financial Overhaul," *Washington Post,* June 23, 2010, http://www.washingtonpost.com/wp-dyn/content/article/2010/06/22/AR2010062205273.html; Pat Garofalo, "Banks Gave Heavily to Scott Brown as He Watered Down Financial Reform," *Think Progress* (blog), December 12, 2010, http://thinkprogress.org/politics/2010/12/12/134614/banks-brown/.

92. David Herszenhorn, "Bill Passed in Senate Broadly Expands Oversight of Wall Street," *New York Times,* May 20, 2010, http://www.nytimes.com/2010/05/21/business/21regulate.html; Donny Shaw, "Dems Win Big Financial Reform Vote," *Open Congress* (blog), May 20, 2010, http://www.opencongress.org/articles/view/1887-Dems-Win-Big-Financial-Reform-Vote; H.R. 4173 (111th): Dodd-Frank Wall Street Reform and Consumer Protection Act (On the Passage of the Bill), undated, http://www.govtrack.us/congress/vote.xpd?vote=s2010-162

At this point, S. 3217 became H.R. 4173, the number of the bill passed by the House in December.

93. David Cho and Binyamin Appelbaum, "Obama's 'Volcker Rule' Shifts Power Away from Geithner," *Washington Post,* January 22, 2010, http://www.washingtonpost.com/wp-dyn/content/article/2010/01/21/AR2010012104935.html; United States Senate Committee on Finance, "Grassley Cloture Vote on Financial Reform," press release, May 20, 2010

http://www.finance.senate.gov/newsroom/ranking/release/?id=c6fd9e8d-7167-4fc9-8cd4-cba95045d19f.

94. Ana Radelat, "Grassley Joins Democrats on Financial Reform Bill," *The Gazette* (Cedar Rapids, IA), May 21, 2010, http://thegazette.com/2010/05/21/grassley-joins-democrats-on-financial-reform-bill/.

95. David Indiviglio, "Scott Brown Helps Democrats Push Through Financial Reform," *The Atlantic,* May 20, 2010, http://www.theatlantic.com/business/archive/2010/05/scott-brown-helps-democrats-push-through-financial-reform/57041/.

96. Eric Dash and Nelson D. Schwartz, "Bank Lobbyists Make a Run at Reform Measures," *New York Times,* June 20, 2010, http://www.nytimes.com/2010/06/21/business/21volcker.html?dbk; Jason Linkins, "Scott Brown's Sweetheart Fin-Reg Deal Needs a Snappy Nickname," *Huffington Post,* June 28, 2010, http://www.huffingtonpost.com/2010/06/28/scott-browns-sweetheart-f_n_627710.html; and Michael Hirsch, "Backroom Deals Weaken Financial-Reform Bill," *The Daily Beast,* July 15, 2010, http://www.thedailybeast.com/newsweek/blogs/the-gaggle/2010/07/15/backroom-deals-weaken-financial-reform-bill.html.

97. Open Secrets and Public Citizen, "Conference Klatch," June 11, 2010, http://www.citizen.org/documents/Conference-Klatch-06-11-2010.pdf.

98. Jim Kuhnhenn, "Key Issues in Paly as Congress Struggles with Financial Rules," *USA Today,* June 13, 2010, http://www.usatoday.com/money/companies/regulation/2010-06-13-financial-overhaul_N.htm.

99. *Side-By-Side Comparison Chart—Key Senate and House Bill Issues* (New York, NY: Davis Polk & Wardwell), June 2, 2010, http://www.davispolk.com/files/Publication/d243b01a-324f-4ccd-85a5-e9bb42d70920/Presentation/PublicationAttachment/c56258f4-0e4e-479e-8632-ea9b08fc2b82/060210_SenateHouseComparisonChart.pdf.

100. Silla Brush, "Frank, Waxman Ironing Out Differences over Financial Regulatory Agency," *The Hill,* December 3, 2009, http://thehill.com/homenews/house/70495-frank-waxman-ironing-out-differences-over-consumer-financial-regulatory-agency.

101. U.S. House of Representatives Committee on Financial Services—Democrats, "Frank Statement on the Energy and Commerce Committee's Manager's Amendment to the CFPA," press release, October 29, 2009, http://democrats.financialservices.house.gov/press/PRArticle.aspx?NewsID=550.

102. Travis Plunkett, interview by the authors, December 21, 2010.

103. Side-By-Side Comparison Chart.

104. Brady Dennis, "Financial Regulation Bill Nears Finish Line with Support from Snowe, Brown," *Washington Post,* July 13, 2010, http://www.washingtonpost.com/wp-dyn/content/article/2010/07/12/AR2010071202628.html.

105. Andrew Ryan, "Popular Brown Also Takes Hits," *Boston Globe,* July 2, 2010, http://www.boston.com/news/local/massachusetts/articles/2010/07/02/popular_brown_also_takes_hits/.

106. H.R. 4173: Dodd-Frank Wall Street Reform and Consumer Protection Act, 111th Cong., http://www.govtrack.us/congress/vote.xpd?vote=s2010-208.

107. The White House, "Remarks by the President at the Singing of Dodd-Frank Wall Street Reform and Consumer Protection Act," press release, Washington, D.C., July 21, 2010, http://www.whitehouse.gov/the-press-office/remarks-president-signing-dodd-frank-wall-street-reform-and-consumer-protection-act.

108. The White House, "Background on the President's Bill Signing Ceremony Today," press release, Washington, D.C., July 21, 2010, http://www.whitehouse.gov/the-press-office/background-presidents-bill-signing-ceremony-today.

109. Nancy Zirkin, interview by authors, Washington, D.C., April 15, 2010.

110. Treasury officials Michael Barr and Eric Stein were praised frequently in our interviews with AFR members.

111. Off-the-record interview by authors.

112. Other constraints included an annual audit by the General Accounting Office, mandatory consultation with other regulators, a requirement to consider the impact of rules on small businesses, and a mandatory cost-benefit analysis of its rules. See Consumer Federation of America, "Accountability of the Consumer Financial Protection Bureau," Washington, D.C., June 11, 2010, http://www.consumerfed.org/pdfs/CFPB-Accountability-fact-sheet-6-11.pdf.

113. Americans for Financial Reform, "Wall Street Reform: The Consumer Financial Protection Bureau," June 30, 2010, http://ourfinancialsecurity.org/2010/06/what-happened-on-wall-street-reform-consumer-financial-protection-bureau/.

Chapter 8

1. Congresssman John Campbell, "Biography," http://campbell.house.gov/index.php?option=com_content&view=article&id=1036&Itemid=37; Anne Schroeder Mullins, "Lawmaking Is Not So Different from Selling Cars," *Politico,* July 15, 2009, http://www.politico.com/news/stories/0709/24929.html.

2. Dena Bunis, "Consumer Groups Blast Rep. Campbell's Car Dealer Exemption," *Orange County Register,* October 22, 2009, http://taxdollars.ocregister.com/2009/10/22/consumer-groups-blast-campbell-amendment-as-a-conflict/40659/; Spencer Kornhaber, "John Campbell Explains His Car Industry Conflict-of-Interest Flip Flop," *OCWeekly Blogs,* June 23, 2010, http://blogs.ocweekly.com/navelgazing/2010/06/john_campbell_explains_his_car.php.

3. "Personal Finances: John Campbell (R-Calif)," accessed September 24, 2012, http://www.opensecrets.org/pfds/candlook.php?CID=N00027565.

4. "Automotive; Money to Congress—All House Candidates, 2010," accessed September 24, 2012, http://www.opensecrets.org/industries/summary.php?ind=M02&cycle=2010&recipdetail=H&mem=N.

5. David Dayen, "CFPA Passes House Committee; Amendment Exempting Auto Dealer Financing Passes, Too," *Firedoglake* (blog), October 22, 2009, http://news.firedoglake.com/2009/10/22/cfpa-passes-house-committee-amendment-exempting-auto-dealer-financing-passes-too/.

6. Catherine Lutz and Anne Lutz Fernandez, "Save Car Buyers from More Bum Rides," *Providence Journal,* June 3, 2010, http://www.projo.com/opinion/contributors/content/CT_lutz3_06-03-10_QQINVND_v8.416b524.html.

7. Delvin Davis and Joshua Frank, "Under the Hood: Auto Loan Interest Rate Hikes Inflate Consumer Costs and Loan Losses," Center for Responsible Lending, (April 19, 2011), http://www.responsiblelending.org/other-consumer-loans/

auto-financing/research-analysis/Under-the-Hood-Auto-Dealer-Rate-Markups-Executive-Summary.pdf.

8. The relationship between dealerships and auto manufacturers' in-house lenders like Ford Credit and GMAC Financial Services is complex. Captive lenders help dealers finance their inventory and purchase loans extended to buyers. Thus, a dealer, acting as a broker for a car buyer, has multiple reasons for considering its manufacturer-based lender when it arranges financing. J.D. Power and Associates reported that in 2010, auto loans from captive lenders outstripped other loan sources by almost 2:1. Consumer advocates claim that dealers often favor captive lenders over credit unions and community bank lenders to the financial detriment of borrowers. Silla Brush, "Auto Exemption Decision Now Lies in Senate Hands," *The Hill,* June 21, 2010, http://thehill.com/business-a-lobbying/104627-auto-exemption-decision-now-lies-in-senate-hands-. Dealers, on the other hand, argue that their relationship to lenders regularly helps customers beat the best deal they can attract on their own. See: National Automobile Dealers Association, "Affordable Auto Finance Preserved in Wall Street Reform Bill," accessed September 24, 2012, http://www.nada.org/legislativeaffairs/economy-financial/dealerfinance.htm.

9. Davis and Frank, "Under the Hood."

10. Raj Date and Brian Reed, "Auto Race to the Bottom," Center Winter Center for Financial Institutions Policy, November 16, 2009, http://www.cambridgewinter.org/Cambridge_Winter/Welcome_files/auto%20finance%20111609.pdf.

11. Raj Date, "Auto Race to the Bottom," *Baseline Scenario* (blog), November 19, 2009, http://baselinescenario.com/2009/11/19/auto-race-to-the-bottom/.

12. National Automobile Dealers Association, "NADA Successful in Effort to Protect Auto Dealer Exclusion in House Financial Reform Bill," press release, December 11, 2009, http://www.nada.org/MediaCenter/News+Releases/2009/NADA+Successful+in+Effort+to+Protect+Auto+Dealer+Exclusion+in+House+Financial+Reform+Bill.htm; Michael Hudson, "Car Dealers Try to Wheedle Their Way Out of Financial Reform," *The Cutting Edge,* June 28, 2010, http://www.thecuttingedgenews.com/index.php?article=12318&pageid=&pagename.

13. Americans for Financial Reform, "Fact Sheet, Car Dealers Are Lenders," May 5, 2010, http://ourfinancialsecurity.org/2010/05/fact-sheet-auto-dealers-are-lenders-pdf/.

14. Americans for Financial Reform, "Fact Sheet: No Carve-Outs for Auto Dealers," May 3, 2010, http://ourfinancialsecurity.org/2010/05/fact-sheet-no-carve-outs-for-auto-dealers/.

15. Ibid.

16. *Regulatory Restructuring: Enhancing Consumer Financial Products Regulation, Hearing Before the Committee on Financial Services,* U.S. House of Representatives, 111th Cong. (2009) Serial 111–49 (Washington, D.C.: Government Printing Office, 2009).

17. Ibid., 2.

18. Discussion Draft of H.R. 3126, September 25, 2009, accessed June 1, 2011, http://democrats.financialservices.house.gov/press/PRArticle.aspx?NewsID=540.

19. Ibid., at section 124(g): Exclusion for Auto Dealers.

20. National Association of Automobile Dealers, "Crisis Timeline: NADA in High Gear," September 16, 2009, accessed December 1, 2011, http://www.nada.org/Advocacy+Outreach/timeline/.

21. David Regan, letter to Hon. Barney Frank regarding H.R. 3126, October 7, 2009, http://newsmanager.commpartners.com/nadah2/downloads/NADA%20on%20CFPA%20dealer%20exemption-final.pdf.

22. A New Way Forward and The Consumer Federation of America and Thirty-Eight Other Organizations, Letter to Reps. Frank and Bachus re H.R. 3126 Consumer Financial Protection Agency: Auto Dealer Exemption, October 7, 2009, http://www.consumerwatchdog.org/resources/cfpaautoloans.pdf.

23. John Campbell and Bill Posey, "Amendment No. 24 to the Discussion Draft of September 25, 2009 of H.R. 3126, October 15, 2009, http://democrats.financialservices.house.gov/Hearings/hearingDetails.aspx?NewsID=801.

24. National Auto Dealers Association, "Crisis Timeline: NADA in High Gear," October 21, 2009, accessed December 1, 2011, http://www.nada.org/Advocacy+Outreach/timeline/.

25. Among the 19 Democrats voting in favor of the Campbell amendment, 11 were members of the Blue Dog or New Democratic Caucuses (or both). The balance was evenly split between members who received higher-than-average campaign contributions from the auto industry (Reps. Ackerman, Maloney, Adler and Clay) and those who received very little (Reps. Green, Cleaver, Driehaus and Kilroy). "Dems Voting to Exempt Auto Dealers from Financial Oversight Receive More Money," (no author), (November 4, 2009). Accessed December 1, 2011, http://maplight.org/dems-voting-to-exempt-auto-dealers-from-financial-oversight-receive-more-money. For an interesting statistical analysis of the association between money and voting (using the Campbell amendment as a case), see, "Probability of Campbell Amendment Yes Vote versus Auto Dealer Industry Contribution," (no author), *Firedoglake* (blog), undated, http://my.firedoglake.com/fhc1/tag/campbell-amendment/.

26. Ryan Grim and Arthur Delaney, "The Cash Committee: How Wall Street Wins on the Hill," *Huffington Post*, December 29, 2009. http://www.huffingtonpost.com/2009/12/29/the-cash-committee-how-wa_n_402373.html.

27. Frank Luntz, "The Language of Financial Reform," theworddoctors, Alexandria, Virginia, January 2010), http://timeswampland.files.wordpress.com/2010/04/languageoffinancialreform.pdf.

28. David Dayen, "CFPA Passes House Committee; Amendment Exempting Auto Dealer Financing Passes, Too," *Firedoglake* (blog), October 22, 2009, http://news.firedoglake.com/2009/10/22/cfpa-passes-house-committee-amendment-exempting-auto-dealer-financing-passes-too/.

29. *Congressional Record—House*, December 11, 2009, p. H14750.

30. U.S. Census Bureau, *Statistical Abstract of the United States: 2011*, Table 1056, http://www.census.gov/compendia/statab/2011/tables/11s1056.pdf.

31. James Surowiecki, "Masters of Main Street," *The New Yorker*, July 12, 2010, http://www.newyorker.com/magazine/bios/james_surowiecki/search?contributorName=james%20surowiecki.

32. Eric Lichtblau, "Auto Dealers Campaign to Fend Off Regulation," *New York Times*, May 16, 2010, http://www.nytimes.com/2010/05/17/business/17dealers. html?_r=0. Dealers combined with their PACs and employees to spend $9.3 million on political contributions in 2008.

33. National Association of Automobile Dealers, "New Survey: Majority of Consumers Say Wall Street Reform Should Not Include Auto Dealers," press release, May 10, 2010, http://www.nada.org/MediaCenter/News+Releases/2010/ Majority+of+Consumers+in+Survey+Say+Wall+Street+Reform+Should+Not+ Include+Auto+Dealers.htm

34. Celinda Lake, David Mermin, Rick Johnson, and Zach Young, "Response to Frank Luntz Memo on Financial Reform," memo, Lake Research Partners, February 22, 2010, http://ourfinancialsecurity.org/2010/01/ lake-research-partners-respond-to-luntz-memo/.

35. A New Way Forward et al., letter to Frank and Bachus.

36. The Leadership Conference on Civil and Human Rights (on behalf of 29 organizations), "Oppose Auto Dealer Carve-Out from Consumer Protection," letter to U.S. senators, May 11, 2010, http://www.civilrights.org/advocacy/letters/ pdfs/auto-dealers.pdf; Consumer Federation of America, "The Hidden Markup of Auto Loans," Washington, D.C., January 26, 2004, http://www.consumerfed.org/ elements/www.consumerfed.org/file/Hidden%20Mark%20Up%20of%20 Auto%20Loans%200104.pdf.

37. National Consumer Law Center, "Racial Disparities in Auto Lending: A State-by-State Reminder Why Auto Dealers Must Be Subject to the Consumer Financial Protection Bureau," Boston, May 4, 2010, http://www.responsiblelending. org/other-consumer-loans/auto-financing/research-analysis/Auto-dealer-racial-disparites-NCLC.pdf.

38. Karen P. Varcoe, Nancy B. Lees, Joan Wright, and Neal Emper, "Financial Issues Faced by Marine Corps Families," *Financial Counseling and Planning* 14, no. 1, 2003: 43–50.

39. Admiral Jan Gaudio, interview by authors, Washington, D.C., April 14, 2011.

40. M. S. Archer, "Motor Vehicle Finance Scams Concerning U.S. Service Members," Camp Lejeune, North Carolina, U.S. Marine Corps Office of the Staff Judge Advocate, Marine Corps Installation East, memorandum, November 22, 2009, https://s3.amazonaws.com/s3.documentcloud.org/documents/225319/marines-auto-scams-against-military.pdf.

41. Brady Dennis and Binyamin Appelbaum, "Dodd, Shelby Hit Impasse, Imperiling Financial System Legislation," *Washington Post*, February 6, 2010, http://www.washingtonpost.com/wp-dyn/content/article/2010/02/05/AR20100 20502157.html.

42. Brady Dennis, "Dodd, Corker to Work Together on Financial Reform," *Washington Post*, February 12, 2010, http://www.washingtonpost.com/wp-dyn/ content/article/2010/02/11/AR2010021102400.html.

43. Jim Kuhnhenn, "Dodd, Corker Regulatory Offer Gets Cool Reception," *Real Clear Politics*, March 2, 2010, http://www.realclearpolitics.com/news/ap/

politics/2010/Mar/02/dodd__corker_regulatory_offer_gets_cool_reception.
html.

44. Travis Plunkett, interview by authors, December 22, 2010.

45. Pat Garofalo, "Shelby and Corker Reject Dodd's Watered-Down Consumer Protection Proposal," *Think Progress* (blog), March 1, 2010, http://thinkprogress.org/economy/2010/03/01/173152/corker-shelby-reject/?mobile=nc.

46. Caren Benjamin, interview by authors, February 10, 2011.

47. Eileen Toback, interview by authors, February 5, 2011.

48. *Congressional Record—Senate,* May 4, 2010, page S3104.

49. The amendment was scheduled for vote on May 13 but was postponed until May 24. In the interim, Senator Brownback accepted the Reed-Brown amendment creating an office of service members' affairs in the CFPB. The industry advanced the argument that the new office obviated the need for CFPB regulation. But here is what Senator Dodd had to say about that point: "Here we have the Reed-Brown amendment that says we will establish within the bureau of consumer financial protection an office to protect the men and women in uniform from the abuses of people who would take advantage of them. Then less than 24 hours later we would take away protection for one of the major problems these young men and women have. What an irony. What is this institution saying? . . . That doesn't make any sense to me." See: U.S. Senate Committee on Banking, Housing, and Urban Affairs, "Dodd on Efforts to Carve Out Auto Dealer Financing," press release, May 13, 2010, http://banking.senate.gov/public/index.cfm?FuseAction=Newsroom.PressReleases&ContentRecord_id=9336526d-06de-8ebd-8ceb-9f6579908d75&Region_id=&Issue_id=

50. Letter from Undersecretary of Defense Clifford Stanley to Assistant Secretary of the Treasure Michael Barr, February 26, 2010, cited in Matthew Jaffe, "Pentagon, Celebrities Call for Consumer Protection Agency," *ABC News,* March 9, 2010, http://abcnews.go.com/Business/pentagon-celebrities-call-consumer-protection-agency/story?id=10055192#.UGSW5KPi58E.

51. Ibid. On November 11, 2009, Rep. Brad Miller wrote to Defense Secretary Gates asking the department to do such a survey.

52. The Military Coalition, letter to Chairman Dodd and Ranking Member Shelby, Alexandria, Virginia, April 15, 2010, http://www.themilitarycoalition.org/library/10letters/04152010.pdf.

53. "Even though DoD found scant evidence of problems between service members and dealers in the portion of the government's own database specifically designed to record consumer complaints by service members, the Pentagon instead decided to justify its policy position based on (i) an informal survey where no inquiry was made to ensure the abusive loans were even made by auto dealers, and (ii) case studies by a special interest group with a known bias against auto dealers." See: National Association of Automobile Dealers, letter to U.S. Senators, Washington, D.C., May 20, 2010, http://www.docstoc.com/docs/78531794/May-20_-2010-Dear-Senator-Re-The-Brownback-Amendment-Retains-.

54. Media conference call with Sen. Richard Durbin (D-IL); Sen. Jack Reed (D-RI); and Holly Petraeus, director, Better Business Bureau Military

Line; Subject: Protections for Military Families against Abusive Lending Practices. *Financial Times Information,* May 12, 2010. David Dayen, "Used Car Salesmen Tap Brownback to Protect their Dealmaking in FinReg," *Firedoglake* (blog), May 12, 2010, http://news.firedoglake.com/2010/05/12/used-car-salesmen-tap-brownback-to-protect-their-dealmaking-in-finreg/.

55. Gaudio, interview. Army Secretary John McHugh (May 12, 2010) and Air Force Secretary Michael Donley (May 13, 2010) sent letters to Senator Dodd highlighting the particular impact of auto lender practices on junior grade enlisted personnel. Both letters can be found at Consumers for Auto Reliability and Safety, http://www.carconsumers.org/military_ripoffs.htm.

56. The White House, "Statement by President Obama on Financial Reform," press release, May 12, 2010, http://www.whitehouse.gov/the-press-office/statement-president-obama-financial-reform.

57. Ed Tonkin, "NADA Response to Obama Statement on Financial Reform," press release, National Automobile Dealers Association, May 12, 2010, http://www.nada.org/MediaCenter/News+Releases/2010/NADA+Response+to+Obama+Statement+on+Financial+Reform.htm.

58. Neil Roland, "Political Showdown Brewing over Dealer Financing Regulation," *Automotive News,* May 10, 2010, http://www.autonews.com/apps/pbcs.dll/article?AID=/20100510/RETAIL02/100519986.

59. Susan Weinstock, "Commentary: Auto Dealers are Part of the Problem, Need to be Included in Overhaul of Financial Regulatory System," *Washington Post,* June 14, 2010, http://www.washingtonpost.com/wp-dyn/content/article/2010/06/11/AR2010061105736.html.

60. David Cho, "Financial Overhaul Pits Military against Car Dealers," *Washington Post,* May 12, 2010, http://www.washingtonpost.com/wp-dyn/content/article/2010/05/11/AR2010051104985.html.

61. Gaudio, interview.

62. Pam Banks, interview by authors, February 1, 2011.

63. Nancy Zirkin, interview by authors, April 15, 2011.

64. National Automobile Dealers Association, "Crisis Timeline: NADA in High Gear," May 19, 2010, accessed December 1, 2011, http://www.nada.org/Advocacy+Outreach/timeline/.

65. Caucus members voting for the Brownback Sense of the Senate measure were: Mark Begich (D-AK); Joseph Lieberman (I-CT); Scott Brown (R-MA); John Kerry (D-MA); Amy Klobuchar (D-MN); Ben Nelson (D-NE); Jean Shaheen (D-NH); Frank Lautenberg (D-NJ); Kay Hagan (D-NC) and Kay Hutchison (R-TX). See: "On the Motion (Brownback Motion to Instruct Conferees Re; H.R. 4173), Senate Vote #163, May 24, 2010, Govtrack.us, accessed, December 1, 2011, http://www.govtrack.us/congress/votes/111-2010/s163.

66. Benjamin, interview.

67. David H. Carpenter, *The Dodd-Frank Wall Street Reform and Consumer Protection Act: Title X, The Consumer Financial Protection Bureau.* (Washington, D.C.; Congressional Research Service, R41338, July 21, 2010).

68. Cora Ganzglass, interview by authors, February 16, 2011.

Chapter 9

1. For greater detail, see Arthur Wilmarth Jr., "The Dodd–Frank Act's Expansion of State Authority to Protect Consumers of Financial Services," *Journal of Corporation Law* 36, no. 4 (2011): 895–954.

2. *Code of Federal Regulations,* title 12, sections 559.3(h), 560.2; *Code of Federal Regulations,* title 12, sec. 7.4000.

3. The assertion of the legal doctrine of preemption by less proactive federal financial regulators such as the Office of the Comptroller of the Currency (OCC) had the practical effect of neutering state law enforcement. See *Consumer Protections in Financial Services: Past Problems, Future Solutions: Hearings Before the Committee on Banking, Housing, and Urban Affairs,* U.S. Senate, 111th Cong., March 3, 2009 (Washington, D.C.: U.S. Government Printing Office, 2009) (statement of Patricia McCoy) and Consumer Federation of America, "The Dodd-Frank Act: How States and the Consumer Financial Protection Bureau Will Work Together to Protect Consumers," Fact Sheet, November 4, 2010, http://www.consumerfed.org/financial-services/credit-and-debt/consumer-financial-protection-bureau. In landmark challenges to the application of preemption by the OCC, the U.S. Supreme Court upheld the agency's authority as applied to national banks and their subsidiaries and to federal savings authorities. See, especially, Barnett Bank of Marion County, N.A. v. Nelson, Florida Insurance Commissioner et al., 517 U.S. 25 (1996), Watters v. Wachovia Bank, N.A., 127 S. Ct. 1559 (2007) and National Consumer Law Center Reports, volume 29, July/August 2010. In 2009, however, the Court revised its stance and opened some partial daylight by ruling, in Cuomo v. Clearing House Association, that New York could investigate national banks for instances of lending discrimination—a liberalization of its earlier, more extreme position on federal preemption. 129 S. Ct. 2710 (2009).

4. Democratic committee member Brad Miller (D-NC) allowed that it was the most contentious issue of any on the Democratic side. Ryan Grim, "Bean Amendment Beaten Back (For Now), A Blow to Wall Street," *Huffington Post,* March 18, 2010, http://www.huffingtonpost.com/2009/10/19/bean-amendment-beaten-bac_n_326145.html. According to Michael Calhoun at the Center for Responsible Lending, one of the early preemption issues that AFR fought (and won) was whether rules promulgated by the CFPB would nullify state laws. Would nonbank lenders like payday or auto title lenders be immunized against state laws by a rule adopted by the CFPB? Ironically, the big national banks lined up with advocates in this matter because they wanted their nonbank competitors to be subject to state as well as federal restrictions. (Michael Calhoun, interview by the authors, February 4, 2012.)

5. Progress Illinois, "Madigan on the Hill," March 20, 2009, accessed February 1, 2012, http://progressillinois.com/2009/3/20/madigan-on-the-hill.

6. *Creating a Consumer Financial Protection Agency: A Cornerstone of America's New Foundation: Hearing Before the Committee on Banking, Housing, and Urban Affairs,* U.S. Senate, 111th Cong., July 14, 2009 (Washington: U.S. Government Printing Office, 2009) (testimony of Travis Plunkett), 38.

7. Edmund Mierzwinski, Testimony on H.R. 4490, the First Accounts Act of 2000 and H.R. 4584, June 27, 2000, http://archives.financialservices.house.gov/banking/62700mie.shtml; Letter from Nineteen Groups to the Office of the Comptroller of the Currency, "Preemption of State Anti-Predatory Lending Laws," October 6, 2003, accessed February 1, 2012, www.responsiblelending.org/media . . . /CRL-OCCsignon100603.pdf. The letter stated: "Your proposal to preempt these state anti-predatory lending laws is, at best, misguided, and at worst, a blatant attempt to increase the power of the OCC at the expense of homeowners, the sovereignty of the states, and the intent of Congress."

8. Predatory and abusive practices included prepayment penalties for loans under $150,000. Additional practices that were prohibited included balloon payments (defined as a scheduled payment of more than twice the regular payment); negative amortization loans (in which monthly payments don't even cover all interest charges, let alone a portion of the principal) were banned; and lending without proper consideration for the borrower's ability to repay. See: Baher Azmy, "Squaring the Predatory Lending Circle: A Case for States as Laboratories of Experimentation," *Florida Law Review* 57 (2005): 295–404.

9. Larry Kirsch, "The State Attorney General as Consumer Advocate: A Recent Effort to Tame Unfair Subprime Lending Practices," Columbia University Law School National State Attorneys General Program, 2010, http://www.law.columbia.edu/null?&exclusive=filemgr.download&file_id=541247&rtcontentdisposition=filename%3DThe%20State%20Attorney%20General%20as%20Consumer%20Advocate.pdf.

10. Eliot Spitzer, "Predatory Lenders' Partner in Crime," *Washington Post,* February 14, 2008, http://www.washingtonpost.com/wp-dyn/content/article/2008/02/13/AR2008021302783.html.

11. Lauren Saunders, "The Role of the States under the Dodd-Frank Wall Street Reform and Consumer Protection Act of 2010," National Consumer Law Center, December 2010.

12. Raphael Bostic et al., "The Impact of State Anti-Predatory Lending Laws: Policy Implications and Insights," July 7, 2008, http://www.fdic.gov/bank/analytical/cfr/2008/jan/CFR_SS_2008McCoy.pdf.

13. National Association of Attorneys General, Letter to President Barack Obama Urging Reconsideration of Office of the Comptroller of the Currency's Interpretation of its Authority Under the National Bank Act, Washington, D.C., February 25, 2009, http://www.consumersunion.org/pdf/AGs-ltr-Obama-209.pdf.

14. *Community and Consumer Advocates' Perspectives on the Obama Administration's Financial Regulatory Reform Proposals: Hearings Before the Committee on Financial Services,* U.S. House of Representatives, 111th Cong. 19, July 16, 2009 (Washington: Government Printing Office, 2009)(statement of Nancy Zirkin), 18.

15. *Community and Consumer Advocates' Perspectives on the Obama Administration's Financial Regulatory Reform Proposals,* statement of Travis Plunkett.

16. *Community and Consumer Advocates' Perspectives on the Obama Administration's Financial Regulatory Reform Proposals,* statement of Edmund Mierzwinski.

17. U.S. Department of Treasury, *Financial Regulatory Reform, A New Foundation: Rebuilding Financial Supervision and Regulation,* June 17, 2009, 14, http://www.treasury.gov/initiatives/Documents/FinalReport_web.pdf.

18. *Banking Industry Perspectives on the Obama Administration's Financial Regulatory Reform Proposals: Hearings Before the Committee on Financial Services,* U.S. House of Representatives, 111th Cong. 62, July 15, 2009 (Washington, D.C.: Government Printing Office, 2010)(statement of Hon. Steve Bartlett), 62.

19. *Banking Industry Perspectives on the Obama Administration's Financial Regulatory Reform Proposals,* statement of R. Michael S. Menzies Sr., 163.

20. According to Barney Frank, "The big banks don't have much political power, and the big banks are the ones that care about preemption because they operate in so many states. The community banks were worried about examinations, and that's why we compromised, appropriately, on the examinations. They have political clout.... They're respected members of the community in everybody's district." Binyamin Applebaum, "Big Financial Firms Losing Power on Capitol Hill," *Washington Post,* October 19, 2009, http://www.washingtonpost.com/wp-dyn/content/article/2009/10/18/AR2009101802156.html

21. "Fast Facts for Congress: Congressional District 8, Illinois," U.S. Census Bureau, accessed February 1, 2012, http://www.census.gov/fastfacts/.

22. "Lawmaker Ratings: Rep. Melissa Bean (D-Ill., 8th)," *The Hill,* accessed February 1, 2012, http://thehill.com/resources/lawmaker-ratings/78795-rep-melissa-bean-d-ill.

23. "Melissa Bean," OpenSecrets, accessed February 1, 2012, http://www.opensecrets.org/politicians/summary.php?cid=N00024875&cycle=2008.

24. Kevin Drawbaugh, "Rep. Frank Extracts Vanilla from Consumer Agency," *Reuters,* September 22, 2009, http://www.reuters.com/article/2009/09/22/us-finan cial-regulation-idUSTRE58L6YR20090922?feedType=RSS&feedName=business News;

Jim Puzzanghera, "Obama Administration Retreats on Key Part of Proposed Financial Overhaul," *Los Angeles Times,* September 24, 2009, http://articles.latimes.com/2009/sep/24/business/fi-reg-reform24.

Although Barr was the originator of the plain vanilla mortgage proposal, Professor Warren was a strong proponent of it. See "Prof. Elizabeth Warren on Why We Need the CFPA, Part 2," *Consumer Reports Consumer News,* August 17, 2009, http://news.consumerreports.org/money/2009/08/consumer-reports-consumer-financial-protection-agency-elizabeth-warren-interview-cfpa-plain-vanilla-mortgage-banks-lenders-fi.html.

25. Pat Garofalo, "Financial Services Lobbyists Banking On Moderate Dems To Push For Federal Preemption," *Think Progress* (blog), September 28, 2009, http://thinkprogress.org/economy/2009/09/28/172948/cfpa-dems-preemption/.

26. Victoria McGrane, "Dems Infight Over Pre-emption," *Politico,* September 30, 2009, http://www.politico.com/news/stories/0909/27727.html.

27. Silla Brush, "Controversial Financial Protection Proposal in Spotlight with Hearing," *The Hill,* September 27, 2009, http://thehill.com/business-a-lobbying/60489-controversial-financial-protection-proposal-in-spotlight-with-hearing-this-week.

28. Americans for Financial Reform, Letter to Members of the House of Representatives Opposing the Bean Preemption Amendment to H.R. 4173, December 9, 2009, http://ourfinancialsecurity.org/2009/12/afr-bean-preemption-amdt-loo/.

29. Susan Saulny and Monica Davey, "Illinois Official Moves to Force Governor Out," *New York Times,* December 12, 2008, http://www.nytimes.com/2008/12/13/us/politics/13illinoiscnd.html?emc=tnt&tntemail0=y.

30. Lisa Madigan, attorney general, State of Illinois, Letter to Hon. Melissa L. Bean, October 14, 2009, http://big.assets.huffingtonpost.com/LtrToBean.pdf.

31. Ibid.

32. Edmund Mierzwinski, interview by authors, December 31, 2010.

33. Eileen Toback, interview by authors, February 5, 2011.

34. Illinois attorney general, "Madigan Continues Push for Federal Consumer Financial Protection Agency," press release, October 14, 2009, http://www.illinoisattorneygeneral.gov/pressroom/2009_10/20091014.html; Illinois Radio Network, "Push for Formation of Consumer Financial Protection Agency," October 14, 2009, http://www.citizenaction-il.org/node/60.

35. Ben Clark, interview by authors, February 18, 2011.

36. Ibid.

37. Bill Swindell, "Finance: Bean to Drop Pre-emption Vote in Markup," *Firedoglake* (blog), October 19, 2009, http://my.firedoglake.com/knoxville/2009/10/19/do-rep-melissa-bean-rep-barney-frank-have-a-deal/; Binyamin Appelbaum, "Big Financial Firms."

38. Stephen Labaton and David Stout, "Compromise Bill Could Block States on Bank Rules," *New York Times,* October 21, 2009, http://www.nytimes.com/2009/10/22/business/22comptroller.html; Ryan Grim, "Bean Amendment."

39. Brady Dennis, "Finance Panel At Odds over Preemption," *Washington Post,* October 21, 2009, http://www.washingtonpost.com/wp-dyn/content/article/2009/10/20/AR2009102003591.html.

40. Ryan Grim, "Bank-Friendly Dems Shut Down House, Threaten to Kill Wall Street Reform," *Huffington Post Politics* (blog), March 18, 2010, http://www.huffingtonpost.com/2009/12/09/bank-friendly-dems-shut-d_n_386200.html.

41. Mike Elk, "Wall Street's Favorite Democrat Melissa Bean Aims to Weaken Current Bank Regulation," *Huff Post Politics* (blog), December 8, 2009, http://www.huffingtonpost.com/mike-elk/wall-streets-favorite-dem_b_384206.html.

42. National Association of Attorneys General, Letter to Senators Christopher Dodd and Richard Shelby and Representatives Barney Frank and Spencer Bachus Regarding Preemption and the Consumer Financial Protection Agency, Washington, D.C., November 4, 2009, http://www.azag.gov/press_releases/nov/2009/Consumer%20Financial%20Protection%20Preemption%20Release.html.

43. Lei Ding, Roberto Quercia, and Alan White, "State Anti-Predatory Lending Laws: Impact and Federal Preemption Phase I Descriptive Analysis," Center for Community Capital, University of North Carolina, Chapel Hill, October 5, 2009, http://www.ccc.unc.edu/documents/Phase_I_report_Final_Oct5,2009_Clean.pdf.

44. Americans for Financial Reform, Letter to Members of the House of Representatives in Opposition to the Bean Preemption Amendment to H.R. 4173, Washington, D.C., December 9, 2009, http://ourfinancialsecurity.org/2009/12/afr-bean-preemption-amdt-loo/http://ourfinancialsecurity.org/2009/12/afr-supports-h-r-4173/. The advocates wrote: "While we support the original Administration preemption provisions, the Watt-Frank amendment strikes an appropriate compromise, allowing preemption of state laws but only when truly necessary to avoid interfering with the business of banking."

45. Ryan Grim, "Bank-Friendly Dems Shut Down House, Threaten To Kill Wall Street Reform," *Huffington Post,* March 18, 2010, http://www.huffingtonpost.com/2009/12/09/bank-friendly-dems-shut-d_n_386200.html.

46. Victoria McGrane, "Moderates Win Wall St. Bill Changes," *Politico,* December 9, 2009, http://www.politico.com/news/stories/1209/30429.html.

47. Michael Calhoun, telephone interview with authors, February 4, 2011.

48. *Perspectives on the Consumer Financial Protection Agency: Hearing Before the Comm. on Financial Services,* U.S. House of Representatives, 111th Cong. 156, September 30, 2009 (Washington, D.C.: U.S. Government Printing Office, 2010) (statement of Edward L. Yingling).

49. Saunders, The Role of the States.

50. Pam Banks, interview by authors, February 1, 2011.

51. Damon Silvers, interview by authors, May 4, 2011.

52. "Lawmakers Ratings: Sen. Tom Carper (D-Del.)," *The Hill,* http://thehill.com/resources/lawmaker-ratings/76069-sen-tom-carper-d-del; Zach Carter, "Tom Carper is Attacking Consumers and Defending Wall Street," OurFuture.org, May 12, 2010, http://institute.ourfuture.org/blog-entry/2010051912/tom-carper-attacking-consumers-and-defending-wall-street. Between 2005 and 2011, Carper's main campaign contributors came from the banking, law, insurance and securities sectors. Citigroup, JP Morgan, Wells Fargo, and Bank of America were among his top five financial supporters. See: "Senator Thomas 'Tom' Carper's Campaign Finances," Project Vote Smart, accessed February 1, 2010, http://votesmart.org/candidate/campaign-finance/22421/tom-carper;

53. As one indication of the growing support for the Carper amendment, a "call for action" put out by a progressive grass roots campaign on May 13 put 20 senators into the "leaning-opposed" or "undecided" categories. When the vote came in, only 3 of the 20 on the list actually voted against the amendment. Interestingly, one of them was Senate Majority Leader Harry Reid who voted against his leadership's position and against Senator Dodd's recommendation. Zephyr Teachout, "Whip the Senate on Carper's Let-Banks-Violate-the-Law Amendment!" A New Way Forward, accessed February 1, 2012, http://www.anewwayforward.org/2010/05/13/whip-the-senate-on-carpers-let-banks-violate-the-law-amendment/.

54. Lauren Saunders, "NCLC: Dodd-Carper Deal on Preemption Does Not Give in to All Banks Demands," Americans for Financial Reform, May 19, 2010, http://ourfinancialsecurity.org/2010/05/nclc-dodd-carper-deal-on-preemption-does-not-give-in-to-all-bank-demands/.

55. David Dayen, "Carper Compromise on Pre-emption Likely to Pass," *Fire-doglake* (blog), May 18, 2010, http://news.firedoglake.com/2010/05/18/carper-com promise-on-pre-emption-likely-to-pass/.

56. Ibid.

57. "AFR's Conference Priorities," Americans for Financial Reform, June 15, 2010, http://ourfinancialsecurity.org/2010/06/afrs-confereence-priorities/.

58. Stacy Kaper and Rob Blackwell, "Endgame: After 20-Hour Session, Reform Talks Yield Final Bill," *American Banker,* June 24, 2010, http://www.americanbanker.com/issues/175_121/reg-reform-1021404–1.html?zkPrintable=1& nopagination=1.

59. Americans for Financial Reform, "Real Reform Won't Allow National Banks to Ignore State Laws Targeting New Abuses Not Yet Addressed in Federal Law," June 2010, accessed February 1, 2012, http://www.nclc.org/images/pdf/regulatory_reform/recommendations-fin-reform.pdf.

60. Lauren Saunders, "The Role of the States." Another assessment of the impact of Dodd-Frank on preemption can be found in: Jared Elosta, "Dynamic Federalism and Consumer Financial Protection: How the Dodd-Frank Act Changes the Preemption Debate," *North Carolina Law Review* 89 (2010–2011): 1273.

61. Lauren Saunders, *The Role of the States,* page 7.

62. David Carpenter, "The Dodd-Frank Wall Street Reform and Consumer Protection Act: Title X, Consumer Financial Protection Bureau," Congressional Research Service, Washington, D.C., July 21, 2010.

63. Lauren Saunders, interview by the authors, Washington, D.C., December 3, 2010.

Chapter 10

1. This is an example of what Harvard professor Theda Skocpol refers to as "multiplex associations." She writes: "Americans need to find ways to extend or build multiplex associations. The biggest challenge, or course, is to recreate associational ties across class lines while progressing toward racial and gender integration." Theda Skocpol, "Advocates without Members: The Recent Transformation of American Civic Life," in *Civic Engagement in American Democracy,* ed. by Theda Skocpol and Morris P. Fiorina (Washington, D.C.: Brookings Institution Press, 1999, 461–510.

2. We use the term "success" advisedly, acknowledging the difficulty of precisely identifying the impact of social movements. Indeed, sociologists and political scientists agonize over the task of measuring movement effects. Some researchers opt for quantitative approaches that measure the results of multiple episodes of social movement activity, whereas others analyze a single campaign in depth. The current study falls in the latter category. For some recent efforts to grapple with the issue of movement impacts, quantitatively, see: Frank R. Baumgartner et al., *Lobbying and Political Change* (Chicago: University of Chicago Press, 2009), and Kay Lehman Schlozman, Sidney Verba, and Henry E. Brady, *The Unheavenly Chorus* (Princeton, NJ: Princeton University Press, 2012).

For recent case studies, see, Daniel M. Cress and David A. Snow, "The Outcomes of Homeless Mobilization: The Influence of Organization, Disruption, Political Mediation, and Framing," *The American Journal of Sociology* 105, no. 4 (2000): 1063–104; William T. Gormley Jr. and Helen Cymrot, "The Strategic Choices of Child Advocacy Groups," *Nonprofit and Voluntary Sector Quarterly* 35, no. 1 (2006): 102–22; and Christopher M. Weible and Paul A. Sabatier, "Comparing Policy Networks: Marine Protected Areas in California," *The Policy Studies Journal* 33, no. 2 (2005): 181–201. For a review of scholarship on social movement impacts, see: Edwin Amenta et al., "The Political Consequences of Social Movements," *Annual Review of Sociology* 36 (2010): 287–307. In addition to the problems of *assigning* credit to social movements, social scientists are increasingly sensitive to the processes by which movements claim credit for political outcomes, often through myths and stories. See: David S. Meyer, "Claiming Credit: Stories of Movement Influences," *Mobilization: An International Journal* 11, no. 3 (2006): 201–29 and David S. Meyer and Deana A Rohlinger, "Big Books and Social Movements: A Myth of Ideas and Social Change," *Social Problems* 59, no. 1 (2012): 136–53.

    3. Ruth Mandell, "What the New Consumer Protection Bureau Means to You," *Market Watch,* July 15, 2010, accessed August 27, 2012. http://articles.marketwatch.com/2010-07-15/finance/30765183_1_consumer-financial-protection-new-consumer-bank-reform-bill

    4. "Consumer Federation of America Applauds Senate Vote on the Dodd-Frank Financial Reform Bill," July 15, 2010, accessed August 27, 2012, http://www.consumerfed.org/pdfs/PR_Senate_Cloture071510.pdf.

    5. Heather Booth, "V-I-C-T-O-R-Y!!!" *Huffington Post,* July 15, 2010, accessed August 28, 2012, http://www.huffingtonpost.com/heather-booth/v-i-c-t-o-r-y_b_648262.html).

    6. Rob Blackwell, "In Surprise Move, Top ABA Exec to Step Down," *American Banker* 175, no. 104, July 8, 2010, 1.

    7. Elizabeth Warren, "Bullshit-Professionally Speaking," accessed August 28, 2012, http://www.creditslips.org/creditslips/2009/01/bullshitprofessionally-speaking.html).

    8. The Credit CARD Act of 2009 was an exception inasmuch as it dealt with a broad range of credit card practices, but like the Dodd-Frank Act, it was passed in the context of a major recession.

    9. *Regulatory Restructuring: Enhancing Consumer Financial Products Regulation: Hearing before the Committee on Financial Services,* U.S. House of Representatives, 111th Cong., June 24, 2009 (Washington, D.C.: Government Printing Office, 2009) (statement of Elizabeth Warren).

    10. John Kingdon, *Agendas, Alternatives, and Public Policies,* 2nd ed. (Boston: Little, Brown & Company, 1995); Michael Mintrom and Phillipa Norman, "Policy Entrepreneurship and Policy Change," *The Policy Studies Journal* 37, no. 4 (2009): 649–67; Nancy C. Roberts and Paula King, "Policy Entrepreneurs: Their Activity Structure and Function in the Policy Process," *Journal of Public Administration Research and Theory* 1, no. 2 (1991): 147–75.

11. Jeff Berry and colleagues argue that the strategy of reframing has succeeded only infrequently. Jeffrey Berry et al., "Washington: the Real No-Spin Zone," paper prepared for delivery at the Annual Meeting of the American Political Science Association, August 30–September 2, 2007, Chicago, Illinois, accessed August 28, 2012, http://ase.tufts.edu/polsci/faculty/berry/NoSpinZone.pdf. Numerous case studies of public policy in the United States and elsewhere, however, do introduce successful examples. See: Zhenhua Chen, "Is the Policy Window Open for High-Speed Rail in the United States: A Perspective from the Multiple Streams Model of Policymaking," *Transportation Law Journal* 38, no. 2 (2011): 116–42; and Nissim Cohen, "Policy Entrepreneurs and the Design of Public Policy: Conceptual Framework and the Case of the National Health Insurance Law in Israel," *Journal of Social Research and Policy* 3, no. 1 (2002): 1–19. Still other cases present a mixed picture, for example, Robert Schwartz and Allan McConnell, "Do Crises Help Remedy Regulatory Failure? A Comparative Study of the Walkerton Water and Jerusalem Banquet Hall Disasters," *Canadian Public Administration* 52, no. 1 (2009): 91–112.

12. According to Mintrom and Norman, "Policy entrepreneurs can be identified by their efforts to promote significant policy change," (p. 651). See note 10 above. They may or may not be successful, depending in large measure on pertinent contextual factors, but they tend to have large rather than smaller, more incremental goals.

13. The similarities include attentiveness to environmental opportunities conducive to change, strategic definition and framing of the problem, expanding and working in teams and networked environments, and attention to the feasibility of proposed solutions.

14. For an interesting case of prolonged and ultimately unfulfilled policy entrepreneurship in which a shift in public support for export-led economic growth failed to materialize, see: John Hogan, "A Comparative Examination of the Nature of Change in Macroeconomic Policies," *Nordic Journal of Political Economy* 36, no. 4 (2010): 1–19.

15. Janice Bowdler, interview by authors, May 9, 2011.

16. Schlozman, Verba, and Brady, *The Unheavenly Chorus*.

17. Albert Hirschman, *Exit, Voice, and Loyalty: Responses to Decline in Firms, Organizations, and States* (Cambridge, MA: Harvard University Press, 1970).

18. Edmund Mierzwinski, interview by authors, December 31, 2010.

19. David S. Meyer and Suzanne Staggenborg, "Thinking About Strategy," paper prepared for delivery at American Sociological Association, Collective Behavior/Social Movement Section's Workshop, "Movement Cultures, Strategies, and Outcomes," August 9–10, 2007, Hofstra University, Hempstead, New York.

20. Bill Ragen, interview by authors, March 17, 2011.

21. Sarah Byrnes, "Is the Consumer Movement a 'Horseless Headman'?" *Caveatemptor* (blog), April 30, 2008, accessed September 9, 2012, http://caveatemptorblog.com/is-the-consumer-movement-a-horseless-headman.

22. Barney Frank, commencement speaker at School of Public Affairs, American University, May 9, 2009, accessed September 9, 2012, http://www.american.edu/media/20090509_School_of_Public_Affairs_Commencement.cfm.

23. U.S. Senate Roll Call Votes of the 111th Congress, 2nd Session, Vote Summary Carper Amendment No. 4071, May 18, 2010, accessed September 9, 2012, http://www.senate.gov/legislative/LIS/roll_call_lists/roll_call_vote_cfm.cfm?congress=111&session=2&vote=00155.

24. Bill Ragen, interview by authors, March 17, 2011.

25. Catherine Rampell, "Young and in Debt," *New York Times,* February 26, 2009, accessed September 6, 2012, http://economix.blogs.nytimes.com/2009/02/26/young-and-in-debt/. Private student loans for college and graduate education have been identified as a major new source of predatory lending abuse. In 2007–2008, 14 percent of students had private loans (up from 5% in 2003–2004). These loans amounted to $15 billion in 2007–2008. Uncapped, variable rate loans, especially those made to low-income students, have resulted in very high default rates, often exceeding 50 percent. A coalition called the Project on Student Debt (many of whose members were also affiliated with AFR) actively sought full enforcement of the private student loan business by the CFPB. See: Project on Student Debt, "Sallie Mae's Private Loans Exempt from Financial Reform Bill?" press release, Washington, D.C., May 3, 2010, http://projectonstudentdebt.org/files/pub/CFPB_NR_May3.pdf (accessed September 7, 2012).

26. Heather McGhee, "Moyers & Company," PBS television program, February 10, 2012, http://billmoyers.com/segment/heather-mcghee-on-the-millennial-generation/ (accessed August 28, 2012).

27. William A. Galston and Elaine C. Kamarck, "Change You Can Believe In Needs A Government You Can Trust," A Third Way Report, November 2008, http://www.agsfoundation.com/data/product/file/176/Third_Way_-_Trust_in_Government_Report.pdf (accessed September 9, 2012).

28. Frank Luntz, "The Language of Financial Reform," theworddoctors, Alexandria, Virginia, January 2010, accessed September 9, 2012, http://timeswampland.files.wordpress.com/2010/04/languageoffinancialreform.pdf.

29. Stanley B. Greenberg, "Why Voters Tune Out Democrats," *The New York Times,* July 30, 2011, http://www.nytimes.com/2011/07/31/opinion/sunday/tuning-out-the-democrats.html?pagewanted=all (accessed September 12, 2012).

30. Andy Kroll, "Occupy Wall Street, Powered by Big Labor," *Mother Jones,* October 5, 2011, http://www.motherjones.com/politics/2011/10/occupy-wall-street-labor-unions (accessed September 8, 2012).

31. "Big Business, Corporte Profits, and the Minimum Wage," Data Brief, National Employment Law Project, New York, New York, July 2012, http://nelp.3cdn.net/e555b2e361f8f734f4_sim6btdzo.pdf (accessed September 9, 2012).

32. Schlozman, Verba, and Brady, *The Unheavenly Chorus.*

33. David Brooks, "Where Are the Liberals?" *The New York Times,* January 9, 2012; Michael McCann, *Taking Reform Seriously: Perspectives on Public Interest Liberalism* (Ithaca, NY: Cornell University Press, 1986).

34. Robert Reich, "Fix Income Inequality, Fix the Economy," *Christian Science Monitor,* November 4, 2011. http://www.csmonitor.com/Business/Robert-Reich/2011/1104/Fix-income-inequality-fix-the-economy (accessed September 9, 2012).

35. Patrick Barry, "Heather Booth and Gale Cincotta: From Grass-Roots Troublemakers to National Leaders," *Illinois Issues* (January 1989), 26.

Afterword

1. Norman I. Silber teaches consumer law and writes about the history of the consumer movement at Hofstra Law School and Yale Law School. Well before the arrival of the "Great Recession" of 2008, he followed Elizabeth Warren's work as a fellow commercial law/consumer law professor, and while serving on the board of *Consumer Reports* he read the arguments she made, together with Professor Oren Bar-Gill, favoring the creation of a commission to regulate the safety of consumer financial products. He and Professor Jeff Sovern at St. John's Law School principally drafted the letter of support for the proposed agency that was endorsed by more than 85 other law teachers and presented to Congress. This Afterword is based on an exchange of correspondence between authors Silber, Kirsch and Mayer, and Elizabeth Warren, during the winter and spring of 2012, and all quotations in this Afterword refer to this correspondence. Special thanks to Dan Geldon for helping to arrange it.

Selected Bibliography

Americans for Financial Reform. "Restoring Oversight and Accountability to Financial Markets." July 10, 2009. Accessed February 1, 2011. http://ourfinancialsecurity.org/2009/07/position-papers/.

Andrews, Suzanna. "The Woman Who Knew Too Much." *Vanity Fair,* November 2011, http://www.vanityfair.com/politics/features/2011/11/elizabeth-warren-201111.

Baker, Dean, et al. "Restoring Oversight and Accountability to Financial Markets." Position paper from Americans for Financial Reform, July 10, 2009. http://ourfinancialsecurity.org/2009/07/position-papers/.

Barr, Michael, Sendhil Mullainathan, and Eldar Shafir. "Behaviorally Informed Financial Services Regulation." New America Foundation, October 2008, Accessed May 17, 2010. http://www.newamerica.net/files/naf_behavioral_v5.pdf.

Battista, Andrew. *The Revival of Labor Liberalism.* Urbana, IL: University of Illinois Press, 2008.

Bernanke, Ben S. "Monetary Policy and the Housing Bubble." Speech presented at the Annual Meeting of the American Economic Association, Atlanta, Georgia, January 3, 2010. http://www.federalreserve.gov/newsevents/speech/bernanke20100103a.htm.

Booth, Heather. "Heather Booth: Living the Movement Life, Memoirs and Biographies." Interview (undated) conducted by Becky Kluchin and edited by Gina Caneva. Chicago Women's Liberation Union Herstory. http://www.uic.edu/orgs/cwluherstory/CWLUMemoir/Booth.html.

Boyte, Harry C., Heather Booth, and Steve Max. *Citizen Action and the New American Populism.* Philadelphia: Temple University Press, 1986.

Caliari, Aldo. "Drawing Lessons from U.S. Financial Reform Efforts: A Civil Society Perspective." Washington, D.C.: Center of Concern, February 2011. www.networkideas.org/featart/mar2011/aldo_caliari.pdf.

Cohen, Lizabeth. "Colston E. Warne Lecture: Is it Time for Another Round of Consumer Protection? The Lessons of Twentieth-Century U.S. History." *Journal of Consumer Affairs* 44, no. 1 (2010): 234–46.

Date, Raj. "Losing the Last War: Evaluating 'Veto' Powers on Consumer Financial Protection." Cambridge Winter Center for Financial Institutions Policy,

March 21, 2010. http://cambridgewinter.org/Cambridge_Winter/Archives/Entries/2010/3/21_LOSING_THE_LAST_WAR_files/cfpa%20veto%20032110_1.pdf.

Doss, Natalie. "The Progressive: For Over Forty Years, Heather Booth has Worked to Build a Small-d Democracy." *Chicago Weekly,* January 7, 2010, http://chicagoweekly.net/2010/01/07/the-progressive-for-over-forty-years-heather-booth-has-worked-to-build-a-small-d-democracy.

Draut, Tamara. "A Financial Product Safety Commission: The Need and the Challenge." Paper presented at the Meeting of the Tobin Project, Harvard University, Cambridge, Massachusetts, May 2009. http://people.hmdc.harvard.edu/~dcarpent/finreg/FPSC-Tobin.pdf.

Draut, Tamara, et al. "The Plastic Safety Net: The Reality behind Debt in America." DEMOS and the Center for Responsible Lending, October 2005, http://www.responsiblelending.org/credit-cards/research-analysis/DEMOS-101205.pdf.

Engel, Kathleen C., and Patricia A. McCoy. *The Subprime Virus.* New York: Oxford University Press, 2011.

Graham, Ann. "The Consumer Financial Protection Agency: Love It Or Hate It, U.S. Financial Regulation Needs It." *Villanova Law Review* 55, no. 3 (2010): 603–26.

Greenberg, Stan. "Why Voters Tune Out Democrats." *New York Times,* July 31, 2011, p. SR-1.

Grim, Ryan, and Arthur Delaney. "The Cash Committee: How Wall Street Wins on the Hill." *Huffington Post,* March 18, 2010, http://www.huffingtonpost.com/2009/12/29/the-cash-committee-how-wa_n_402373.html.

Hamscher, Jane. "Americans for Financial Reform: Waste. Of. Time." *Firedoglake,* June 29, 2009, http://fdlaction.firedoglake.com/2009/06/29/americans-for-financial-reform-waste-of-time/.

Kamenetz, Anya. "It's Banks vs. Families, Who Will Come Out on Top? Q&A with Elizabeth Warren." *Fast Company,* March 11, 2010, http://www.fastcompany.com/1578370/elizabeth-warren-its-banks-vs-families.

Kesselman, Amy, Heather Booth, Vivian Rothstein, and Naomi Weisstein. "Our Gang of Four: Friendships and Women's Liberation." In *The Feminist Memoir Project: Voices from Women's Liberation,* edited by Rachel Blau DePlessis and Ann Snitow, 25–53. New York: Three Rivers Press, 1998.

Kirsch, Larry. "The State Attorney General as Consumer Advocate: A Recent Effort to Tame Unfair Subprime Lending Practices." Columbia Law School, National State Attorneys General Program, 2010. http://www.law.columbia.edu/null?&exclusive=filemgr.download&file_id=541247&rtcontentdisposition=filename%3DThe%20State%20Attorney%20General%20as%20Consumer%20Advocate.pdf.

Klein, Ezra. "Elizabeth Warren on Elizabeth Warren." *Washington Post,* September 17, 2010. http://voices.washingtonpost.com/ezra-klein/2010/09/elizabeth_warren_on_elizabeth.html.

Lake Research Partners. "Response to Frank Luntz Memo on Financial Reform." Memorandum, February 22, 2010. http://ourfinancialsecurity.org/blogs/wp-content/ourfinancialsecurity.org/uploads/2010/01/luntz_response.f.022210.pdf

Levitin, Adam J. "The Consumer Financial Protection Agency." Pew Financial Reform Project Briefing Paper No. 3. Washington, D.C., 2009. http://www.pew trusts.org/uploadedFiles/wwwpewtrustsorg/Reports/Financial_Reform/Pew-Levitan-CFPA.pdf

Luntz, Frank. "The Language of Financial Reform." theworddoctors, Alexandria, Virginia, January 2010. http://timeswampland.files.wordpress.com/2010/04/languageoffinancialreform.pdf.

Lusardi, Annarmaria, Daniel Schneider, and Peter Tufano. "Financially Fragile Households: Evidence and Implications." Brookings Papers on Economic Activity (Spring 2011): 83–134. http://www.brookings.edu/~/media/projects/bpea/spring%202011/2011a_bpea_lusardi.

McGhee, Heather C., and Tamara Draut. "Why We Need an Independent Consumer Financial Protection Agency Now." DEMOS Briefing Paper, March 1, 2010. http://www.demos.org/publication/why-we-need-independent-consumer-protection-agency

Mierzwinski, Edmund. "Consumer Protection 2.0—Protecting Consumers in the 20th Century." Journal of Consumer Affairs 44, no. 3 (2010): 578–97.

National Association of Automobile Dealers. "Crisis Timeline: NADA in High Gear." September 16, 2009. Accessed December 1, 2011. http://www.nada.org/Advocacy+Outreach/timeline/.

Plunkett, Travis. "The Regulatory Structure and Consumer Credit Protections." Harvard University Joint Center for Housing Studies, August 2010. http://www.jchs.harvard.edu/sites/jchs.harvard.edu/files/mf10-13.pdf.

Reitzes, Donald C., and Dietrich C. Reitzes. The Alinsky Legacy: Alive and Kicking. Greenwich, CT: JAI Press Inc., 1987.

Saunders, Lauren. "The Role of the States under the Dodd-Frank Wall Street Reform and Consumer Protection Act of 2010." Boston: National Consumer Law Center, December 2010.

Sullivan, Teresa, Elizabeth Warren, and Jay L. Westbrook. As We Forgive Our Debtors: Consumer Credit and Bankruptcy in America. New York: Oxford University Press, 1989.

Surowiecki, James. "Masters of Main Street." The New Yorker, July 12, 2010, http://www.newyorker.com/magazine/bios/james_surowiecki/search?contributorName=james%20surowiecki.

Tomasky, Michael. "The Elizabeth Warren Story." Guardian.co.uk, July 20, 2010. http://www.guardian.co.uk/commentisfree/michaeltomasky/2010/jul/20/obama-administration-finreg-consumers-warren.

Warren, Elizabeth. "The Economics of Race: When Making It to the Middle Is Not Enough." Washington & Lee Law Review 61 (2004): 1777–99.

Warren, Elizabeth. "A Fair Deal for Families: The Need for a Financial Products Safety Commission." Paper presented at Risk Working Group Meeting of the Tobin Project, Harvard University, Cambridge, Massachusetts, May 6, 2007. http://www.tobinproject.org/news-article/may-2007-risk-working-group-meeting.

Warren, Elizabeth. "Joanne Alter Women in Government Lecture." Presentation at the Chicago Humanities Festival, Chicago, Illinois, February 23, 2011. http://

www.consumerfinance.gov/speech/joanne-alter-women-in-govern
ment-lecture/.

Warren, Elizabeth. "Three Myths about the Consumer Financial Product Agency."
The Baseline Scenario, July 21, 2009. http://baselinescenario.com/2009/07/21/
three-myths-about-the-consumer-financial-product-agency/.

Warren, Elizabeth. "Unsafe at any Rate." *Democracy* 5 (Summer 2007): 8–19.

Warren, Elizabeth, Teresa A. Sullivan, and Jay Lawrence Westbrook. *The Fragile
Middle Class: Americans in Debt.* New Haven: Yale University Press, 2000.

Warren, Elizabeth, and Amelia Warren Tyagi. *The Two-Income Trap.* New York:
Basic Books, 2003.

Zywicki, Todd J., and Stefanie Haeffele-Balch. "Loans are Not Toasters: The Problem with a Consumer Financial Protection Agency." *Mercatus on Policy,* no.
60, Mercatus Center, George Mason University, October 2009. http://mercatus.
org/sites/default/files/publication/MOP_-_60_Loans_are_not_Toasters_
web.pdf.

Congressional and Other Public Documents

*Addressing the Need for Comprehensive Regulatory Reform: Hearing before the
Committee on Financial Services,* U.S. House of Representatives, 111th Cong.,
March 26, 2009 (Washington, D.C.: Government Printing Office, 2009) (state-
ment of Timothy Geithner, Secretary of the Treasury).

*Banking Industry Perspectives on the Obama Administration's Financial Regulatory
Reform Proposals: Hearings Before the Committee on Financial Services,* U.S.
House of Representatives, 111th Cong., July 15, 2009 (Washington, D.C.:
Government Printing Office, 2010) (statements of Hon. Steve Bartlett, John
Courson, R. Michael S. Menzies Sr., Chris Stinebert, Edward L. Yingling,
Steven I. Zeisel, and Todd J. Zywicki).

Carpenter, David. The Dodd-Frank Wall Street Reform and Consumer Protection
Act: Title X, the Consumer Financial Protection Bureau, Congressional Research Service R41338, Washington, D.C., July 21, 2010.

*Community and Consumer Advocates' Perspectives on the Obama Administration's
Financial Regulatory Reform Proposals: Hearings Before Committee on Financial
Services,* U.S. House of Representatives, 111th Cong., June 16, 2009 (Washington, D.C.: Government Printing Office, 2009) (statements of Edmund Mierzwinski, Janet Murguia, Travis Plunkett, John Taylor, Nancy Zirkin).

Congressional Oversight Panel, Special Report on Regulatory Reform, January,
2009, http://cybercemetery.unt.edu/archive/cop/20110401232141/http://cop.
senate.gov/reports/library/report-012909-cop.cfm.

*Creating a Consumer Financial Protection Agency: A Cornerstone of America's New
Foundation: Hearing Before the Committee on Banking, Housing, and Urban
Affairs,* U.S. Senate, 111th Cong., July 14, 2009 (Washington, D.C.: U.S. Gov-
ernment Printing Office) (statements of Michael S. Barr, Richard Blumen-
thal, Sendhil Mullainathan, Travis B. Plunkett, Peter Wallison, and Edward L.
Yingling).

The Credit Cardholders' Bill of Rights (H.R. 5244): Hearing of the Sub-Committee on Financial Institutions and Consumer Credit of the Committee on Financial Services, U.S. House of Representatives, 110th Cong., April 17, 2008 (Washington, D.C.: Government Printing Office, 2008 (statements Edmund Mierzwinski, Travis Plunkett, and Linda Sherry).

Credit Card Practices: Current Consumer and Regulatory Issues: Hearing before the Committee on Financial Services, U.S. House of Representatives, 110th Cong., April 26, 2007 (Washington, D.C.: Government Printing Office, 2007) (statement of Arthur Wilmarth Jr.).

Credit Card Practices that Undermine Consumer Safety: Hearing Before the Sub-Committee on Financial Institutions and Consumer Credit Of the Committee on Financial Services, U.S. House of Representatives, 110th Cong., March 13, 2008 (statement of Elizabeth Warren), http://archives.financialservices.house.gov/hearing110/warren031308.pdf.

Economic Outlook: Hearing before the Joint Economic Committee, U.S. Congress, 110th Cong., March, 28, 2007 (Washington, D.C.: U.S. Government Printing Office, 2007) (statement of Ben Bernanke, Chair Board of Governors, Federal Reserve System).

The Effect of Current Credit Card Industry Practices on Consumers: Hearing before the Committee on Banking, Housing and Urban Affairs, U.S. Senate, 110th Cong., January 25, 2007 (statement of Travis Plunkett). http://bank ing.senate.gov/public/index.cfm?FuseAction=Files.View&FileStore_id= 766faff0-2501-43ac-ae39-791b0d883585.

Examining the Billing, Marketing, and Disclosure Practices of the Credit Card Industry and Their Impact on Consumers: Hearing Before the Committee on Banking, Housing and Urban Affairs, U.S. Senate, 110th Cong., January 25, 2007 (Washington, D.C.: Government Printing Office, 2009) (statement of Elizabeth Warren).

Improving Federal Consumer Protection in Financial Services: Hearing before the Committee on Financial Services, U.S. House of Representatives, 110th Cong., June 13, 2007 (Washington, D.C.: Government Printing Office, 2007) (statement of Hon. Sheila C. Bair).

Legislative Proposals On Reforming Mortgage Practices: Hearing before the Committee on Financial Services, U.S. House of Representatives, 110th Cong., October 24, 2007 (Washington, D.C.: Government Printing Office, 2008) (statement of Hon. Sheila C. Bair).

Medical Bankruptcy: Middle Class Families at Risk: Hearing before the Judiciary Committee, U.S. House of Representatives, 110th Cong., July 17, 2007 (Washington, D.C.: Government Printing Office, 2008) (statement of Elizabeth Warren).

Perspectives on the Consumer Financial Protection Agency: Hearing Before the Committee on Financial Services, U.S. House of Representatives, 111th Cong., September 30, 2009 (Washington, D.C.: Government Printing Office, 2010) (statements of Janis Bowdler, Michael Calhoun, Hilary O. Shelton, and Edward L. Yingling).

The Proposed Consumer Financial Protection Agency: Implications for Consumers and FTC: Hearings of the Subcommittee on Commerce, Trade and Consumer

Protection of the Committee on Energy and Commerce. U.S. House of Representatives, 111th Cong., July 8, 2009 (Washington, D.C.: U.S. Government Printing Office, 2012) (statements of Rachel E. Barkow, Michael Barr, Gail Hillebrand, Jon Leibowitz, and Chris Stinebert).

Regulatory Perspectives on the Obama Administration's Financial Regulatory Reform Proposals, Part II: Hearing Before the Committee on Financial Services, U.S. House of Representatives, 111th Cong., July 24, 2009 (Washington, D.C.: Government Printing Office, 2010) (statements of Hon. Sheila C. Bair, Hon. Ben S. Bernanke, Hon. John C. Dugan, and Hon. Timothy F. Geithner).

Regulatory Restructuring: Enhancing Consumer Financial Products Regulation: Hearing Before the Committee on Financial Services, U.S. House of Representatives, 111th Cong., June 24, 2009 (Washington, D.C.: Government Printing Office, 2009) (statements of Hon. William Delahunt, Kathleen E. Keest, Edmund Mierzwinski, Travis Plunkett, Hon. Ellen Seidman, Elizabeth Warren, and Edward L. Yingling).

Strengthening and Streamlining Prudential Bank Supervision: Hearing Before the Committee on Banking, Housing, and Urban Affairs, U.S. Senate, 111th Cong. 407, August 4, 2009 (Washington, D.C.: Government Printing Office, 2010) (statement Sheila C. Bair).

U.S. Department of the Treasury, Blueprint for a Modernized Financial Structure, Washington D.C: Government Printing Office, March 2008. http://www.treasury.gov/press-center/press-releases/Documents/Blueprint.pdf.

U.S. Department of Treasury, Financial Regulatory Reform, A New Foundation: Rebuilding Financial Supervision and Regulation, June 17, 2009, http://www.treasury.gov/initiatives/Documents/FinalReport_web.pdf.

U.S. Financial Crisis Inquiry Commission, Final Report of the National Commission on the Causes of the Financial and Economic Crisis in the United States, January 2011, http://www.gpo.gov/fdsys/pkg/GPO-FCIC/pdf/GPO-FCIC.pdf.

The White House, "Remarks by the President at the Signing of Dodd-Frank Wall Street Reform and Consumer Protection Act," press release, Washington, D.C., July 21, 2010, http://www.whitehouse.gov/the-press-office/remarks-president-signing-dodd-frank-wall-street-reform-and-consumer-protection-act.

The White House, "Statement by President Obama on Financial Reform," press release, May 12, 2010, http://www.whitehouse.gov/the-press-office/statement-president-obama-financial-reform.

The White House, "Weekly Address: President Obama Promotes Tougher Rules on Wall Street to Protect Consumers," press release, September 19, 2009, http://www.whitehouse.gov/the_press_office/Weekly-Address-President-Obama-Promotes-Tougher-Rules-on-Wall-Street-to-Protect-Consumers/.

Index

About the Authors

LARRY KIRSCH is an economist and managing partner of IMR Health Economics, a consulting firm in Portland, OR. His consulting practice focuses on health insurance financing and market practices and consumer protection. He has published extensively in the areas of consumerism and health care, including "Do Product Disclosures Inform and Safeguard Insurance Policyholders?" and "The State Attorney General as Consumer Advocate: A Recent Effort to Tame Unfair Subprime Lending Practices."

ROBERT N. MAYER, PhD, is professor in the Department of Family and Consumer Studies at the University of Utah. His published works include ABC-CLIO's *Encyclopedia of the Consumer Movement* and *The Consumer Movement: Guardians of the Marketplace* (Twayne Publishing). He serves or has served on the editorial boards of multiple journals and on boards of directors of numerous organizations, including the Consumer Federation of America, the Consumer WebWatch Program of Consumers Union, the National Consumers League, and DebtorWise Foundation. Mayer holds a doctorate in sociology from the University of California, Berkeley.